W0018256

Best Kept Secrets in .NET

DEBORAH KURATA

Best Kept Secrets in .NET
Copyright © 2004 by Deborah Kurata

All rights reserved. No part of this work may be reproduced or transmitted in any form or by any means, electronic or mechanical, including photocopying, recording, or by any information storage or retrieval system, without the prior written permission of the copyright owner and the publisher.

ISBN (pbk): 1-59059-426-6

Printed and bound in the United States of America 9 8 7 6 5 4 3 2 1

Trademarked names may appear in this book. Rather than use a trademark symbol with every occurrence of a trademarked name, we use the names only in an editorial fashion and to the benefit of the trademark owner, with no intention of infringement of the trademark.

Lead Editor: Dominic Shakeshaft

Technical Reviewer: David McCarter

Editorial Board: Steve Anglin, Dan Appleman, Ewan Buckingham, Gary Cornell, Tony Davis, Jason Gilmore, Chris Mills, Steve Rycroft, Dominic Shakeshaft, Jim Sumser, Gavin Wray

Project Manager: Laura Cheu

Copy Edit Manager: Nicole LeClerc

Copy Editor: Marilyn Smith

Production Manager: Kari Brooks

Production Editor: Katie Stence

Compositor and Artist: Point 'n Click Publishing LLC

Proofreader: Greg Teague

Indexer: Ann Rogers

Cover Designer: Kurt Krames

Manufacturing Manager: Tom Debolski

Distributed to the book trade in the United States by Springer-Verlag New York, LLC, 233 Spring Street, 6th Floor, New York, NY 10013 and outside the United States by Springer-Verlag GmbH & Co. KG, Tiergartenstr. 17, 69112 Heidelberg, Germany.

In the United States: phone 1-800-SPRINGER, e-mail orders@springer-ny.com, or visit http://www.springer-ny.com. Outside the United States: fax +49 6221 345229, e-mail orders@springer.de, or visit http://www.springer.de.

For information on translations, please contact Apress directly at 2560 Ninth Street, Suite 219, Berkeley, CA 94710. Phone 510-549-5930, fax 510-549-5939, e-mail info@apress.com, or visit http://www.apress.com.

The information in this book is distributed on an "as is" basis, without warranty. Although every precaution has been taken in the preparation of this work, neither the author(s) nor Apress shall have any liability to any person or entity with respect to any loss or damage caused or alleged to be caused directly or indirectly by the information contained in this work.

The source code for this book is available to readers at http://www.apress.com in the Downloads section.

To my daughters, Jessica and Krysta. You are both growing up so fast, and sadly there is no way to slow that down. As Gandalf says in The Lord of the Rings: The Fellowship of the Ring, *"All we have to decide is what to do with the time we are given." I cherish every moment of time that I am given to spend with both of you.*

Contents at a Glance

Contents

About the Author

 Deborah Kurata is a professional software architect, designer, and developer. She has authored several books, including the *Doing Objects in Visual Basic* series (SAMS) and *Doing Web Development: Client-Side Techniques* (Apress), and is currently working on *Doing Objects in VB 2005* (Addison-Wesley). She also writes for MSDN and *CoDe* magazine (www.code-magazine.com).

Deborah speaks at .NET user groups all over the country as a member of the INETA Speaker's Bureau (www.ineta.org) and at conferences, such as VSLive, DevDays, and TechEd. She enjoys participating in the local .NET community as a member of the Bay.NET board and co-chair of the East Bay.NET user group (www.baynetug.org). For her work in support of software development and software developers, she has been recognized with the Microsoft Most Valuable Professional (MVP) award.

Deborah is cofounder and President of InStep Technologies Inc. (www.insteptech.com), a professional consulting firm that focuses on turning business vision into reality using Microsoft .NET technologies. InStep architects, designs, and develops object-oriented and service-oriented software for Windows and the Web. InStep provides premier software consulting services to the most successful companies in Silicon Valley, the San Francisco Bay area, and nation-wide. Reach InStep at (925) 224-7280 or info@insteptech.com.

Deborah holds degrees in Physics and Mathematics from the University of Wisconsin—Eau Claire and an MBA from the College of William and Mary.

About the Technical Reviewer

David McCarter is a senior software engineer in San Diego. He is the editor-in-chief of VSDN Tips & Tricks (formerly VB Tips & Tricks, started in 1994), a web site dedicated to helping programmers in all aspects of programming (www.vsdntips.com).

David has written for magazines like the *Visual Basic Programmers Journal* and has published two books (*David McCarter's VB Tips and Techniques* and *VB Tips and Tricks*). He is one of the founders of the 10-year-old San Diego Visual Basic User Group, now called the San Diego .NET Developers Group (www.sdvbug.org).

David gives talks on programming at colleges, high schools, and conferences such as VSLive, and he teaches at the University of California, San Diego. He also runs his own software/consulting company called NicheWare.

Acknowledgments

THIS BOOK IS BASED ON a presentation that I offer as a member of the International .NET Association (INETA) Speakers Bureau. I would like to acknowledge the many developers who have attended my INETA talks and contributed suggestions and additional .NET secrets. I would particularly like to thank the members of the Northern New Jersey .NET User Group, who first suggested that I convert the presentation into a book.

This book was great fun to write, and part of what made the process fun was the amazing team of people working with me on this endeavor. I want to thank Gary Cornell at Apress for his interest in this book. I would especially like to thank Dominic Shakeshaft, the Apress editorial director, for his insights on the content and presentation of the material. Your opinions were quite helpful—thanks, Dominic!

I would also like to thank the Apress project manager, Laura Cheu; the copy editor, Marilyn Smith; and the production editor, Katie Stence. You were all great at smoothly moving the chapters through the editing and production process. I sincerely appreciate your assistance on this project.

A special thanks goes to David McCarter for his role as the official technical editor. I appreciate all of your time and great advice, David!

I also had a fabulous team of technical reviewers. Mary Jane Beddow and Stephen Hahn meticulously reviewed all of the chapters and provided detailed comments and valuable suggestions. I thank you both for your feedback. Jim Butler, Cheryl Phipps, and Ken Smith reviewed every chapter and offered corrections and suggestions. Gerald Smith focused on both the usability and layout of the information. Thanks for all of your great ideas, Jerry. In addition to reviewing chapters, Chi-Wei Lee verified every shortcut key and command. Thanks for all of your hard work, Chi-Wei. I would also like to thank Sam Gill, Julie Lerman, Gerhard Macek, Les Pinter, Marcie Robillard, Chris Rucci, Samuel Santiago, and Fred Yano, who all gave of their free time to review and comment on chapters.

Finally, I would like to thank my family for their understanding and support. To my husband and business partner, Jerry, thanks for helping me allocate time during work hours for writing this book. It was so much easier that way, instead of writing nights and weekends. To my 14-year-old daughter, Jessica, thank you for your positive outlook and encouragement. To my 11-year-old daughter, Krysta, thanks for helping me keep this project in perspective. And to my parents, Jerre and Virginia Cummings, thanks for always being there for me.

—Deborah Kurata, June 2004

Introduction

WANT TO KNOW MORE ABOUT your favorite tools and technologies? This book reveals many secret treasures hiding within Visual Studio and the .NET Framework.

As professional and semiprofessional developers, we build Windows and web applications; fat-client, thin-client, and smart-client applications; and applications to run businesses, devices, and our homes. We learned .NET so we could get the job done. But what if we could get the job done faster and better?

By using the hidden treasures of .NET that are revealed in this book, you can be more productive, create better code, and produce superior software. You will work more efficiently, so you have more time to focus on the business issues.

Who Should Read This Book?

Whether you have been working with .NET for several years now or you are just beginning to move from VB or C/C++ to VB.NET or C#, this book is for you.

This book reveals the information you need to reach the next level of expertise with Visual Studio and the .NET Framework.

What This Book Is

This book is a collection of very valuable but lesser-known features of Visual Studio and the .NET Framework. It provides detailed information about how to use each of these features to improve the efficiency of your software development process and the quality of the resulting software.

You'll uncover hidden treasures in Visual Studio and learn how to get the most from your development environment. You'll discover how to organize a snippet library, see how to manage your development tasks, learn 12 different ways to find the code you need within Visual Studio, and much more. By leveraging the full power of Visual Studio, you'll greatly enhance your productivity.

You'll discover tips for building Windows Forms applications. For example, you'll learn how to implement Enter and Leave events so you can highlight the current control, use GDI+ to draw lines and resize controls to their contents, and display validation errors to the end users using the ErrorProvider control. Using these tips, you can develop a better user interface with less code.

You'll learn coding tricks for both Visual Basic .NET (VB) and C#. For example, you'll discover how to improve your type casting, build regular expressions, define regions to organize your code, and expand your debugging skills. You can apply these techniques to more easily develop code that has better performance and higher quality.

You'll discover the secrets of working with data in Visual Studio. You'll learn how to use the Server Explorer to build your database structure and edit your data, and how to use a database project to manage your stored procedures. By using Visual Studio to work with your database, rather than using external database management tools, you won't need to swap between tools to accomplish your objective.

You'll find out why there is much ado over ADO.NET as some of the exceptionally useful but lesser-known features of ADO.NET are presented. For example, you'll learn how to use the XML features to view or store your dataset, how to sort and filter your dataset with a data view, and how to make your dataset smarter using extended properties. These features improve the way you work with data in your application.

Finally, secrets of defensive development will be revealed. You'll learn how to prevent unauthorized application access, manage application failures, implement a notification mechanism, and perform unit testing. You'll also discover tips about agile methodologies and software development best practices. These techniques help prevent failures in your application.

The primary goal of this book is to let you in on the secrets and hidden treasures that you can discover in Visual Studio and the .NET Framework. If, as you read through this book, you say to yourself, "I didn't know I could do that with .NET," then this book has met its objective.

NOTE   All of the code in this book is presented in both VB and C#, except in cases where only one language supports a feature. For example, DirectCast is VB-only and operator overloading is a C#-only feature (until Visual Studio 2005).

What This Book Is Not

To further understand what this book is, it is important to know what this book is not. This book is not any of the following:

- A tutorial. This book does not provide a beginner's tutorial on how to use Visual Studio or the .NET Framework. Rather, it provides useful but lesser-known Visual Studio and .NET techniques, expanding on your existing knowledge.

- A detailed reference manual. This book does not provide the level of detail found in a reference manual. When it covers a feature, it does not describe every parameter set, option, and technique for using the feature. Rather, it provides the key information you need to use the feature in your daily work.

- An in-depth exposé on internals. This book does not expose all of the secrets of compiler and language internals. Rather, it provides pragmatic tips and tricks that you can use in your everyday software development tasks.

What Will This Book Tell Me?

This book is organized as follows:

- **Chapter 1, Hidden Treasures in Visual Studio:** You may use your cell phone every day, yet don't know all of its hidden features. So, too, you may be using Visual Studio every day and yet not know every feature hiding in the many menus and dialog boxes. This chapter uncovers some of the exceptionally useful, yet lesser-known, features of Visual Studio that can make you more productive.

- **Chapter 2, Doing Windows Forms:** In this chapter, you will discover how to do better Windows Forms applications. This chapter presents some of the lesser-known Windows Forms features to improve both the visual aesthetics of your forms and the code behind the forms.

- **Chapter 3, Code Tricks:** This chapter presents some VB and C# code tricks to make your coding easier, more productive, and just better. It uncovers information on short-circuiting, type casting, data type aliasing, regular expressions, regions, XML commenting, and much more. Some debugging tips are also included.

- **Chapter 4, Much ADO:** Most applications work with some type of data. This chapter presents some of the lesser-known but extremely useful features of ADO.NET, such as viewing datasets as XML and building smart datasets using extended properties. It also demonstrates the many database tools provided within Visual Studio to help you create your database structure, edit database data, and manage your stored procedures, without leaving the comfort of your development environment.

- **Chapter 5, Defensive Development:** The key to a good offense is a good defense. This chapter reveals the secrets of how to design and develop your .NET application so it can defend itself against the perils awaiting it in production. Topics include implementing a methodology for design, preventing unauthorized application access, managing application failures using exception handling, and performing unit testing.

How Do I Use This Book?

You can read this book from cover to cover to discover all of the secrets it reveals. Or, you can use this book as a reference to tips, tricks, and best practices in the areas of most interest to you. You can use this book as it best suits your needs.

As I was working through the examples included in this book, I developed a sample application with components in both VB and in C#. This sample application is available from the Downloads section of the Apress web site (www.apress.com).

I have made every effort to describe the concepts presented in this book in a clear and concise fashion. I have tried to ensure it is up-to-date as of this writing. If you have suggestions for improving the content of the book, have secrets to share, or find something that is incorrect or unclear, I would like to hear from you. I can then incorporate your comments in future editions of this book. You can reach me via e-mail at deborahk@insteptech.com.

Hidden Treasures in Visual Studio

WHEN YOU HAVE A GREAT tool and learn the basics of using it, you get quite comfortable with it. Take your cell phone, for example. Once you learn the basics of how to make phone calls and store and retrieve phone numbers, your cell phone quickly becomes a part of your daily routine. But if you take a moment to read through the manual, you may find that your phone has many hidden treasures—many features that you didn't even know you had available.

The same is true with your Visual Studio interactive development environment (IDE). You know how to use Visual Studio to create projects, edit code, and build an executable. Since your focus is on getting the job done, you might not have time to explore the numerous features hiding in the many menus and dialog boxes. This chapter exposes these hidden treasures.

What Will This Chapter Cover?

This chapter uncovers the following Visual Studio secrets:

- Laying out windows

- Organizing code snippets

- Managing your to-do list

- Finding code

- Using shortcut keys

- Executing Visual Studio commands

- Accessing external tools

By the end of this chapter, you will have discovered many of the hidden treasures in the Visual Studio IDE. You will be able to lay out your code windows for optimal access to the routines you are working on. You will see how to manage your code snippets so the code you need is always close at hand. You will learn how to use the Task List window to manage your development tasks. You will discover a dozen different ways to get to the code you need to find. You will see how easy it is to access the many features of Visual Studio using shortcut keys and Visual Studio commands, so there is no need for your hands to ever leave the keyboard. Finally, you will learn how to hook your favorite external tools directly into Visual Studio.

Laying Out Windows

When preparing to work on a project, such as building a doghouse, you can make the process more productive by laying out your materials and tools so you can easily find what you need. The same is true for your development projects. You can lay out your code windows, designers, and toolboxes in the Visual Studio IDE so they are where you need them.

Managing the Tabs

By default, when you open a file from the Solution Explorer window, such as a code file or Windows Forms file, it appears in the IDE as a tabbed document. Each open file appears with a separate tab at the top of the editor.

You can easily switch between the documents by clicking the tabs or by pressing Ctrl+Tab or Shift+Ctrl+Tab. You can also change the order of the documents by dragging the tabs.

Viewing Multiple Documents

Visual Studio makes it easy to open multiple files and click a tab to work with each one as a document in the IDE. But working with one document at a time is not always sufficient. You may need to compare code from two different code files. You may find it more efficient to view a Windows form or web page at the same time you are working on the code for that form or page.

You can view two or more documents side by side, either vertically or horizontally, by creating a tab group. To create a new vertical tab group, drag one of the tabs to the right. The new tab group will appear as shown in Figure 1-1. To create a new horizontal tab group, drag one of the tabs to the bottom. The new tab group will appear as shown in Figure 1-2.

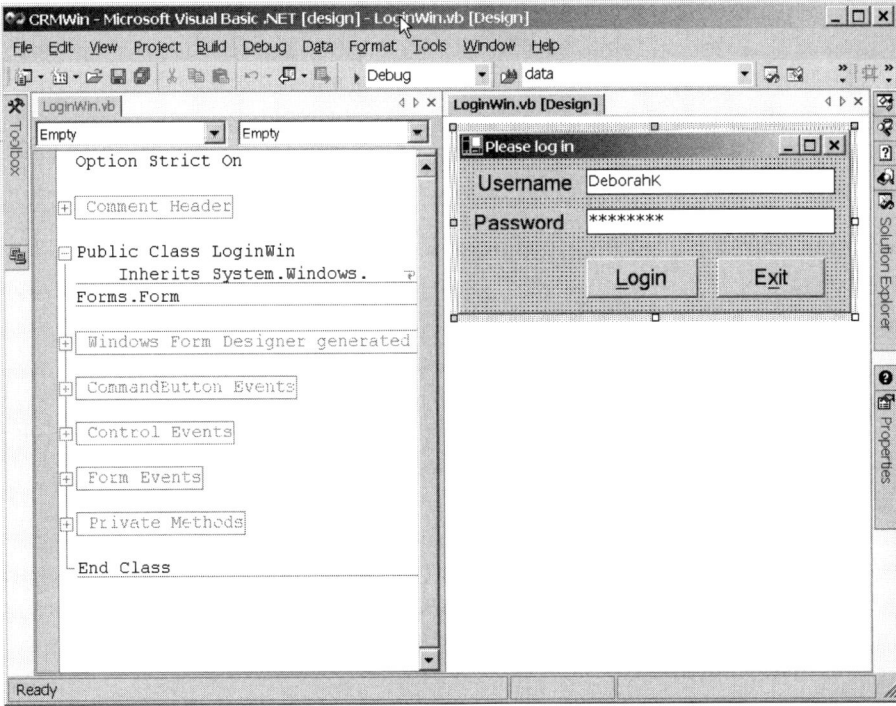

Figure 1-1. Drag a tab to the right to create another vertical tab group.

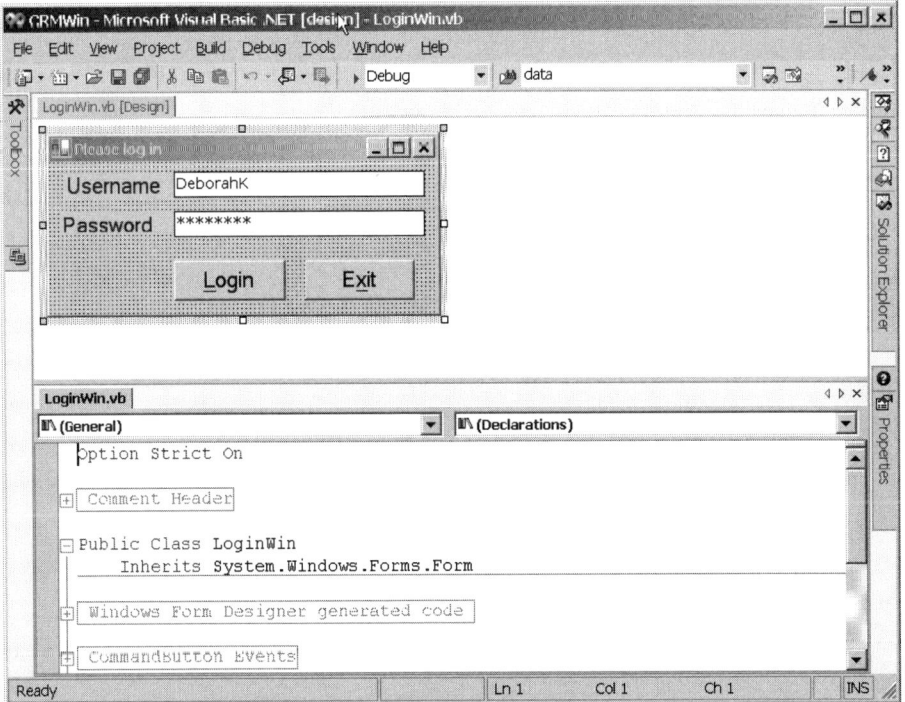

Figure 1-2. Drag a tab to the bottom to create another horizontal tab group.

If you don't like to drag tabs, right-click a tab and select New Horizontal Tab Group or New Vertical Tab Group from the context menu. These options are also available from the Window menu. Once you have your tabs in a tab group, you can move them back to the prior tab group by right-clicking the tab and selecting Move to Previous Tab Group from the context menu.

Viewing Different Parts of the Same Document

Sometimes, it is useful to view two parts of the same document. This allows you to easily compare two different methods in a code file or work concurrently on an event procedure and a related subroutine.

When working with code files, you can split a single document into two horizontal panes to view two parts of the same code file by using the splitter bar. The splitter bar is a small, horizontal bar in the upper-right corner of the document, just above the vertical scroll bar. To split the document, drag the splitter bar downward. This produces two views of the same code file, as shown in Figure 1-3. The menu option Window ➤ Split performs the same function. Double-click the splitter bar or select the menu option Window ➤ Remove Split to remove the split.

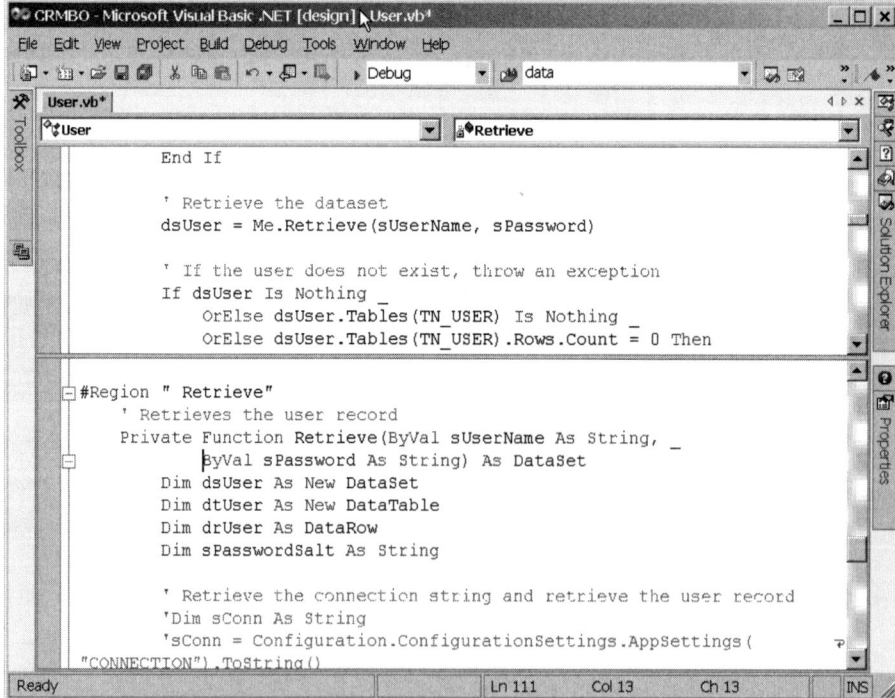

Figure 1-3. Use the splitter bar to view two parts of the same code file.

NOTE Splitting a document causes all of the regions to be closed. For more information about regions, see the "Exploring Undiscovered Regions" section in Chapter 3.

In some cases, such as C# code files and help files (not VB code files), you can view two different parts of the same file simultaneously in full-sized windows, as shown in Figure 1-4. To open a new window containing a second view of a file, select the tab containing the desired file, and then select the menu option Window ➤ New Window.

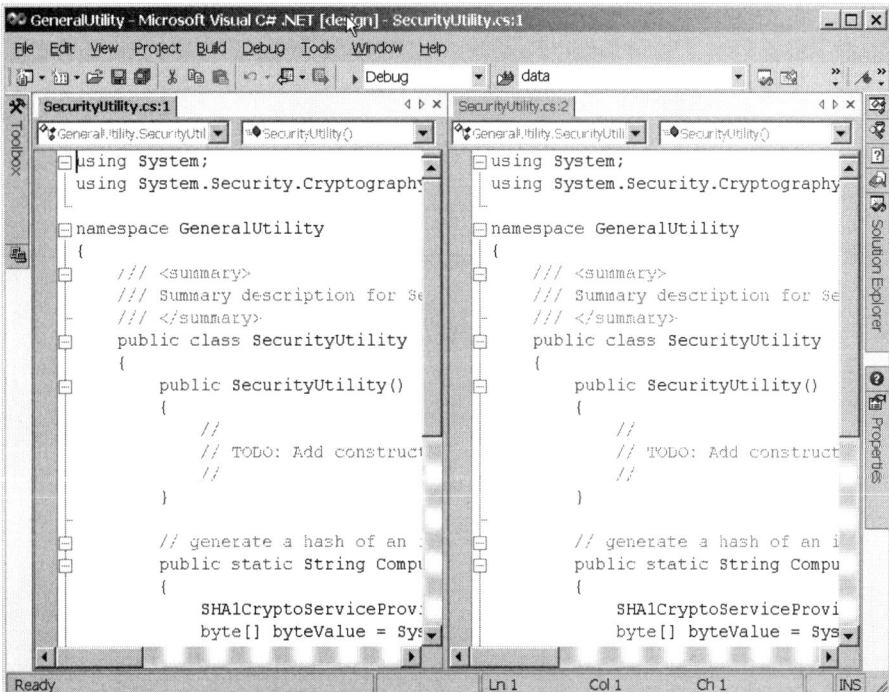

Figure 1-4. For some file types, you can work with two windows for the same file.

Viewing Only the Code

Full Screen mode hides all tool windows and expands the document windows, giving you the maximum view of your code or other document windows. This is useful when you want to concentrate on just the code. It is also great for giving code presentations.

To toggle Full Screen mode, press Shift+Alt+Enter or select View ➤ Full Screen from the menu. When toggled on, Full Screen mode hides the toolbars, toolboxes, and all other support windows, leaving only the menu and the tabbed document windows open, as shown in Figure 1-5.

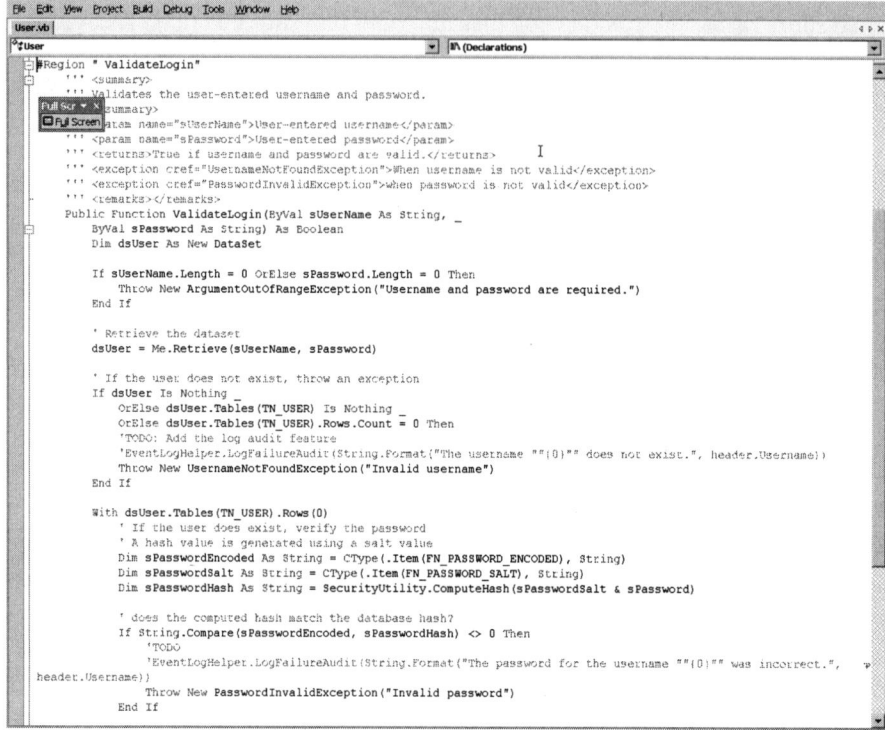

Figure 1-5. Full Screen mode clears away the tool windows, allowing you more space for working with the code.

Wrapping Code

If you have long code lines, you'll find that you do a lot of horizontal scrolling to view the entire line. As an alternative, you can wrap the code lines so you can view the code without needing to scroll.

The easiest way to toggle word wrapping is by pressing Ctrl+R and then Ctrl+R again or by selecting Edit ➤ Advanced ➤ Word Wrap from the menu. When word wrapping is turned on, the horizontal scroll bar is removed and any lines of code that exceed the width of the code window will automatically wrap to the next line, as shown in Figure 1-6. This wrapping does not require any additional line-continuation characters (for VB), nor does it affect how the code is compiled.

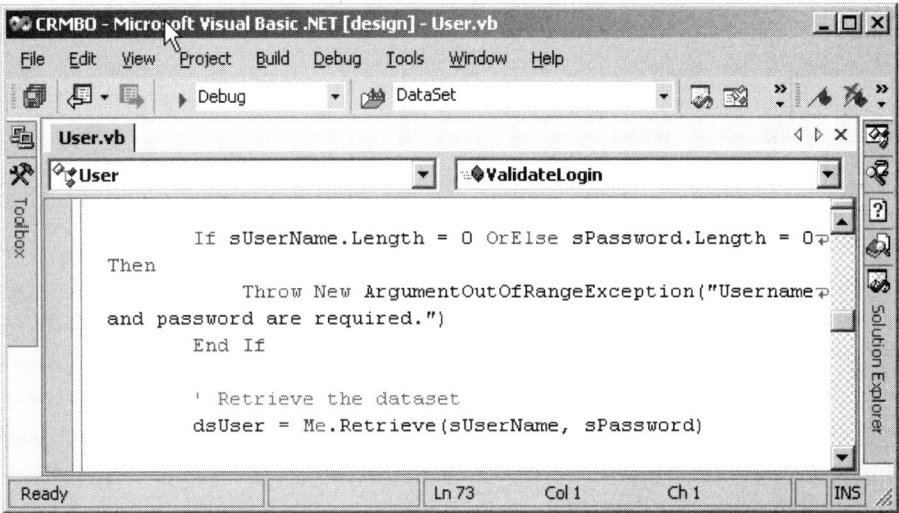

Figure 1-6. Enabling word wrapping makes it easier to work with long code lines.

You can also set word wrapping by selecting Tools ➤ Options and opening the Text Editor folder. Set word wrapping for one specific programming language or for all .NET programming languages, as shown in Figure 1-7.

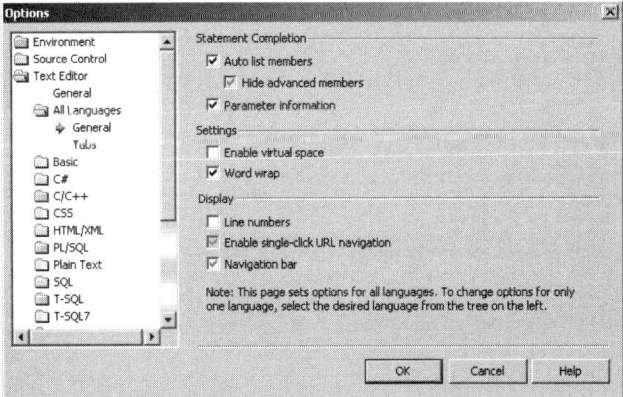

Figure 1-7. Set Text Editor Options, such as word wrap, for a specific language or all languages.

Undocking Windows

If you know this secret, you can undock any tool window without worrying about how to get it to dock back correctly. Just double-click the title bar of the window. It will then undock, and you can use it for your work. When you are fin-ished with the window, simply double-click the title bar of the window again, and it will automatically redock where it had been.

If you really mess up your window layout, you can reset it back to the default Visual Studio windows layout. Select Tools ➤ Options to open the Options dialog box, and then click the Reset Window Layout button. After you confirm the operation and close the Options dialog box, the window layout will be reset to the default.

Organizing Code Snippets

You may often find that you write a little piece of code that you want to reuse again and again. These pieces of code are called *code snippets*. Wouldn't it be great to have a place to organize these snippets and easily find and use them when you need them? The Visual Studio Toolbox provides such a place.

Storing Code Snippets

Before you can use code snippets, you need to store them. Any bit of code that you want to reuse can be stored as a code snippet.

Store your snippets on the General tab of the Visual Studio Toolbox. (If your Toolbox is not displayed in the IDE, choose the View ➤ Toolbox option to dis-play it.) Or, if you prefer to categorize your snippets, create additional tabs on the Visual Studio Toolbox by right-clicking a tab and selecting Add Tab from the context menu. Then store your snippets on your new tabs.

Add a code snippet to a tab of the Toolbox as follows:

1. Select the code snippet (or any text) in the code file.

2. Copy the text to the Clipboard.

3. Click the desired tab of the Toolbox.

4. Right-click the area below the tab.

5. Select Paste from the context menu.

Alternatively, simply select the text from the code file and drag it to the desired tab of the Toolbox. An example of the Toolbox with code snippets is shown in Figure 1-8.

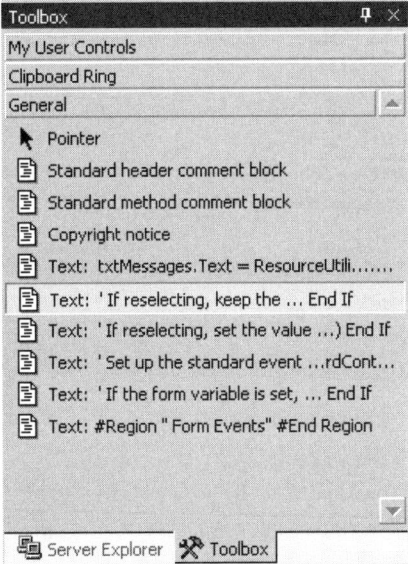

Figure 1-8. The Toolbox provides a great place for organizing your snippet library.

After you have snippets in the Toolbox, you can sort, rename, or delete them using the context menu. You can also reorganize them by dragging and dropping them onto a different tab.

The snippets in the Toolbox are retained as part of the IDE, so you can access the snippets from any solution. The contents of the Toolbox are stored in the toolbox.tbd file, located under Local Settings\Application Data\Microsoft\Visual Studio\7.1.

Store any piece of code that you may reuse as a code snippet in the Toolbox. This will greatly aid your productivity, because the next time you need the code, you can locate it quickly and insert it into your code file.

Using Code Snippets

Once you have stored a set of code snippets, you will want to use them in your code files. You can use them in any code file in any solution.

To use the code from your snippet library, follow these steps:

1. Right-click the desired snippet in the Toolbox.

2. Select Copy from the context menu.

3. Place the cursor at the desired insertion point in the code file.

4. Select Paste from the Edit menu (or the code window's context menu).

You don't need to use the Clipboard to access your snippets. Instead, place the cursor at the desired insertion point in the code file, and then double-click the snippet in the Toolbox. Alternatively, drag the snippet from the Toolbox to the desired location in the code file.

Organizing Comment Blocks

In addition to using the Toolbox to maintain a set of code snippets, you can keep comment blocks as text snippets in the Toolbox as well. For example, you can create a standard comment block for the header of every class and one for the header of every method, and store them as text snippets. This simplifies and standardizes your commenting tasks. To store and use a text snippet, follow the same techniques as defined for code snippets in the previous sections.

Organizing the Clipboard

If you have ever wished that you could have multiple items on the Clipboard, your wish has come true. The Clipboard Ring tab of the Toolbox, shown in Figure 1-9, displays the last set of items added to the Clipboard using the Cut or Copy commands within Visual Studio.

Items on the Clipboard Ring tab can be dragged and dropped onto the active editing or design surface. If you prefer to use the keyboard, cycle through the contents of the Clipboard Ring tab while you work in an editor or designer by pressing Ctrl+Shift+V. This pastes an item from the Clipboard Ring tab at the current insertion point. Press Ctrl+Shift+V again to replace the pasted item with the next item from the Clipboard Ring tab. Repeat this process until you paste the desired item.

Figure 1-9. The Clipboard Ring tab gives you access to the last set of items added to the Clipboard from within Visual Studio.

Managing Your To-Do List

As with most developers, you probably don't finish every detail of a routine before moving along to another piece of code. Rather, you finish a "rough draft" of the routine and perform some testing to ensure that it works before adding all of the detail work. Even then, you may find that you need to wait for another developer or wait for a response from the user, or you just want to go home for the evening before the routine is finished. Visual Studio provides an easy way to mark unfinished code or unfinished tasks so you can easily come back to them later.

The Task List window in Visual Studio provides a way to manage your to-do list. You are probably most familiar with the Task List window as the window that displays your syntax errors, as shown in Figure 1-10. But the Task List window can be used for so much more. It can help you organize and manage the work of building your application.

If the Task List window is not displayed in your IDE, show it by selecting View ➤ Show Tasks, and then picking the category of tasks to be displayed. The long list of task categories gives you an idea of the utility of this feature.

NOTE   By default, the Task List window will list only build errors. To view all categories of tasks, select View ➤ Show Tasks ➤ All from the menu.

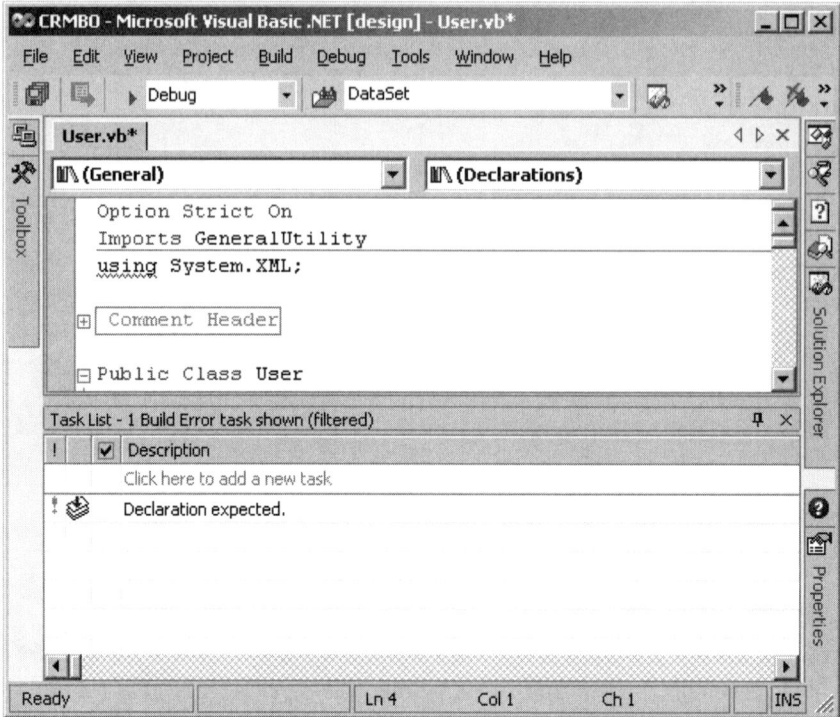

Figure 1-10. The Task List window displays syntax errors.

Creating Comment Tasks

One of the most useful features of the Task List window is the ability to display links to comments in your code. This feature allows you to easily mark a section of code that you want to return to later and provides a mechanism for linking directly back to that code.

To define a comment in your code that will appear as a link in the Task List window, insert a token string immediately following the comment mark. The default token strings are TODO, UNDONE, and HACK.

In VB, use an apostrophe followed by the token string:

```
' TODO: Add the rest of the controls here
```

In C#, use two slashes and then the token string:

```
// TODO: Add constructor logic here
```

Comments marked with a token string will appear in the Task List window, as shown in Figure 1-11. Double-click any of the comments in the Task List window to open the appropriate code file, automatically positioned at the comment line in the code. When a task is complete, remove the comment from your code, and the task will be automatically removed from the Task List window.

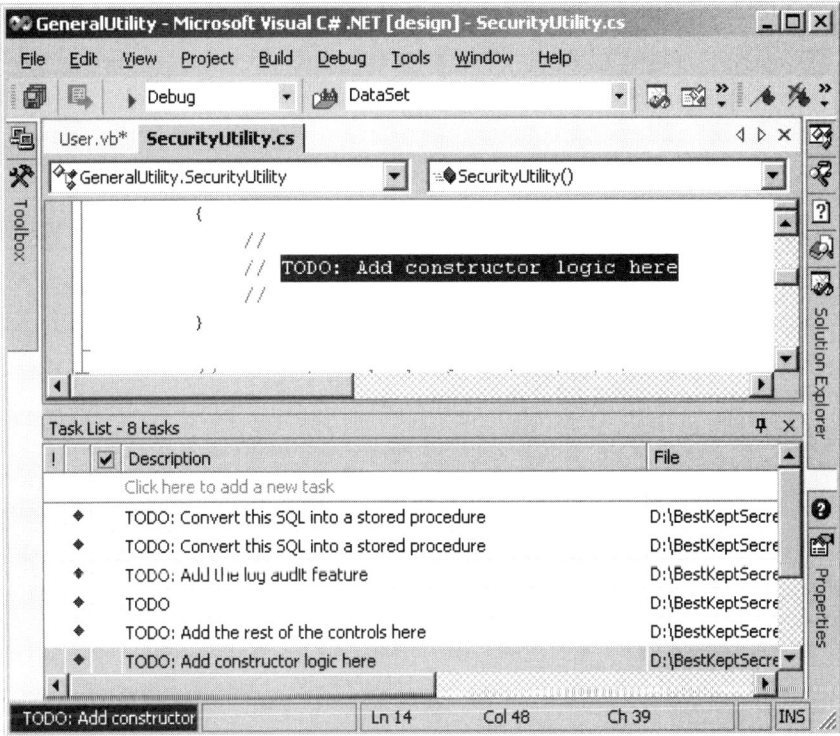

Figure 1-11. The Task List window displays any code comments defined with a token string and provides a quick way to return to the code marked with the comment.

NOTE   In C#, the comments will not appear in the Task List window unless the code file is open in the editor.

NOTE   Comments in HTML, CSS, and XML markup don't appear in the Task List window.

13

To add your own custom tokens, select Tools ➤ Options, open the Environment folder, and then choose the Task List item, as shown in Figure 1-12. For example, if you are working with a team, you could define a token for each member of your team, such as SteveFix or JessicaToDo.

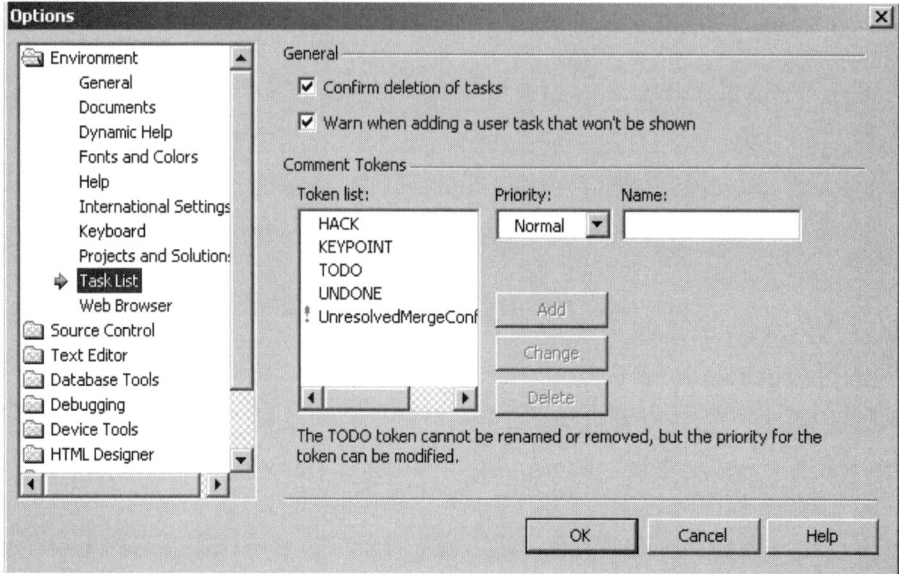

Figure 1-12. Define your own code comment token strings for display in the Task List window.

Viewing Build Error Tasks

Build errors are the category of tasks in the Task List window with which you are probably already familiar. Build error tasks include the syntax and build errors for the current solution.

Errors are automatically assigned a High priority, and warnings are assigned a Normal priority in the Task List window. Double-click any error or warning to open the appropriate code file, automatically positioned at the appropriate line in the code.

The only way to remove a build error item from the Task List window is to fix the error.

Adding User Tasks

Sometimes, you have a task to do that is not directly related to any particular piece of code. You can add these tasks to the Task List window to keep all of your development tasks in one place.

Add your own user tasks by entering the task in the first line of the Task List window, as shown in Figure 1-13. Enter a description and set a priority. When you have finished the task, mark it as complete by clicking the Checked column. You can delete a user task by right-clicking the task and selecting Delete from the context menu.

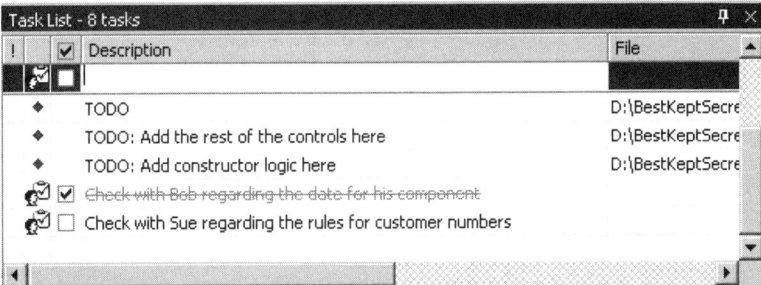

Figure 1-13. You can add any number of user tasks to the Task List window. Use the check box column on the left to mark the task as complete.

Separate sets of user tasks are stored for each user within each solution. You can edit and delete only your own user tasks.

Defining Shortcut Tasks

If you don't want to create a code comment, but still want a quick link to a particular code line, define a Task List shortcut. This bookmarks a line of code and creates a link to the bookmark in the Task List window.

To define a Task List shortcut, place the insertion point in the desired line of code, and then select Edit ➤ Bookmarks ➤ Add Task List Shortcut or press Ctrl+K, Ctrl+H. The line of code will then be marked in the Code Editor with a shortcut icon in the left margin, and a link to the code will be listed in the Task List window marked with the same icon, as shown in Figure 1-14.

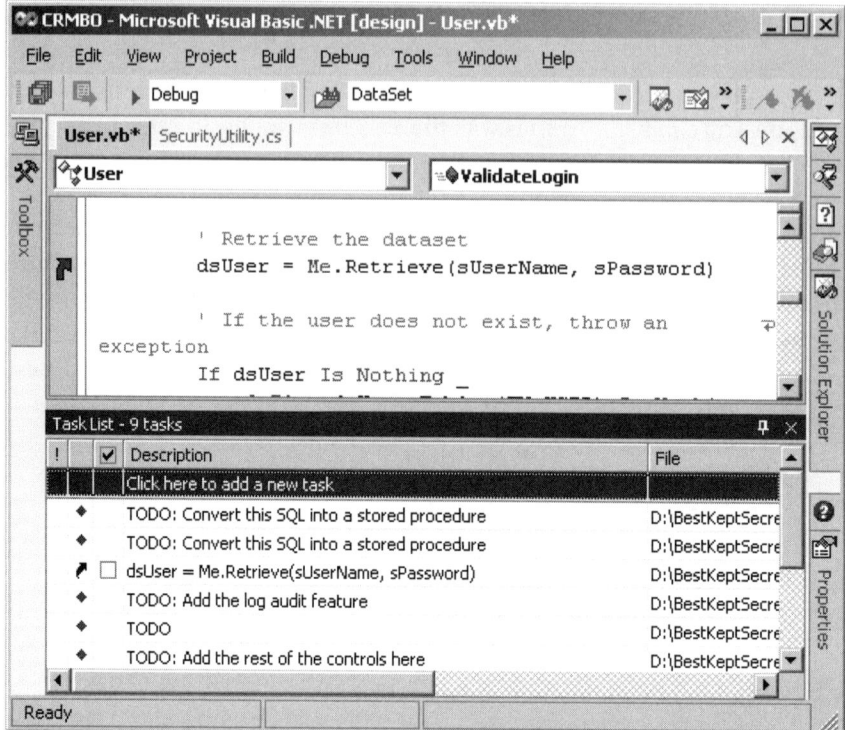

Figure 1-14. Code marked with a Task List shortcut appears with a shortcut icon. The Task List window contains a link to the code associated with the Task List shortcut.

By default, the code line text itself will appear as the task description in the Task List window. You can change the description by clicking in the Description column, and then editing the text. You can update the priority in the Priority column. Double-click any of the shortcuts in the Task List window to open the appropriate code file, automatically positioned at the code marked with the shortcut. Mark a task as complete by clicking the Checked column.

To remove the shortcut item from the Task List window, right-click the shortcut item in the Task List and select Delete from the context menu. This will remove the shortcut icon from the code file as well.

To remove the shortcut when you are in the code file, place the insertion point on the line of code containing the shortcut and select Edit ➤ Bookmarks ➤ Remove Task List Shortcut or press Ctrl+K, Ctrl+H. When you remove the shortcut from the code file, it will also be deleted from the Task List window.

Viewing Policy Tasks

The Policy category in the Task List window links to problems in the code as defined by the Template Description Language (TDL) compiler as *Enterprise Template* policies are applied. These templates aid in ensuring that enterprise standards and best practices are followed.

If you have the Enterprise Edition of Visual Studio, you can create Enterprise Templates to define coding standards and policies. When projects, folders, and other solution items are added or deleted within the project hierarchy, the Enterprise Templates perform validation and apply defined policies. If any problems are found, such as a defined Enterprise Template constraint or policy is not met, a policy reminder is added to the Task List window explaining the problem. The Task List window will also contain a link to a line in a code file or to the policy definition related to the violation, where appropriate.

NOTE For more information about Enterprise Templates, search for "Enterprise Templates" on http://msdn.microsoft.com.

Filtering and Sorting Tasks

To filter the tasks in the Task List window to any of the defined categories, right-click any column header in the Task List window, select Show Tasks from the context menu, and select the desired category. You can also filter to the current file to list only those tasks associated with the code file that has focus.

To sort the tasks in the task list, click the header of the column to sort in the Task List window. You can also sort by right-clicking a column header in the Task List window, selecting Sort By from the context menu, and selecting the desired sort column.

Selecting and sorting tasks allow you to arrange those tasks in the order you prefer to work on them or to view their status. You can then navigate through the items in the list by double-clicking each one or by pressing F8 and Shift+F8 to move to the next and previous items, respectively.

By using the Task List window to create and view your tasks, you can manage your to-do list from within Visual Studio. This will give you better control over your development tasks, helping you be more productive.

Finding Code

You have undoubtedly found several ways to find the code you are looking for within your code files, but did you know that there are at least 12 ways to find code within Visual Studio? By understanding all of the different ways to search for code, you can use the most efficient technique to find the code you need.

The following sections cover the many ways to find code, starting with the most obvious. You may want to skip the first few if you have done a lot of searching within the IDE and move directly on to the lesser-known techniques.

Finding a Text String Interactively

The most obvious way to find a text string within a code file is with the Find option. This option searches for a specified text string and then allows you to interactively review matches. Access this option by selecting Edit ➤ Find and Replace ➤ Find or by pressing Ctrl+F.

Selecting the Find option displays the Find dialog box, as shown in Figure 1-15. You can limit your search to a specific method, the current document, all open documents, or the current project. It also provides for wildcard searching.

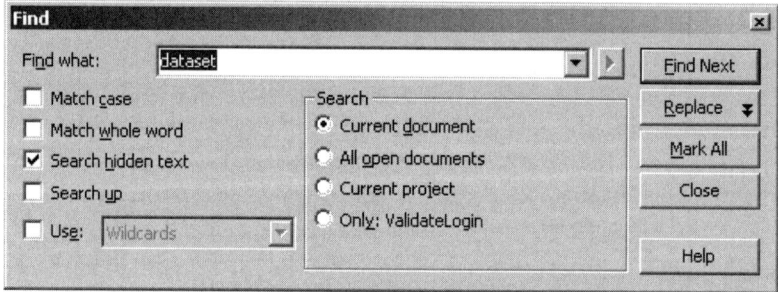

Figure 1-15. The Find dialog box allows you to find a text string within your documents.

NOTE If you are using *regions*, as defined in the "Exploring Undiscovered Regions" section in Chapter 3, be sure to check the Search hidden text check box in this dialog box. Otherwise, the Find operation will not look in any closed regions.

When you click the Find Next button, the next occurrence of the defined string is found and selected in the document. If you don't want the Find dialog box in your way, close the dialog box and continue to find the next occurrence by pressing the F3 key or find the previous occurrence by pressing Shift+F3.

Use the Find option to quickly find a text string within an open code file or within the current project and interactively review the matches. Associated with the Find is a Replace feature to find and replace a specific text string.

Finding a Text String in Files

The Find option is missing one key feature: the ability to find text strings in any file in a solution. That is where the Find in Files option is useful.

Access the Find in Files option by selecting Edit ➤ Find and Replace ➤ Find in Files or by pressing Ctrl+Shift+F. Selecting the Find in Files option displays the Find in Files dialog box, as shown in Figure 1-16. You can limit your search to the current document, all open documents, or the current project, or you can search in all files in the solution.

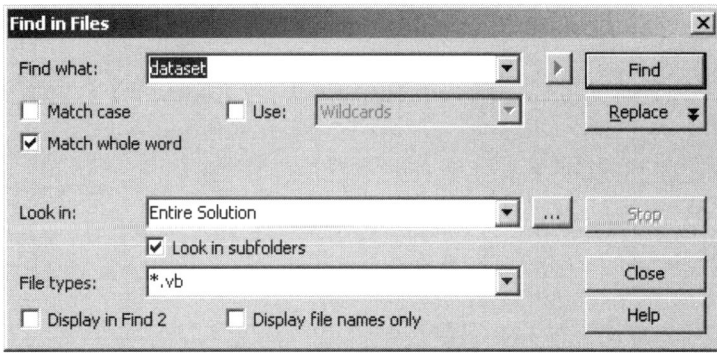

Figure 1-16. The Find in Files dialog box allows you to find a specified text string within your files.

When you click the Find button, the specified files are searched and all occurrences of the defined string are listed in the Find Results window, as shown in Figure 1-17. Double-click an entry in the Find Results window to open the appropriate code file, automatically positioned at the selected occurrence of the defined string.

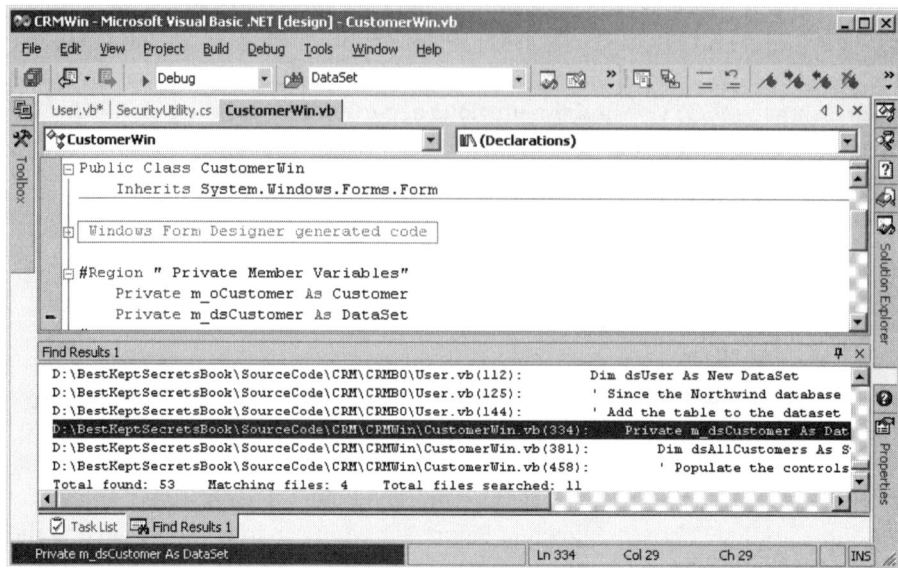

Figure 1-17. The Find Results window displays each occurrence of the defined string.

Use the Find in Files option to quickly find a text string anywhere within your solution. It is also useful for obtaining a list of all occurrences of a particular text string without needing to navigate through each occurrence. Associated with the Find in Files option is a Replace in Files feature to find and replace a specific text string in a set of files.

 CAUTION   You can modify all of the files in your solution with the Replace in Files feature. In some cases, an undo operation is not possible. Therefore, take extreme care when using Replace in Files.

Using the Find/Command Box

Another frequently unnoticed treasure is the Find/Command box in the standard toolbar. The Find/Command box lists the last set of text strings used as search strings and allows you to select one of these strings or enter another string to find. Basically, it provides a shortcut to the Find feature. For example, the Find/Command box shown here contains the text "DataSet."

To minimize the number of times you need to use your mouse, jump to the Find/Command box by pressing Ctrl+D. After you select or enter the string to find in the Find/Command box, press the Enter or F3 key to find each occurrence of the specified text in the current file.

In addition to a Find feature, the Find/Command box allows you to execute Visual Studio commands. To identify text as a command instead of search text, preface the command with a greater than (>) character. You can jump to the Find/Command box and automatically put it into Command mode by pressing Ctrl+/. See the "Executing Visual Studio Commands" section later in this chapter for more information about using Visual Studio commands.

Use the Find/Command box option to quickly find a text string within the current file without opening a dialog box. This provides an efficient shortcut when you want to search in the current file.

Searching for Properties and Methods with Find Symbol

If you are searching for a specific property or method in your code, you may want to limit your search to only property and method names. That is the primary use of the Find Symbol option. To use this option, select Edit ➤ Find and Replace ➤ Find Symbol or press Alt+F12. Selecting the Find Symbol option displays the Find Symbol dialog box, as shown in Figure 1-18.

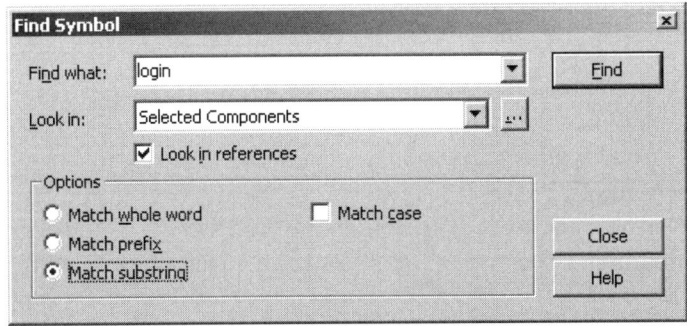

Figure 1-18. The Find Symbol dialog allows you to find a defined text string in only property and method names.

When you click the Find button, the definition of any symbol that matches the entered text will be listed in the Find Symbol Results window, as shown in Figure 1-19. This search will ignore any comments or other code syntax in your code files.

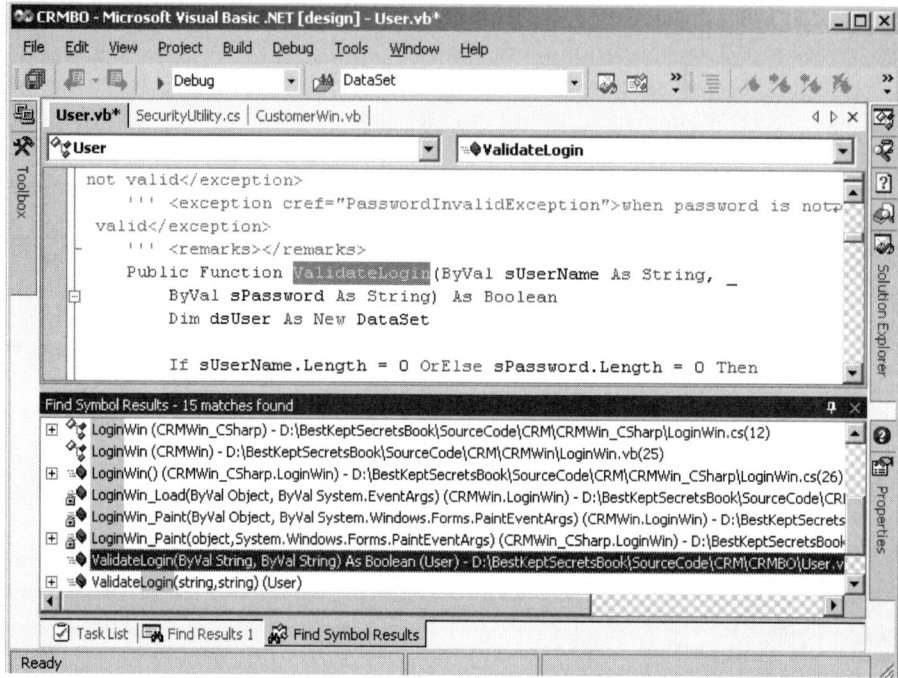

Figure 1-19. The Find Symbol Results window displays each occurrence of the defined string found in a property or method name.

Double-click an entry in the Find Symbol Results window to open the appropriate code file, automatically positioned at the selected occurrence of the symbol. If the symbol is not defined in your solution, double-clicking the entry will display the Object Browser.

To quickly find a symbol without going through the Find Symbol dialog box, press Alt+Shift+F12 on the selected symbol. This invokes the Quick Find Symbol feature.

Use the Find Symbol option to quickly find a text string within a property or method name. This prevents finding extraneous comments and other code syntax containing the desired text string.

Performing an Incremental Search

The Incremental Search feature allows you to search by entering text, character by character. Matching text is found as the characters accumulate. To be honest, I don't know how useful this is, but it is definitely fun to play with.

It is hard to explain how this works, so your best bet is to try it:

1. Open a code file.

2. Select Edit ➤ Advanced ➤ Incremental Search or press Ctrl+I. The cursor icon will change to binoculars with an arrow indicating the search direction. This indicates that you are in Incremental Search mode.

3. Start to type. The characters you are entering are shown in the status bar, and as you type, the entered characters are found and highlighted in the Code Editor.

4. When you have found the text you want, press Esc, and the search will be terminated.

The incremental search begins at the current location in the document and searches in the defined direction. To move to the next match for the search text, press Ctrl+I to search forward or Ctrl+Shift+I to search backward. An error is displayed in the status bar if no text is found matching the entered text.

The search is limited to the current document or window. It won't search any hidden text; that is, text that is within a closed region. It also does not support wildcard characters. The search will use the matching criteria, such as the Match Case option, last defined in the Find, Replace, Find in Files, or Replace in Files dialog box.

Use the Incremental Search feature to quickly find a text string within the current file without opening a dialog box or using the Find/Command box.

Finding a Routine with the Code Window Combo Boxes

At the top of the code window, just below the tabs, are two combo boxes. These combo boxes provide a quick way to find particular routines in your code file.

The names of these combo boxes depend on the language used in the code window. For VB, the left combo box is called the Class Name, because you can select any class defined in the code file. The right combo box is called the

Method Name, because you can select any method within the class selected in the left combo box. Note that properties and events are included in this combo box for VB.

In C#, the left combo box is called Type, because you can select any type (another name for class) defined in the code file. The right combo box is called Members, because it defines all of the members of the type selected in the left combo box. This includes both properties and methods, but not events.

Regardless of their names, these two combo boxes are useful for finding a specific routine within the current code file. Simply select the appropriate class/type from the left combo box and method/member from the right combo box to view the code for that method/member. To jump to the class/type combo box using the keyboard, press Ctrl+F2.

As an example, Figure 1-20 shows these combo boxes for the User.vb code file. To find the ValidateLogin routine in the User class, select User from the left combo box and ValidateLogin from the right combo box.

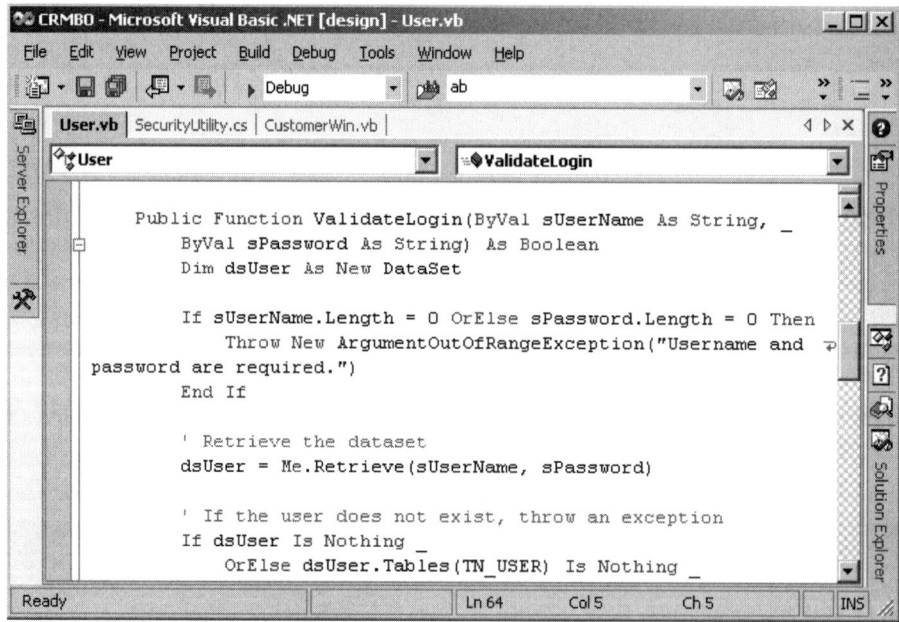

Figure 1-20. Use the combo boxes at the top of the code window to quickly navigate to a desired routine.

Use the code window combo boxes whenever you want to quickly navigate to a particular routine in a code file. When coding in VB, you can also use these combo boxes to view the set of available events. The events that have defined event procedures are shown in bold.

Finding Symbols Using the Class View

The Class View window (View ➤ Class View) displays each component in your application, each class in each component, and each property and method in each class, as shown in Figure 1-21. This provides a hierarchical view of your solution. Using the Class View window, you can examine and navigate to any symbol in your solution by double-clicking the symbol.

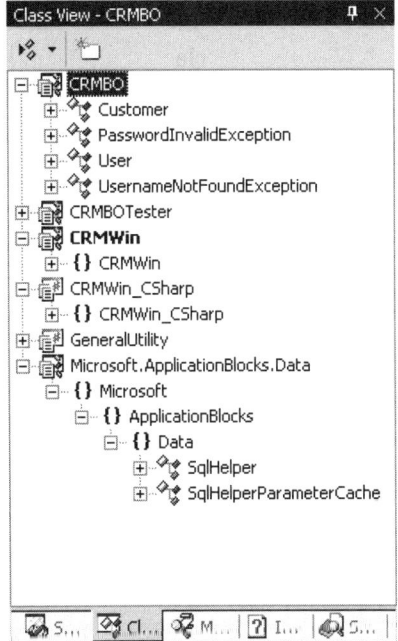

Figure 1-21. The Class View window allows you to navigate to any property or method in any class in your solution.

Use the Class View window to quickly find code for a particular routine when you don't have the associated code file open or when you don't know which code file contains the desired routine.

Finding Code Using the Task List

Earlier in this chapter, you saw the many features of the Task List window. These features include the ability to immediately find code that was marked with a task comment or a Task List shortcut bookmark.

To find code from the Task List, double-click the task associated with the desired code. The appropriate code file is opened, automatically positioned at the comment line or bookmark. See the "Managing Your To-Do List" section in this chapter for more information about using the Task List window to find code.

Marking Code with Bookmarks

Bookmarks work somewhat like the standard bookmarks that you use in the books you read. They allow you to mark your place while you look up something else in the book.

Bookmarks in the IDE allow you to mark lines of code and navigate through those code lines. This allows you to mark areas of the code you are working on, look up something else, and then return to where you were.

To bookmark a code line, ensure the insertion point is on the line, and then select Edit ➤ Bookmarks ➤ Toggle Bookmark or click the Toggle Bookmark button (shown with a flag icon) on the Text Editor toolbar. Navigate through your bookmarks within a code file using Edit ➤ Bookmarks ➤ Next Bookmark or Edit ➤ Bookmarks ➤ Previous Bookmark, or by clicking the Next or Previous Bookmark buttons on the Text Editor toolbar.

NOTE   The bookmarks are not retained when the code file is closed.

Use bookmarks to mark code that you want to come back to while you are editing your code files.

Navigating to Referenced Methods with Go To Definition

When you are working with code, you may want to quickly navigate to a referenced method. That's the purpose of the Go To Definition feature.

View the referenced method by right-clicking the method name and selecting Go To Definition from the context menu or by placing the insertion point in the method name and pressing F12. This will immediately open the appropriate code file, automatically positioned at the method.

As an example, say that your button Click event calls a ProcessClick method. Right-click the ProcessClick method name and select Go To Definition from the context menu. The code file containing the ProcessClick method is opened, and the ProcessClick method is displayed. If the method is not a part of your solution, the method definition is displayed in the Object Browser.

If you want to return to the code where the method was called, click the Navigate Backward button on the standard toolbar. See the next section for more information about the Navigate buttons.

Use the Go To Definition feature when you want to navigate to a method from the method call or to a property definition from where the property is used.

Navigating with the Navigate Buttons

Two very useful but frequently unnoticed buttons on the standard toolbar are the Navigate Forward and Navigate Backward buttons. These buttons take you backward and forward through the last several places you were in the solution, allowing you to retrace your steps through the code files.

Select the Navigate Backward button to move back to the last location in which you were working in your code files. Click the down arrow to the right of the Navigate Backward button to see the list of code files and the locations in each file, as shown in Figure 1-22. Then select the desired location to navigate to that location. Select the Navigate Forward button to return to where you started.

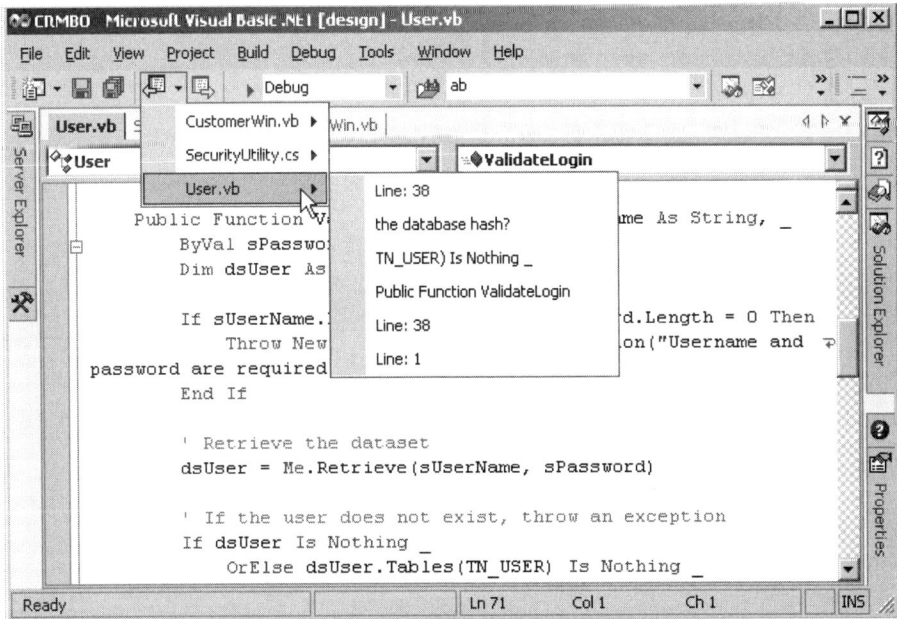

Figure 1-22. The Navigate Forward and Navigate Backward buttons allow you to retrace your steps through your code files.

You can also access the Navigate Forward and Navigate Backward options from the View menu or with shortcut keys: Ctrl+- (hyphen) to navigate backward and Ctrl+Shift+- to navigate forward.

The Navigate Forward and Navigate Backward feature is most useful when you have navigated away from where you are working. For example, if you used the Go To Definition or Go To Line feature to go to another place in the code and now want to return to your original point, use the Navigate Backward button. If you then want to get back to where you were before selecting Navigate Backward, select Navigate Forward.

Navigating with Go To Line

Visual Studio, by default, does not display line numbers in the Code Editor. However, there are times when you need to view or find line numbers. When in Debug mode, for example, any exceptions will provide the number of the line that generated the exception.

The number of the current line is displayed in the status bar at the bottom of the Code Editor. So, to find a particular line number, you could navigate through the code file, watching the current line number until you get to the line you want.

A better option is to select Edit ➤ Go To or press Ctrl+G to go to a specified line. When you select this option, the Go To Line dialog box is displayed. Enter the desired line number and click OK. The code file is then automatically positioned at the selected line number.

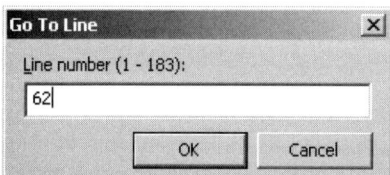

Visual Studio also gives you the option to display line numbers on every line. Turn on line numbers by setting Text Editor Options (Tools ➤ Options). You can turn on line numbers for one specific programming language or for all programming languages, as shown earlier in Figure 1-7.

NOTE If you want the line numbers to print, you must select File ➤ Page Setup and check the Line numbers check box.

Use Go To Line when you know the line number of the code you want to find.

Using Shortcut Keys

Shortcut keys provide a quick way to get to the features that you use most often. Visual Studio defines several sets of shortcut keys to access everything from text editor features to help topics.

The shortcut keys available to you depend on the keyboard scheme you selected when you installed Visual Studio. To change your keyboard scheme, select Tools ➤ Options, open the Environment folder, choose Keyboard, and then change the keyboard scheme using the Keyboard mapping scheme drop-down list, as shown in Figure 1-23. You can also redefine any of the predefined shortcut keys using this dialog box. This allows you to define your shortcut keys to match your working style.

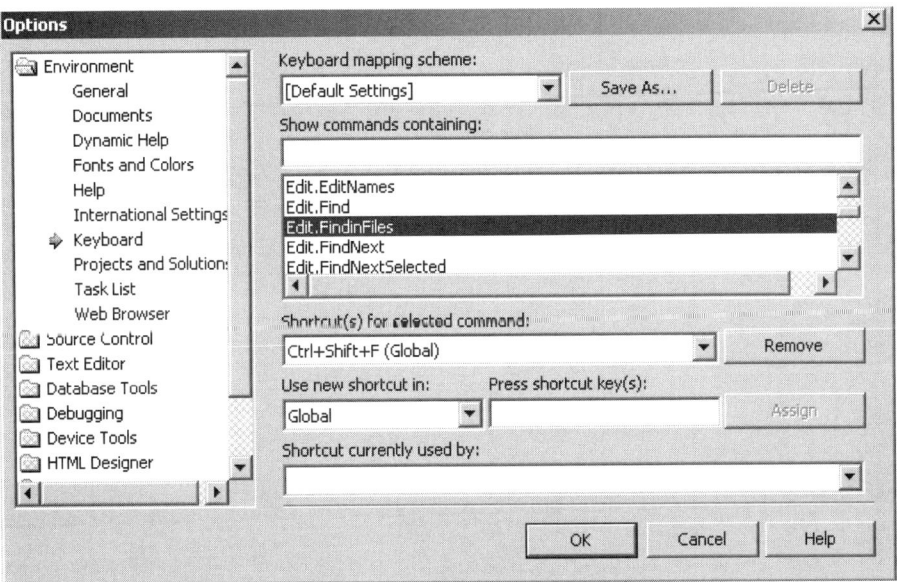

Figure 1-23. Change your keyboard scheme, or reassign, add, or delete shortcut keys associated with Visual Studio commands to tailor the shortcut keys to your preferences.

The following sections list the most useful key combinations available for the Default Settings keyboard scheme, along with their associated commands. Check out the help system for the full list of shortcut keys.

 **NOTE**   This section lists the shortcut keys for the Default Settings keyboard scheme. If you are using the Visual Basic 6.0, Visual Studio 6.0, or another keyboard scheme, your shortcut keys may be different from those listed here.

Accessing Commonly Used Features with General Shortcuts

General shortcuts are shortcut key combinations that can be used in many places throughout Visual Studio. They provide quick access to Edit, File, and View menu options, as shown in Table 1-1.

Table 1-1. General Shortcuts for Common Visual Studio Features

COMMAND	MENU	SHORTCUT	DESCRIPTION
Edit.Copy	Edit ➤ Copy	Ctrl+C Ctrl+Insert	Copies the currently selected item to the system Clipboard.
Edit.Cut	Edit ➤ Cut	Ctrl+X Shift+Delete	Copies the currently selected item to the system Clipboard and then deletes the item.
Edit.Cycle-Clipboard Ring	Edit ➤ Cycle-Clipboard Ring	Ctrl+Shift+Insert Ctrl+Shift+V	Pastes an item from the Clipboard Ring tab of the Toolbox at the insertion point in the file and automatically selects the pasted item. You can overwrite the pasted item with each item on the Clipboard by repeatedly pressing the shortcut keys. See the "Organizing Code Snippets" section of this chapter for more information.
Edit.Delete	Edit ➤ Delete	Delete	Deletes one character to the right of the cursor.
Edit.Delete-Backwards		Backspace Shift+Backspace	Deletes one character to the left of the cursor.

(continued)

Table 1-1. General Shortcuts for Common Visual Studio Features (continued)

COMMAND	MENU	SHORTCUT	DESCRIPTION
Edit.Paste	Edit ➤ Paste	Ctrl+V Shift+Insert	Inserts the Clipboard contents at the insertion point.
Edit.Redo	Edit ➤ Redo	Ctrl+Shift+Z Ctrl+Y Shift+Alt+ Backspace	Restores the previously undone action.
Edit.Undo	Edit ➤ Undo	Alt+Backspace Ctrl+Z	Reverses the last editing action.
File.Print	File ➤ Print	Ctrl+P	Displays the Print dialog box, where you can choose printer settings.
File.SaveAll	File ➤ Save All	Ctrl+Shift+S	Saves all documents in the current solution.
File.Save- SelectedItems	File ➤ Save	Ctrl+S	Saves the selected items in the current project.
Tools.GoTo- CommandLine		Ctrl+/	Jumps to the Find/Command line on the standard toolbar and puts it in Command mode. See the "Using the Find/Command box" section earlier in this chapter for more information.
View.ViewCode	View ➤ Code	F7	When accessed from the Solution Explorer or the Design view of the editor, this displays the Code view.
View.ViewDesigner	View ➤ Designer	Shift+F7	When accessed from the Solution Explorer or the Code view of the editor, this displays the Design view.
View.FullScreen	View ➤ Full Screen	Shift+Alt+Enter	Toggles Full Screen mode on and off.
View.Navigate- Backward	View ➤ Navigate Backward	Ctrl+-	Goes back to the previous location in the navigation history. This is also accessible with the Navigate Backward button on the standard toolbar.

(continued)

Table 1-1. General Shortcuts for Common Visual Studio Features (continued)

COMMAND	MENU	SHORTCUT	DESCRIPTION
View.Navigate-Forward	View ➤ Navigate Forward	Ctrl+Shift+-	Moves forward to the location next in the navigation history. This is also accessible with the Navigate Forward button on the standard toolbar.
View.Web-NavigateBack	View ➤ Web Browser ➤ Back	Alt+Left Arrow	Displays the previous page in the viewing history. This is used most frequently to go back to a prior help topic when viewing help.
View.Web-NavigateForward	View ➤ Web Browser ➤ Forward	Alt+Right Arrow	Displays the next page in viewing history. This is used most frequently to go forward when viewing help.

Working with Controls Using Design View Shortcuts

Design view shortcut key combinations can be used to move, select, and change the size of controls on design surfaces, as shown in Table 1-2. They offer keyboard access to features that are not available on the menus and provide a way to work with controls without using the mouse.

Table 1-2. Design View Shortcuts for Designer Editing Features

COMMAND	SHORTCUT	DESCRIPTION
Edit.MoveControlDown	Ctrl+Down Arrow	Moves the selected control down in increments of one on the design surface.
Edit.MoveControlDownGrid	Down Arrow	Moves the selected control down by one grid unit on the design surface.
Edit.MoveControlLeft	Ctrl+Left Arrow	Moves the control to the left in increments of one on the design surface.
Edit.MoveControlLeftGrid	Left Arrow	Moves the control to the left by one grid unit on the design surface.

(continued)

Table 1-2. Design View Shortcuts for Designer Editing Features (continued)

COMMAND	SHORTCUT	DESCRIPTION
Edit.MoveControlRight	Ctrl+Right Arrow	Moves the control to the right in increments of one on the design surface.
Edit.MoveControlRightGrid	Right Arrow	Moves the control to the right by one grid unit on the design surface.
Edit.MoveControlUp	Ctrl+Up Arrow	Moves the control up in increments of one on the design surface.
Edit.MoveControlUpGrid	Up Arrow	Moves the control up by one grid unit on the design surface.
Edit.SelectNextControl	Tab	Moves to the next control on the page.
Edit.SelectPreviousControl	Shift+Tab	Moves back to the previously selected control on the page.
Edit.SizeControlDown	Ctrl+Shift+Down Arrow	Increases the height of the control in increments of one on the design surface.
Edit.SizeControlDownGrid	Shift+Down Arrow	Increases the height of the control by one grid unit on the design surface.
Edit.SizeControlLeft	Ctrl+Shift+Left Arrow	Reduces the width of the control in increments of one on the design surface.
Edit.SizeControlLeftGrid	Shift+Left Arrow	Reduces the width of the control by one grid unit on the design surface.
Edit.SizeControlRight	Ctrl+Shift+Right Arrow	Increases the width of the control in increments of one on the design surface.
Edit.SizeControlRightGrid	Shift+Left Arrow	Increases the width of the control by one grid unit on the design surface.
Edit.SizeControlUp	Ctrl+Shift+Up Arrow	Decreases the height of the control in increments of one on the design surface.
Edit.SizeControlUpGrid	Shift+Up Arrow	Decreases the height of the control by one grid unit on the design surface.

 **NOTE** All of the Grid commands, such as Edit.MoveControlUpGrid and Edit.SizeControlRightGrid, produce an "unavailable" message in the Forms Designer and do not move or size the controls, though the associated shortcut keys do work.

Using Text Editor Navigation Shortcuts

Text editor navigation shortcut key combinations can be used in the Code Editor to move within an open document. These shortcuts are shown in Table 1-3.

Table 1-3. Text Editor Navigation Shortcuts

COMMAND	SHORTCUT	DESCRIPTION
Edit.CharLeft	Left Arrow	Moves the cursor one character to the left.
Edit.CharRight	Right Arrow	Moves the cursor one character to the right.
Edit.DocumentEnd	Ctrl+End	Moves the insertion point to the end of the last line of the document.
Edit.DocumentStart	Ctrl+Home	Moves the insertion point to the beginning of the first line of the document.
Edit.GoTo	Ctrl+G	Displays the Go To Line dialog box.
Edit.GoToBrace	Ctrl+]	Moves the insertion point to the next brace in the document. This feature helps you to match the braces ({}) in your code. (C#)
Edit.LineDown	Down Arrow	Moves the cursor down one line.
Edit.LineEnd	End	Moves the cursor to the end of the current line.
Edit.LineStart	Home	Moves the cursor to the beginning of the line.
Edit.LineUp	Up Arrow	Moves the cursor up one line.
Edit.NextBookmark	Ctrl+K, Ctrl+N	Moves to the next bookmark in the document.

(continued)

Table 1-3. Text Editor Navigation Shortcuts (continued)

COMMAND	SHORTCUT	DESCRIPTION
Edit.PageDown	Page Down	Scrolls down one screen in the editor window.
Edit.PageUp	Page Up	Scrolls up one screen in the editor window.
Edit.PreviousBookmark	Ctrl+K, Ctrl+P	Moves to the previous bookmark.
Edit.QuickInfo	Ctrl+K, Ctrl+I	Displays Quick Info, based on the current language.
Edit.ScrollLineDown	Ctrl+Down Arrow	Scrolls text down one line.
Edit.ScrollLineUp	Ctrl+Up Arrow	Scrolls text up one line.
Edit.WordNext	Ctrl+Right Arrow	Moves the insertion point to the right one word.
Edit.WordPrevious	Ctrl+Left Arrow	Moves the insertion point to the left one word.

Selecting with Text Editor Selection Shortcuts

Text editor selection shortcut key combinations can be used in a Code Editor to select text within an open document. These shortcuts are shown in Table 1-4.

Table 1-4. Text Editor Selection Shortcuts

COMMAND	SHORTCUT	DESCRIPTION
Edit.CharLeftExtend	Shift+Left Arrow	Moves the cursor to the left one character, extending the selection.
Edit.CharRightExtend	Shift+Right Arrow	Moves the cursor to the right one character, extending the selection.
Edit.DocumentEndExtend	Ctrl+Shift+End	Selects the text from the insertion point to the end of the last line of the document.
Edit.DocumentStartExtend	Ctrl+Shift+Home	Selects the text from the insertion point to the beginning of the first line of the document.
Edit.GoToBraceExtend	Ctrl+Shift+]	Moves the insertion point to the next brace, extending the selection. (C#)

(continued)

Table 1-4. Text Editor Selection Shortcuts (continued)

COMMAND	SHORTCUT	DESCRIPTION
Edit.LineDownExtend	Shift+Down Arrow	Extends text selection down one line, starting at the location of the insertion point.
Edit.LineEndExtend	Shift+End	Selects text from the insertion point to the end of the current line.
Edit.LineStartExtend	Shift+Home	Selects text from the insertion point to the start of the line.
Edit.LineUpExtend	Shift+Up Arrow	Selects text up line by line starting from the location of the insertion point.
Edit.PageDownExtend	Shift+Page Down	Extends selection down one page.
Edit.PageUpExtend	Shift+Page Up	Extends selection up one page.
Edit.SelectAll	Ctrl+A	Selects everything in the current document.
Edit.SelectCurrentWord	Ctrl+W	Selects the word containing the insertion point or the word to the right of the insertion point.
Edit.SelectToLastGoBack	Ctrl+=	Selects from the current location in the editor back to the previous location in the editor.
Edit.ViewBottomExtend	Ctrl+Shift+Page Down	Moves the cursor to the last line in view, extending the selection.
Edit.ViewTopExtend	Ctrl+Shift+Page Up	Extends the selection to the top of the current window.
Edit.WordNextExtend	Ctrl+Shift+Right Arrow	Extends the selection one word to the right.
Edit.WordPreviousExtend	Ctrl+Shift+Left Arrow	Extends the selection one word to the left.

Using Text Editor Manipulation Shortcuts

Text editor manipulation shortcut key combinations can be used in a Code Editor to delete, move, or format text within an open document. These shortcuts are shown in Table 1-5.

Table 1-5. Text Editor Manipulation Shortcuts

COMMAND	SHORTCUT	DESCRIPTION
Edit.BreakLine	Enter Shift+Enter	Inserts a new line.
Edit.CharTranspose	Ctrl+T	Swaps the characters on either side of the insertion point. For example, AC|BD becomes AB|CD.
Edit.ClearBookmarks	Ctrl+K, Ctrl+L	Removes all unnamed bookmarks in the current document.
Edit.ColllapseToDefinitions	Ctrl+M, Ctrl+O	Automatically determines logical boundaries for creating regions in code, such as procedures, and then hides them.
Edit.CommentSelection	Ctrl+K, Ctrl+C	Marks the current line of code as a comment, using the correct comment syntax for the programming language.
Edit.CompleteWord	Alt+Right Arrow Ctrl+Spacebar	Displays Word Completion based on the current language.
Edit.DeleteHorizontal-Whitespace	Ctrl+K, Ctrl+\	Collapses white space in the selection, or deletes white space adjacent to the cursor if there is no selection.
Edit.FormatDocument	Ctrl+K, Ctrl+D	Applies the indenting and space formatting for the language as specified in the Options dialog box. You can change the formatting using Tools ➤ Options, opening the Text Editor folder, selecting the desired programming language, and then selecting the Format item (C#).

(continued)

Table 1-5. Text Editor Manipulation Shortcuts (continued)

COMMAND	SHORTCUT	DESCRIPTION
Edit.FormatSelection	Ctrl+K, Ctrl+F	Indents the selected lines of code based on the surrounding lines of code. In most cases, VB does this when you leave the line. This is more useful in C#.
Edit.HideSelection	Ctrl+M, Ctrl+H	Hides the selected text. A signal icon marks the location of the hidden text in the file.
Edit.InsertTab	Tab	Indents the line of text a specified number of spaces, such as four. You can set the number of spaces for a tab by selecting Tools ➤ Options, opening the Text Editor folder, selecting the desired programming language, and then choosing the Tabs item.
Edit.LineCut	Ctrl+L	Cuts all selected lines, or the current line if nothing has been selected, to the Clipboard. Note that this does not put the cut text onto the Clipboard Ring.
Edit.LineDelete	Ctrl+Shift+L	Deletes all selected lines, or the current line if nothing has been selected.
Edit.LineOpenAbove	Ctrl+Enter	Inserts a blank line above the insertion point.
Edit.LineOpenBelow	Ctrl+Shift+Enter	Inserts a blank line below the insertion point.
Edit.LineTranspose	Shift+Alt+T	Moves the line containing the insertion point below the next line.
Edit.MakeLowercase	Ctrl+U	Changes the selected text to lowercase characters. If no text is selected, changes the character after the insertion point.

(continued)

Table 1-5. Text Editor Manipulation Shortcuts (continued)

COMMAND	SHORTCUT	DESCRIPTION
Edit.MakeUppercase	Ctrl+Shift+U	Changes the selected text to uppercase characters. If no text is selected, changes the character after the insertion point.
Edit.OverTypeMode	Insert	Toggles between insert and overtype insertion modes.
Edit.StopHidingCurrent	Ctrl+M, Ctrl+U	Removes the outlining information for the currently selected region.
Edit.StopOutlining	Ctrl+M, Ctrl+P	Removes all outlining information from the entire document.
Edit.SwapAnchor	Ctrl+R, Ctrl+P	Swaps the anchor and end points of the current selection.
Edit.TabLeft	Shift+Tab	Moves selected lines to the left one tab stop.
Edit.ToggleAllOutlining	Ctrl+M, Ctrl+L	Toggles all previously marked hidden text sections between hidden and display states.
Edit.ToggleBookmark	Ctrl+K, Ctrl+K	Sets or removes a bookmark at the current line.
Edit.ToggleOutliningExpansion	Ctrl+M, Ctrl+M	Toggles the currently selected hidden text section between the hidden and display state.
Edit.ToggleTaskListShortcut	Ctrl+K, Ctrl+H	Sets or removes a shortcut at the current line.
Edit.ToggleWordWrap	Ctrl +R, Ctrl+R	Enables or disables word wrap in an editor.
Edit.UncommentSelection	Ctrl+K, Ctrl+U	Removes the comment syntax from the current line of code.
Edit.ViewWhiteSpace	Ctrl+R, Ctrl+W	Shows or hides spaces and tab marks.
Edit.WordDeleteToEnd	Ctrl+Delete	Deletes the word to the right of the insertion point.

(continued)

Table 1-5. Text Editor Manipulation Shortcuts (continued)

COMMAND	SHORTCUT	DESCRIPTION
Edit.WordDeleteToStart	Ctrl+Backspace	Deletes the word to the left of the insertion point.
Edit.WordTranspose	Ctrl+Shift+T	Transposes the words on either side of the insertion point. For example, End Sub would be changed to read Sub End.

Searching with Find Shortcuts

The shortcut key combinations shown in Table 1-6 can be used with the Find, Replace, Find in Files, and Replace in Files features. See the "Finding Code" section in this chapter for more information about using the Find features in Visual Studio.

Table 1-6. Find Shortcuts

COMMAND	SHORTCUT	DESCRIPTION
Edit.Find	Ctrl+F	Displays the Find dialog box.
Edit.FindInFiles	Ctrl+Shift+F	Displays the Find in Files dialog box.
Edit.FindNext	F3	Finds the next occurrence of the previous search text.
Edit.Find-NextSelected	Ctrl+F3	Finds the next occurrence of the currently selected text in the document.
Edit.FindPrevious	Shift+F3	Finds the previous occurrence of the search text.
Edit.FindPreviousSelected	Ctrl+Shift+F3	Finds the previous occurrence of the currently selected text, or the word at the insertion point.
Edit.GoToFindCombo	Ctrl+D	Jumps to the Find/Command line on the standard toolbar. See the "Using the Find/Command box" section earlier in this chapter for more information.
Edit.HiddenText	Alt+F3, H	Selects or clears the Search Hidden Text option in the Find dialog box.

(continued)

Table 1-6. Find Shortcuts (continued)

COMMAND	SHORTCUT	DESCRIPTION
Edit.IncrementalSearch	Ctrl+I	Starts an incremental search. If an incremental search is started, but you have not typed any characters, recalls the previous pattern. If text has been found, searches for the next occurrence.
Edit.MatchCase	Alt+F3, C	Selects or clears the Match Case option for Find and Replace operations.
Edit.RegularExpression	Alt+F3, R	Selects or clears the Regular Expression option so that special characters can be used in Find and Replace operations.
Edit.Replace	Ctrl+H	Displays the Replace dialog box.
Edit.ReplaceInFiles	Ctrl+Shift+H	Displays the Replace in Files dialog box.
Edit.Reverse-IncrementalSearch	Ctrl+Shift+I	Changes the direction of an incremental search to progress from the current insertion point toward the top.
Edit.StopSearch	Alt+F3, S	Halts the current Find in Files operation.
Edit.Up	Alt+F3, B	Selects or clears the Search Up option for Find and Replace operations.
Edit.WholeWord	Alt+F3, W	Selects or clears the Match Whole Word option for Find and Replace operations.
Edit.Wildcard	Alt+F3, P	Selects or clears the Wildcard option for Find and Replace operations.

Debugging Code with Shortcuts

The shortcut key combinations in Table 1-7 can be used while debugging code, see also "Expanding Your Debugging Techniques" in Chapter 3.

Table 1-7. Debugging Shortcuts

COMMAND	SHORTCUT	DESCRIPTION
Debug.Autos	Ctrl+Alt+V, A	Displays the Auto window to view the values of variables currently in the scope of the current line of execution within the current procedure.
Debug.BreakAll	Ctrl+Alt+Break	Temporarily stops execution of all processes in a debugging session. Available only in Run mode.
Debug.Breakpoints	Ctrl+Alt+B	Displays the Breakpoints dialog box, where you can add and modify breakpoints.
Debug.CallStack	Ctrl+Alt+C	Displays the Call Stack window to display a list of all active procedures or stack frames for the current thread of execution. Available only in Run mode.
Debug.ClearAll-Breakpoints	Ctrl+Shift+F9	Clears all of the breakpoints in the project.
Debug.Disassembly	Ctrl+Alt+D	Displays the Disassembly window.
Debug.EnableBreakpoint	Ctrl+F9	Sets a breakpoint at the current line of code.
Debug.Exceptions	Ctrl+Alt+E	Displays the Exceptions dialog box.
Debug.Immediate	Ctrl+Alt+I	Displays the Immediate window, where you can evaluate expressions and execute individual commands.
Debug.Locals	Ctrl+Alt+V, L	Displays the Locals window to view the variables and their values for each procedure in the current stack frame.
Debug.Memory1	Ctrl+Alt+M, 1	Displays the Memory 1 window to view large buffers, strings, and other data that do not display clearly in the Watch or Variables window.
Debug.Memory2	Ctrl+Alt+M, 2	Displays the Memory 2 window to view large buffers, strings, and other data that do not display clearly in the Watch or Variables window.

(continued)

Table 1-7. Debugging Shortcuts (continued)

COMMAND	SHORTCUT	DESCRIPTION
Debug.Memory3	Ctrl+Alt+M, 3	Displays the Memory 3 window to view large buffers, strings, and other data that do not display clearly in the Watch or Variables window.
Debug.Memory4	Ctrl+Alt+M, 4	Displays the Memory 4 window to view large buffers, strings, and other data that do not display clearly in the Watch or Variables window.
Debug.Modules	Ctrl+Alt+U	Displays the Modules window, which allows you to view the .dll or .exe files used by the program. In multiprocess debugging, you can right-click and select Show Modules for All Programs.
Debug.NewBreakpoint	Ctrl+B	Inserts or clears a breakpoint in the current line of code.
Debug.QuickWatch	Ctrl+Alt+Q	Displays the Quick Watch dialog box with the current value of the selected expression. Available only in Break mode. Use this command to check the current value of a variable, property, or other expression for which you have not defined a watch expression.
Debug.Registers	Ctrl+Alt+G	Displays the Registers window, which displays registers content for debugging native code applications.
Debug.Restart	Ctrl+Shift+F5	Terminates a debugging session, rebuilds, and then starts running the application from the beginning. Available in Break and Run modes.
Debug.Running-Documents	Ctrl+Alt+N	Displays the Running Documents window that shows the set of documents that you are in the process of debugging. Available in Run mode.

(continued)

Table 1-7. Debugging Shortcuts (continued)

COMMAND	SHORTCUT	DESCRIPTION
Debug.RunToCursor	Ctrl+F10	In Break mode, resumes execution of your code from the current statement to the selected statement. The Current Line of Execution margin indicator appears in the Margin Indicator bar. In Design mode, starts the debugger and executes your code to the cursor location.
Debug.SetNextStatement	Ctrl+Shift+F10	Sets the execution point to the line of code you choose.
Debug.Show-NextStatement	Alt+NUM * (asterisk on the number keypad)	Highlights the next statement to be executed.
Debug.Start	F5	Automatically attaches the debugger and runs the application from the startup project specified in the Project Properties dialog box. Changes to Continue if in Break mode.
Debug.Start-WithoutDebugging	Ctrl+F5	Runs the code without invoking the debugger.
Debug.StepInto	F11	Executes code one statement at a time, following execution into function calls.
Debug.StepOut	Shift+F11	Executes the remaining lines of a function in which the current execution point lies.
Debug.StepOver	F10	Executes the next line of code, but does not follow execution through any function calls.
Debug.StopDebugging	Shift+F5	Stops running the current application in the program. Available in Break and Run modes.
Debug.This	Ctrl+Alt+V, T	Displays the This window (C#) or Me window (VB), which allows you to view the data members of the object associated with the current method.
Debug.Threads	Ctrl+Alt+H	Displays the Threads window to view all of the threads for the current process and information about them.

(continued)

Table 1-7. Debugging Shortcuts (continued)

COMMAND	SHORTCUT	DESCRIPTION
Debug.ToggleBreakpoint	F9	Sets or removes a breakpoint at the current line.
Debug.ToggleDisassembly	Ctrl+F11	Displays the disassembly information for the current source file. Available only in Break mode.
Debug.Watch1	Ctrl+Alt+W, 1	Displays the Watch 1 window to view the values of selected variables or watch expressions.
Debug.Watch2	Ctrl+Alt+W, 2	Displays the Watch 2 window to view the values of selected variables or watch expressions.
Debug.Watch3	Ctrl+Alt+W, 3	Displays the Watch 3 window to view the values of selected variables or watch expressions.
Debug.Watch4	Ctrl+Alt+W, 4	Displays the Watch 4 window to view the values of selected variables or watch expressions.
Tools.DebugProcesses	Ctrl+Alt+P	Displays the Processes dialog box, which allows you to debug multiple programs at the same time in a single solution.

Using Visual Database Tool Shortcuts

The shortcut key combinations shown in Table 1-8 can be used with the Database Designer and Query Designer.

Table 1-8. Visual Database Tool Shortcuts for Working with the Database Designer and Query Designer

COMMAND	SHORTCUT	DESCRIPTION
Database.Run	Ctrl+E	Runs the currently active database object.
Database.RunSelection	Ctrl+Q	Runs the current selection in the SQL editor.
Database.StepInto	Alt+F5	Steps into Debug mode for the currently active database object.

(continued)

Table 1-8. Visual Database Tool Shortcuts for Working with the Database Designer and Query Designer (continued)

COMMAND	SHORTCUT	DESCRIPTION
Query.Run	Ctrl+R	Executes the query. Available only in the Query Designer.
View.Diagram	Ctrl+1	Displays the Diagram pane of the Query Designer. Available only in the Query Designer.
View.Grid	Ctrl+2	Displays the Grid pane of the Query Designer. Available only in the Query Designer.
View.Results	Ctrl+4	Displays the Results pane of the Query Designer. Available only in the Query Designer.
View.SQL	Ctrl+3	Displays the SQL pane of the Query Designer. Available only in the Query Designer.

Using Help Shortcuts

The shortcut key combinations shown in Table 1-9 can be used to view and move among help topics.

Table 1-9. The Help Shortcuts

COMMAND	SHORTCUT	DESCRIPTION
Help.Contents	Ctrl+Alt+F1	Displays the Contents window for the documentation contained in MSDN.
Help.DynamicHelp	Ctrl+F1	Displays the Dynamic Help window, which displays different topics depending on what items currently have focus in the product.
Help.F1Help	F1	Displays a topic from help that corresponds to the current selection.
Help.Index	Ctrl+Alt+F2	Displays the Index window for the documentation contained in MSDN.

(continued)

Table 1-9. The Help Shortcuts (continued)

COMMAND	SHORTCUT	DESCRIPTION
Help.Indexresults	Shift+Alt+F2	Displays the Index Results window, which lists the topics that contain the keyword selected in the Index window.
Help.Nexttopic	Alt+Down Arrow	Displays the next topic in the table of contents.
Help.Previoustopic	Alt+Up Arrow	Displays the previous topic in the table of contents.
Help.Search	Ctrl+Alt+F3	Displays the Search window, which allows you to search for words or phrases in the documentation contained in MSDN.
Help.Searchresults	Shift+Alt+F3	Displays the Search Results window, which displays a list of topics that contain the string searched for from the Search window.
Help.WindowHelp	Shift+F1	Displays a topic from help that corresponds to the current user interface selected.

Executing Visual Studio Commands

The fewer times you need to take your hands off the keyboard and use the mouse, the more efficient you can be. To aid you with this goal, Visual Studio provides direct access to most features of the system through commands accessible from the keyboard. Commands can do everything from searching the help system to moving controls around in a designer.

The commands are defined in a *subject.feature* format, such as Help.WindowHelp and Edit.MoveControlDown. Some common commands are included in the shortcut key tables presented in the previous "Using Shortcut Keys" section, but there are many more. You can find the list of all available commands by selecting Tools ➤ Options, opening the Environment folder, and then selecting the Keyboard item (as shown earlier in Figure 1-23).

Commands are often easier to use than their corresponding shortcut keys. Shortcut keys require memorization, whereas commands are discoverable and the tools for entry of the commands support IntelliSense.

NOTE The IntelliSense for the commands is not based on the context, meaning that all of the commands are always shown, even if they don't make sense in a particular context. If you select a command that is not available based on your context, a message is displayed in the status bar.

The Find/Command box in the standard toolbar, shown in Figure 1-24, provides a quick way to execute commands. Jump to the Find/Command box and put it into Command mode by pressing Ctrl+/, or click in the Find/Command box and put it into Command mode manually by typing a greater than symbol (>). Then type in a command subject, such as Edit, and IntelliSense will list the many Edit commands available for you.

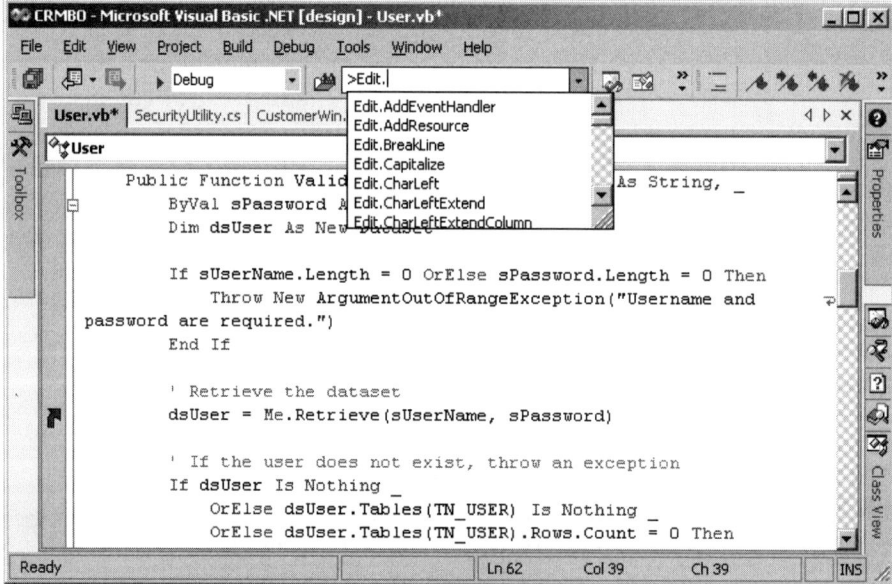

Figure 1-24. The Find/Command box interprets entered text strings as commands if they are prefixed with the greater than character (>).

The Command mode of the Command window provides an editing window for your commands, as shown in Figure 1-25. To put the Command window into Command mode, type >cmd or open the window in Command mode by pressing Ctrl+Alt+A. To toggle the Command window back to Immediate mode for debugging, type immed.

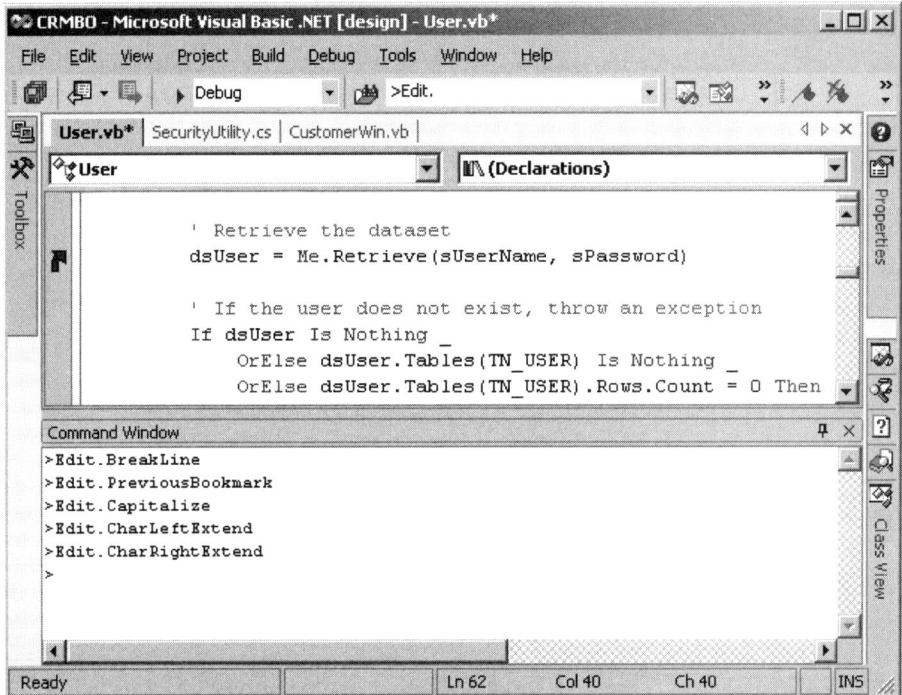

Figure 1-25. The Command window allows you to enter sets of commands and arrow up and down to reexecute any of the commands.

Some commands provide a wealth of arguments, options, and switches. To view the help topic listing the valid syntax available for a command, type /? after the command. For example, typing >`Edit.FindinFiles/?` will display the help topic with the options available for the Edit.FindinFiles command.

By using switches, you can bypass any dialog box associated with the command. To try this, type >`Edit.FindinFiles`, and you'll see that the Find in Files dialog box is displayed. But, if you type in the full set of options and switches, the command will execute without displaying the Find in Files dialog box. The following command will find the text *dataset* as a whole word in all files with a .vb extension without displaying the Find in Files dialog box:

```
>Edit.FindinFiles dataset /ext:*.vb /w
```

Visual Studio comes with a set of aliases that provide shortcuts to the commands. For example, ? is a shortcut for the Debug.Print command. For example, when debugging an application, type >`? sConnection` to display the contents of the sConnection variable.

 **NOTE** You must put a space after the question mark character for the alias to work correctly when in Command mode.

To view the list of available aliases, type >`alias` as the command. Create your own aliases for commands that you use frequently or change predefined aliases using the Alias command with appropriate parameters. For example, to create an alias of `mvd` for the Edit.MoveControlDown command, you would enter the following command:

```
>alias mvd Edit.MoveControlDown
```

Using commands, instead of menu options or mouse movements, provides quick access to the features of Visual Studio, thereby increasing your productivity.

Accessing External Tools

Although Visual Studio can do a lot, you can further expand its abilities using external tools. You can find many helpful (and often free) external tools at web sites such as `sourceforge.net` or `gotdotnet.com`. The good news is that you can hook any external tool into Visual Studio, so you don't need to leave the comfort of the IDE to access them.

Add an external tool to Visual Studio by selecting Tools ➤ External Tools from the menu. The External Tools dialog box is displayed, as shown in Figure 1-26. In this dialog box, enter a title for use in the Visual Studio Tools menu and define the associated command to execute the desired tool. You can even add parameters and switches to the command line and define arguments.

For example, to add the NUnit test tool (`http://sourceforge.net/projects/nunit`) to the Visual Studio IDE, specify a title of **NUnit Testing Tool** and the following command:

```
C:\Program Files\Nunit V2.0\bin\nunit-gui.exe
```

The Visual Studio Tools menu will then contain the NUnit Testing Tool option. Selecting this option will execute the NUnit testing tool.

Hooking external tools directly into Visual Studio makes them easier to access and expands the capabilities of IDE.

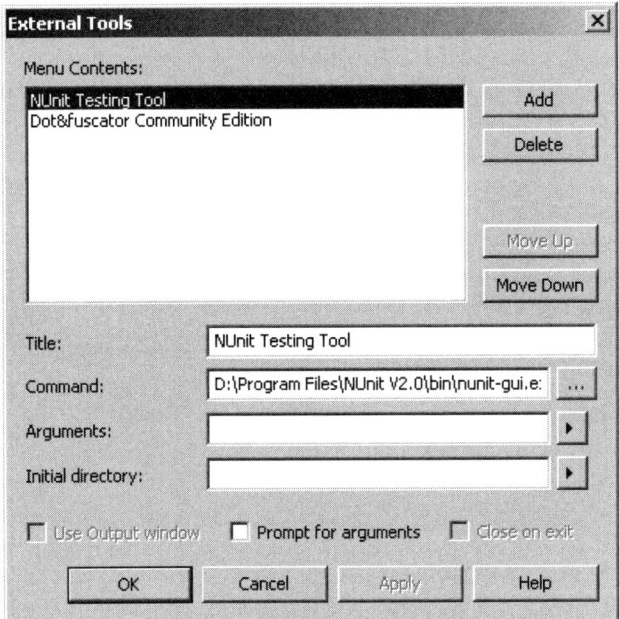

Figure 1-26. The External Tools dialog box allows you to insert external tools into the Visual Studio Tools menu, such as a unit testing tool.

What Did This Chapter Cover?

There are many hidden treasures that can improve how you work with Visual Studio and make you more productive.

You can save time in switching between windows by laying out your windows as effectively as possible. You can keep a snippet library to quickly insert commonly used routines or comment blocks into your application. The Task List window provides many features for managing your set of coding tasks and tracking those that are incomplete, making your task management more efficient.

You can use one of the 12 different techniques to rapidly find a specific location in your code. You can use shortcut keys and Visual Studio commands to quickly access the Visual Studio features that you need. And you can hook external tools into Visual Studio to provide easy access to those tools without leaving Visual Studio.

The next chapter looks at secrets for working with Windows Forms.

Doing Windows Forms

IF YOU ARE DOING Windows Forms applications with .NET, you know the basics of building forms. You know how to use the basic controls, such as text boxes and labels. You know how to put the controls on the forms and write code to access the controls.

The purpose of this chapter is to present some of the lesser-known Windows Forms features. You may already be familiar with some of these treasures because they are reasonably discoverable. Others, such as how to draw a simple line when there is no line control, are buried treasures that are much harder to discover.

What Will This Chapter Cover?

This chapter uncovers the following Windows Forms secrets:

- Docking for better layout

- Anchoring for better resizing

- Aligning for a clean look

- Editing controls with the keyboard

- Centering a form without using code

- Iterating through the controls on a form

- Implementing Enter and Leave events

- Leveraging the DialogResult property

- Drawing simple lines

- Resizing controls for contents

- Displaying validation errors with the ErrorProvider control

By the end of this chapter, you will know the secrets of how to do more with Windows Forms.

Using the Windows Forms Designer, you will discover how to apply docking and anchoring to enable end-user resizing of your forms without writing a single line of code. You will be able to improve the visual aesthetics of your forms using the alignment features. You will see how to edit controls on the Windows Forms Designer without moving your hands from the keyboard, and you will learn how to center a form without writing code.

But there are some Windows Forms features for which you do need to write code. You will see how to use recursion to iterate through all of the controls on your form. You will learn how to implement Enter and Leave events on controls to highlight the active control. You will discover how the DialogResult property can help you work with dialog boxes. You will observe the code you need to write to draw simple lines and resize controls to the size of their contents. Finally, you will see how to display validation errors using the ErrorProvider control.

Docking for Better Layout

Docking defines how a control will be attached to its container, such as a form or panel. You can dock a control to the edges of your form (or other container control) or have it fill the entire container.

The primary use of docking is to separate a form into sections to make it easier for the end user to work with the form. For example, you can dock a TreeView or ListView control to the left edge of the form. You can then fill the remainder of the form with a Panel control containing details of the item selected in the TreeView or ListView control. Since the controls are docked, they will remain attached to the defined edge of the form and will automatically resize as the form is sized.

Figure 2-1 provides an example of another common scenario, where the end user makes a selection, and then reviews or edits the information pertaining to that selection. In this case, a panel was docked to the top of the form to contain the controls for end user selection. Specifically, the end user selects the company name of the customer to review or edit. Other selection criteria could be added to this panel. A second panel was docked to fill the remainder of the form and is used to display the details of the selected entry, which is the information for the selected customer. Using panels in this situation provides a visual separation of the selection criteria from the display results, making the form easier to work with for the end user.

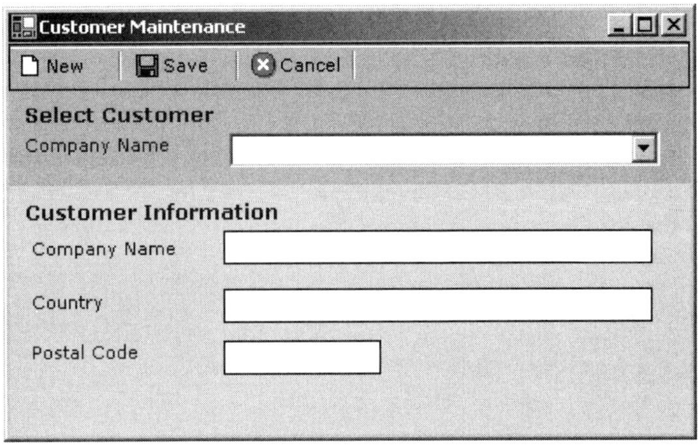

Figure 2-1. This form has one panel docked to the top and another panel filling in the remainder of the form to provide visual separation of selection criteria and the details displayed based on the selection.

To set the docking for a particular control, select the control and use the Dock property in the Properties window. The value of the Dock property is set using a graphic that shows how the control will be docked. The selections allow for Left, Right, Top, Bottom, and Fill. You can also select None to remove any docking.

NOTE If you add another docked control to your form later, you may need to undock some of the existing controls by setting their docking to None before adding the new control, especially if one of the existing controls is docked to fill the form.

TIP If you have a lot of panels on your form, you may want to set the background color of each of them to a different color during development, so you can work with them more easily in the designer.

Anchoring for Better Resizing

Anchoring defines how a control will be resized and repositioned as its container is resized at runtime. The primary use of anchoring is to provide automatic resizing and repositioning of controls as the end user resizes a form. If your form has a fixed size, no anchoring is required.

You can anchor controls in any combination of the four directions: left, right, top, or bottom. When a control is anchored in a particular direction, the control remains a predefined distance from the container in that direction. For example, when a control is anchored to the left, the left side of the control will remain a predefined distance from the left side of the container. That will keep the control in the same basic position as the form is resized.

More interesting, however, is anchoring to the right. When a control is anchored to the right, the right side of the control will remain a predefined distance from the right side of the container. When the container is resized horizontally, the control will be repositioned such that the space between the right edge of the control and the right edge of the container will remain constant. A control anchored to both the left and the right will automatically expand or contract to keep its left and right edges the same distance from the left and right edge of its container when the container is resized horizontally.

Anchoring to the top or bottom of the form works similarly. However, not all controls can expand vertically. For example, a TextBox control is a fixed height based on the font (unless you define it to be multiline). So, if you anchor a TextBox to the top and bottom, the control will not expand vertically.

To set the anchoring for a particular control, select the control and use the Anchor property in the Properties window. The value of the Anchor property is set using a graphic that shows how the control will be anchored. The property allows you to select any combination of Left, Right, Top, or Bottom. Deselect in each direction for no anchoring.

TIP For many properties, such as the Anchor property, you can set the property for multiple controls simultaneously by selecting the set of controls, and then setting the property.

Figure 2-2 presents an anchoring example. The first TextBox control (Company Name) is anchored to the top, left, and right, so it grew as the form was enlarged. The second TextBox control (Country) is anchored to the top and right, so it moved to the right as the form was enlarged. The third TextBox control (Postal Code) is anchored to the bottom and left, so it moved down as the form was enlarged.

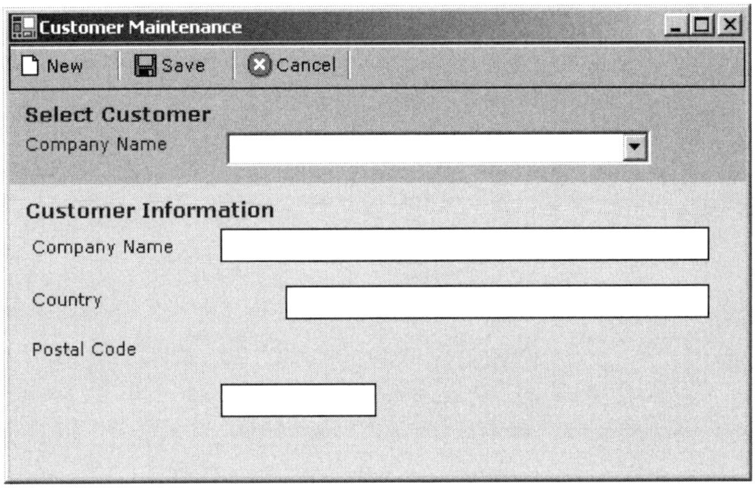

Figure 2-2. All of the TextBox controls on this form started at the same left margin, but have different values for the Anchor property, so they moved differently when the form was resized.

A single screenshot cannot really demonstrate anchoring. The best way to understand how anchoring works is to try it. Add some controls to a form and try different settings for the anchoring values.

Combine docking and anchoring by docking panels to divide the form, like the two panels shown in Figure 2-2. Then anchor the combo boxes, text boxes, and other controls that reside on the panels to define how those controls should resize when the panel is resized. The resulting form is easier for end users to work with, and allows the end users to size the form to match their preferences and working style.

Aligning for a Clean Look

Aligning assists you with laying out the controls on your forms in a consistent manner. Use the alignment options to align all of the labels, align all of the controls, and align each control with its associated label. This gives your forms a cleaner, more professional look.

The many options provided to assist you with alignment are located on the Format menu. Select two or more controls to align by holding down the Ctrl key as you click each control, and then select the desired alignment option. The alignment will always be with respect to the last-selected control. This is shown visually with black (instead of white) sizing handles, as illustrated in Figure 2-3.

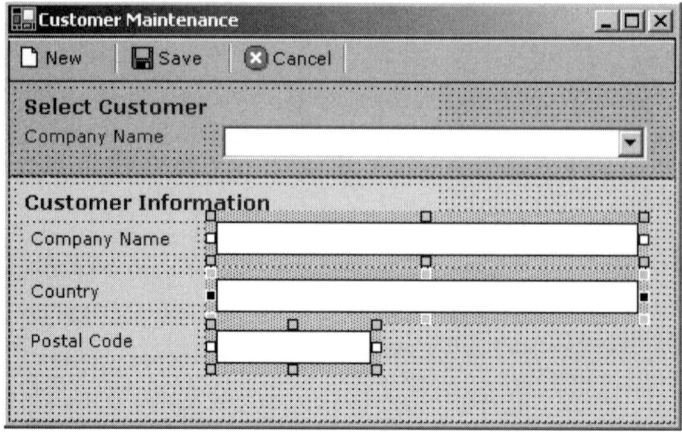

Figure 2-3. The last control selected in this form was the TextBox control associated with the Country label. Notice how its sizing handles are different from the handles of the other two selected TextBox controls.

The following Format menu options are useful for aligning controls:

- **Format ➤ Align:** Use these options to line up a set of controls with the left, right, center, top, middle, or bottom of the last-selected control, or to align the controls to the grid. The alignment options are valuable for aligning a set of controls to the left so they appear vertically aligned, as shown in Figure 2-3. The Align Middle option is useful for aligning the middle of a label with the middle of its associated data-entry control, such as a TextBox control.

> **TIP** Many controls, including labels, also have a TextAlign property that allows you to define how text should be aligned within the control. To align text within a Label control so it appears centered with its associated data-entry control, set the TextAlign property to MiddleLeft.

- **Format ➤ Make Same Size:** Use these options to consistently size controls. This also aids in giving a form a clean look. However, don't make the controls the same size if that does not make sense from the end user's perspective. For example, in Figure 2-3, the Postal Code text box is not the same size as the other text boxes because the content is much shorter.

- **Format ➤ Horizontal Spacing:** Use these options to set a consistent horizontal space between the controls.

- **Format ➤ Vertical Spacing:** Use these options to set a consistent vertical space between the controls. Since most forms are laid out in a vertical style, such as the one shown in Figure 2-3, the consistency of the vertical spacing is frequently more important than the horizontal spacing.

- **Format ➤ Center in Form:** Use these options to center a set of controls either vertically or horizontally within the form.

The alignment options don't make the coding any easier or the form easier to work with for the end user, just as combing your hair and polishing your shoes do not impact how well you code. But using alignment does add professionalism and visual appeal to the look of the forms, and provides a sense that care was taken in the development of the application.

Editing Controls with the Keyboard

The Windows Forms Designer is a very visual tool, which makes it easy to work with and easy to see your results. But sometimes, you may want to do some quick editing of the controls in the designer without needing to use the mouse. You'll be glad to know that most features for working with the controls are available on the keyboard through shortcut keys, Visual Studio commands, or both.

For example, move a control on the form from the keyboard by pressing Ctrl+an arrow key. Or use Visual Studio commands in the Find/Command box by pressing Ctrl+/ to move the cursor to the Find/Command box, and then typing **Edit** to see the list of available editing commands. See the "Using Shortcut Keys" and "Executing Visual Studio Commands" sections in Chapter 1 for more information about some of the most common shortcut keys and Visual Studio commands.

Centering a Form Without Using Code

The code for centering a form on the screen or over another form is not that difficult, but why write code at all if you can use form properties?

Using the StartPosition property of a form in the Properties window (or in code), you can define that a form should be positioned centered on the screen or centered on a parent form. Or, you can define that the form should be positioned in its Windows default location, which will place the form shifted slightly down and to the right of the last-displayed form.

Iterating Through the Controls on a Form

There are many reasons why you may want to iterate through all of the controls on a form. You may want to move all of the controls due to a user action, resize each control to its contents at runtime, or set a particular property for the controls at runtime, for example.

The seemingly obvious (but potentially incorrect) solution for iterating through the controls on the form is as follows:

In VB:

```
For Each ctrl As Control In me.Controls
    ' Do whatever here
Next
```

In C#:

```
foreach (Control ctrl in this.Controls)
{
    // Do whatever here
}
```

This code iterates through all of the controls *on* the form. But this won't always iterate through all of the controls that appear on the form, because all of those controls may not technically be *on* the form.

For example, Figure 2-4 displays a form that contains two Panel controls. The first Panel control contains a Toolbar control, two Label controls, and a ComboBox control. The second Panel control contains four Label controls and three TextBox controls. The form itself contains only the two Panel controls.

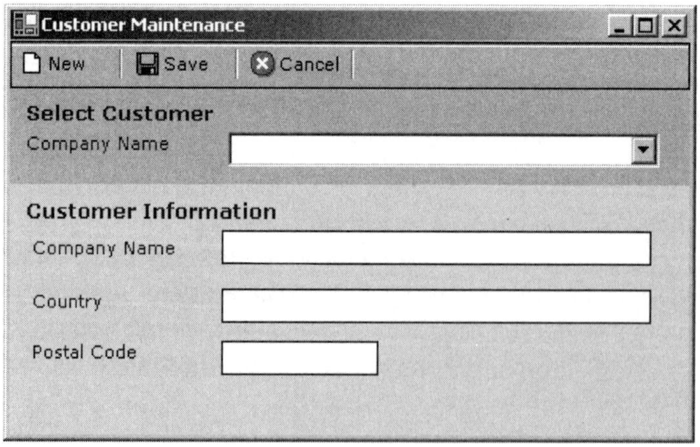

Figure 2-4. Even though all of the controls look like they are on the form, only the two panels actually reside on the form. All of the other controls reside on one of the two panels.

The prior sample code will process only the two Panel controls, because those are the only controls actually on the form, and therefore the only controls in the form's controls collection. To confirm this for yourself, add that sample code to a form with controls on panels (as in Figure 2-4), put a breakpoint in the loop, and display me.Controls.Count or this.Controls.Count.

To ensure that you process every control that appears on the form, you need to add the code that iterates through the controls to a method and call the method recursively for each control that contains other (child) controls.

In VB:

```vb
Private Sub MyMethod(ByVal pnl As Control)
    For Each ctrl As Control In pnl.Controls
        ' Do whatever here

        If ctrl.HasChildren Then
            MyMethod(ctrl)
        End If
    Next
End Sub
```

In C#:

```csharp
private void MyMethod(Control pnl)
{
    foreach (Control ctrl in pnl.Controls)
    {
        // Do whatever here
        if (ctrl.HasChildren)
        {
            MyMethod(ctrl);
        }
    }
}
```

These routines use the HasChildren property of each control to determine if the control contains other controls. If so, it recursively calls the method to process the child controls. This code will then process every control that appears on the form. If more controls are added later, those controls will also be processed.

Use this technique whenever you want to iterate through all of the controls that appear on a form when you have controls that contain other controls, such as Panel, GroupBox, or Tab controls.

Implementing Enter and Leave Events

An often-requested feature in applications is to change the background color of the control that has focus. This highlights the active control for the end user. When a form has many controls, this feature allows the end users to more easily see where they are on the form.

This feature is best implemented using the Enter and Leave events for the controls. When the user enters the control, the background color is changed to a defined value. When the user leaves the control, the background color is changed back to the Windows standard color.

The following sections take you through the process of implementing the Enter and Leave events.

An Introduction to Event Procedures

If you are new to .NET, it is important to understand how event procedures work. Applications written using .NET are *event-driven*; that is, they execute based on a response to an event. For example, when the user clicks a button, the application receives a Click event. The code that is written to respond to an event is called an *event procedure* or *event handler*.

You can write an event procedure to respond to any event generated by a control. For example, you can write an event procedure to respond to the TextChanged or Enter event for a TextBox control or the Click event for a Button control.

To write a procedure that responds to an event generated by a control, you must do the following:

- Write the procedure. The event procedure contains the code you wish to execute when a specific event occurs.

- Wire up the procedure to the appropriate control(s) and event(s). The process of wiring up the procedure to the desired control and event ensures that the code is executed when the event occurs.

The "Implementing Enter and Leave Events" section in this chapter demonstrates how to write procedures to respond to the Enter and Leave events. You can use this information as a guide for writing procedures that respond to any events.

Writing the Enter and Leave Event Procedures

To meet the objective of changing the background color of the control that has focus, you need to write event procedures for the Enter and Leave events. In these procedures, you need to change the background color of the control.

In VB:

```
Private Sub txt_Enter(ByVal sender As Object, _
    ByVal e As System.EventArgs)
    DirectCast(sender, TextBox).BackColor = Color.BlanchedAlmond
End Sub
```

```
Private Sub txt_Leave(ByVal sender As Object, _
    ByVal e As System.EventArgs)
    DirectCast(sender, TextBox).BackColor = _
        Color.FromKnownColor(KnownColor.Window)
End Sub
```

In C#:

```
private void txt_Enter(object sender, System.EventArgs e)
{
    TextBox tb = (TextBox)sender;
    tb.BackColor = Color.BlanchedAlmond;
}
```

```
private void txt_Leave(object sender, System.EventArgs e)
{
    TextBox tb = (TextBox)sender;
    tb.BackColor = Color.FromKnownColor(KnownColor.Window);
}
```

The control that generated the event is passed as an object, represented by sender, to the event procedure. Since sender is defined as an object, it has only the properties and methods defined for an object. To access the properties and methods of the actual control, you need to cast the sender object to the correct control data type. In this example, the code is specifically designed to work with TextBox controls. It could be revised to work with any type of control.

The DirectCast statement in the above VB code casts the sender object to a TextBox control. The BackColor property of the TextBox control is then accessible and is set to the desired color.

TIP   The VB DirectCast statement performs better than using CType when casting from an object. See the "Improving Type Casting" section in Chapter 3 for more information about DirectCast.

In C#, the casting is done using the C# casting operator: ( ). After the control is cast to a TextBox control, the code sets the TextBox control's background color.

TIP   With C#, if there is a possibility that the casting will result in a cast exception, use the as operator instead. The as operator will yield a null on a conversion failure, instead of raising an exception. See the "Improving Type Casting" section in Chapter 3 for more information about the as operator.

The Color object from the System.Drawing namespace is used to set the BackColor property of the TextBox control to blanched almond when the end user enters the control. This highlights the control, making it easier for the end user to see which control has focus.

When the end user leaves the control, you could set the BackColor property to white, but this would not take into consideration the end user's Windows scheme. The end user can set the Windows scheme such that the window color, used for the background color of TextBox controls, is something other than white. To ensure that the BackColor property of the TextBox control is set to the appropriate end user-defined Windows scheme color, use the FromKnownColor method of the Color object.

The event procedures in these code examples won't execute at this point because this code is not yet wired up to any control or event. You need to associate the appropriate control(s) and event(s) with each event procedure. After the event procedures are wired up, they will be executed when a defined control's event occurs. In this example, the txt_Enter procedure will be wired up to the Enter event for TextBox controls, so the procedure will be executed when the end user enters a TextBox control. The txt_Leave procedure will be wired up to the Leave event for TextBox controls, so the procedure will be executed when the end user leaves a TextBox control.

Wiring Up the Event Procedures

Once you have the event procedures written, you need to wire them up to the appropriate controls and events. The technique that you use for this depends on the programming language that you are using and the number of controls that are to be wired to the event procedure.

The following sections demonstrate how to wire up one control, a small set of controls, and all of the controls on a form. If you are familiar with these techniques and just want to see how to wire up the Enter and Leave events to complete this scenario, skip to the "Wiring Up All Controls on a Form" section of this chapter.

Wiring Up One Control

You can write an event procedure that will execute for only one particular event for one particular control. This is most often used for controls that have unique behavior, such as buttons. For example, a click on an OK button performs a different action from a click on a Cancel button.

In VB, there are two ways to associate an event procedure with a specific control and event. The Handles clause can be added as part of the event procedure signature. This clause defines the exact control and event that the event procedure will handle.

```
Private Sub txt_Enter(ByVal sender As Object, _
    ByVal e As System.EventArgs) Handles txtUserName.Enter
```

The Handles clause in this example defines that this event procedure should be executed when the Enter event is generated for the TextBox control named txtUserName.

Instead of using the Handles clause, you can associate the event procedure with the control and event it handles using the VB AddHandler statement, as follows:

```
AddHandler txtUserName.Enter, AddressOf txt_Enter
```

The AddHandler statement associates the control and event with the name of the procedure that will be executed when the event occurs. In this example, when the Enter event is generated for the TextBox control named txtUserName, the procedure named txt_Enter will be executed.

The AddHandler statement is frequently added to the Load event code for the form so that the event is wired up as soon as the form is loaded. However, you can add this statement anywhere in the code if you want to manage when the event handler is active.

> **NOTE** There is also a RemoveHandler statement, which removes the association between the event procedure and the event. This prevents the event procedure from being executed for the defined control and event.

In C#, you can associate the event procedure with the control and event it handles in the Properties window. Select the control in the designer, click the Events icon in the Properties window, and then select the procedure for the desired event, as shown in Figure 2-5.

Figure 2-5. When coding Windows Forms with C#, you can use the Properties window to associate a method with the control and the event it handles.

After you select the procedure, the following line of code is automatically added to the Windows Forms Designer-generated code in your Windows Forms code file.

```
this.txtUserName.Enter += new System.EventHandler(this.txt_Enter);
```

This statement associates the Enter event for the TextBox control named txtUserName with the event handler named txt_Enter.

If you don't want to use the Properties window, add this code line directly into your code file. Normally, you would add it to the constructor code for the form, but it could be added anywhere in the code if you want to manage when the event handler is active.

Regardless of language, by setting the background color in the Enter event, the background color will change when the end user enters the control. When the end user leaves the control, the code in the Leave event will set the color back to the standard Windows control color.

But this feature is not very useful in this scenario if it works for only one control. You want the background color to change for a set of controls.

Wiring Up a Set of Controls

Since you already have the Enter and Leave event procedures defined, all you need to do is associate these procedures with multiple controls on the form.

In VB, there are two ways to associate an event procedure with multiple controls on the form. One way is to simply add the other controls to the Handles clause of the event procedure, as follows:

```
Private Sub txt_Enter(ByVal sender As Object, _
    ByVal e As System.EventArgs) Handles txtUserName.Enter, txtPassword.Enter
```

The second way to associate an event procedure with multiple controls on the form in VB is to use the AddHandler statement for each control, as follows:

```
AddHandler txtUserName.Enter, AddressOf txt_Enter
AddHandler txtPassword.Enter, AddressOf txt_Enter
```

In C#, there are also two ways to associate an event procedure with multiple controls on the form. One way is to simply pick the method in the Properties window for each of the controls, as shown earlier in Figure 2-5.

The second way to associate an event procedure with multiple controls on the form in C# is to use the EventHandler method for each control, as follows:

```
this.txtUserName.Enter += new System.EventHandler(this.txt_Enter);
this.txtPassword.Enter += new System.EventHandler(this.txt_Enter);
```

These techniques allow you to have the same event procedure execute for a set of controls. But you (and the maintenance developer) will need to remember to handle the Enter and Leave events for each control added to the form.

Wiring Up All Controls on a Form

The best choice when implementing events for all of the controls on the form is to loop through all of the controls and associate the event with each control. As controls are added to the form, they will automatically be associated with the defined event. This makes it easier for you (and the maintenance developer) to handle the events.

Implementing this solution involves leveraging the technique described in the "Iterating Through the Controls on a Form" section earlier in this chapter. Start with the code from that section, and add the code to wire up event procedures.

In VB:

```vb
Private Sub AddEventHandlers(ByVal pnl As Control)
    For Each ctrl As Control In pnl.Controls
        If TypeOf ctrl Is TextBox Then
            AddHandler ctrl.Enter, AddressOf txt_Enter
            AddHandler ctrl.Leave, AddressOf txt_Leave
        End If
        If ctrl.HasChildren Then
            AddEventHandlers(ctrl)
        End If
    Next
End Sub
```

In C#:

```csharp
private void AddEventHandlers(Control pnl)
{
    foreach (Control ctrl in pnl.Controls)
    {
        if (ctrl is TextBox)
        {
            ctrl.Enter += new System.EventHandler(this.txt_Enter);
            ctrl.Leave += new System.EventHandler(this.txt_Leave);
        }
        if (ctrl.HasChildren)
        {
            AddEventHandlers(ctrl);
        }
    }
}
```

The AddEventHandlers method loops through all of the controls on the form. If the control is a TextBox, it wires up the Enter and Leave events to their appropriate event procedures. You could change this code to support other types of controls as well. If the control contains other controls, it recursively calls AddEventHandlers again and processes the child controls.

This method can be called from the Load event or constructor of the form to add the event handlers as soon as the form is loaded. To wire up the controls for the Login form, for example, you call AddEventHandlers as shown next.

In VB:

```
Private Sub LoginWin_Load(ByVal sender As Object, _
    ByVal e As System.EventArgs) Handles MyBase.Load
    AddEventHandlers(me)
End Sub
```

In C#:

```
public LoginWin()
{
    //
    // Required for Windows Form Designer support
    //
    InitializeComponent();

    AddEventHandlers(this);
}
```

Wiring Up All Controls on All Forms

The previous section implied that the AddEventHandlers code that wired up the Enter and Leave events for all of the controls on the form resided in the form. To produce a consistent user interface, you will want to implement the Enter and Leave event code for all controls on *all* forms.

The most straightforward way to reuse the AddEventHandlers code for each form is to put that code into a utility component and call AddEventHandlers from the Load event or constructor for each form. When you add a form to your project, you can simply call the AddEventHandlers utility function from that form, and all of the TextBox controls on the form will change background color when the end user enters the control.

If you are familiar with inheritance, an alternative solution is to leverage form inheritance. You could put the AddEventHandlers code in a base form class, and then every form that you add to your project can inherit from that base form class.

NOTE For more information about using form inheritance for coding Enter and Leave events, see the March/April 2004 *CoDe Magazine* article "Give Your Forms a Base" (http://www.devx.com/codemag/Article/20643).

Regardless of which of these two techniques you choose, once you have the AddEventHandlers code in place, you can easily access it from any form in your application. You can also extend it to handle other important events in your application, such as the Validating event.

Leveraging the DialogResult Property

The term *dialog* is normally used to refer to a form that is brought up modally, meaning that the end user must respond to the dialog before continuing. For example when you select to print from most products, such as Microsoft Word or Visual Studio, the Print form that is displayed is a dialog.

The number of dialogs that you use in your application depends on the application. Your Login form is most likely a dialog, because you want the end user to log in before continuing. If you need the end user to specify reporting or printing criteria, or provide confirmation of an operation, those forms may be dialogs as well. To display a form as a dialog, use the ShowDialog method in place of the Show method: `frmLogin.ShowDialog()`.

When the end user has responded to a dialog, your code needs to proceed based on that response. For example, in a dialog that requests end-user confirmation of an operation, your application needs to know whether the end user selected OK to proceed or Cancel to abort the operation. The DialogResult property of the form provides an easy way for the code in the dialog form to specify the end user's action and for the code that displayed the dialog to retrieve that result.

To set the DialogResult property of the dialog form, you can set this property for the buttons on the dialog using the Properties window. The DialogResult property of the form is then automatically set to the value defined for the button selected by the end user. Alternatively, you can set the DialogResult property of the form directly in the code. Both methods are described in the following sections.

Setting the DialogResult Property for a Button

Button controls have a DialogResult property. You can use the Properties window to set the DialogResult value for a button on a dialog. When the end user clicks a dialog button, the value of the button's DialogResult property is automatically assigned to the DialogResult property of the form.

For example, you could set the DialogResult property to OK for an OK button and to Cancel for a Cancel button. If the end user clicks the OK button, the DialogResult property for the form is set to OK, and the dialog is automatically hidden. If the end user clicks the Cancel button, the DialogResult property for the form is set to Cancel, and the dialog is automatically hidden. If the user clicks the Close button of the dialog (the button with an x in the top-right corner of the form), the form is hidden, and the DialogResult property is set to Cancel.

The code that displayed the dialog can then access the DialogResult property of the dialog form to determine how to proceed.

In VB:

```
frmConfirm.ShowDialog()
If frmConfirm.DialogResult = DialogResult.OK Then
    ' Do whatever operation
End If
frmConfirm.Dispose()
```

In C#:

```
frmConfirm.ShowDialog();
if (frmConfirm.DialogResult == DialogResult.OK)
{
    // Do whatever operation
}
frmConfirm.Dispose();
```

This example displays a confirmation dialog containing an OK and Cancel button. The DialogResult property is set for each of these buttons. If the end user clicks the OK button, the dialog is hidden, processing returns to the calling code, and the operation is performed. If the end user clicks the Cancel button, the dialog is hidden, processing returns to the calling code, and the operation is skipped. In either case, the dialog is then disposed of. This is necessary because setting the DialogResult property will hide the dialog, not close and dispose of it.

Setting the DialogResult Property in Code

When you need to perform some processing to determine the appropriate DialogResult property, you can set the DialogResult property of the dialog form in your code.

In this example, a Login form is displayed with Login and Exit buttons. The Exit button has its DialogResult property set to Cancel. The Login button needs to confirm the username and password before setting the DialogResult property to OK. The following code in the dialog validates the end-user login and set the form's DialogResult property to OK if the login validation was successful.

In VB:

```
Private Sub cmdLogin_Click(ByVal sender As Object, _
    ByVal e As System.EventArgs) Handles cmdLogin.Click
    Dim bValid As Boolean
    Dim oUser As New User
    bValid = oUser.ValidateLogin(txtUserName.Text, txtPassword.Text)
    If bValid Then
      me.DialogResult = DialogResult.OK
    End If
End Sub
```

In C#:

```
private void cmdLogin_Click(object sender, System.EventArgs e)
{
    bool bValid = false;
    User oUser = new User();
    bValid = oUser.ValidateLogin(txtUserName.Text, txtPassword.Text);
    if (bValid == true)
    {
        this.DialogResult = DialogResult.OK;
    }
}
```

NOTE   Notice that this code did not close the form. Setting the DialogResult property to DialogResult.OK hides the dialog and returns execution to the calling form.

On returning from the dialog, you can check the DialogResult property for the form as shown in the previous section.

Using the DialogResult property provides an easy way to know how to proceed after displaying a dialog, without needing to create your own form properties.

Drawing Simple Lines

The real mystery to drawing simple lines on a Windows form is why there is no Line control. You can fake a line by using a Panel control and setting its width or height to a few pixels. But if you want a real line, the secret is in understanding the correct set of library methods you need.

To draw a line with code you need to use GDI+, which is the .NET graphics library.

In VB:

```
Private Sub LoginWin_Paint(ByVal sender As Object, _
    ByVal e As System.Windows.Forms.PaintEventArgs) _
    Handles MyBase.Paint
    Dim g As Graphics = e.Graphics
    Dim penLine As Pen = New Pen(Color.CornflowerBlue, 12)
    g.DrawLine(penLine, 15, 0, 15, Me.Height)
    penLine.Dispose()
End Sub
```

In C#:

```
    private void LoginWin_Paint(object sender,
    System.Windows.Forms.PaintEventArgs e)
{
    Graphics g = e.Graphics;
    Pen penLine = new Pen(Color.CornflowerBlue, 12);
    g.DrawLine(penLine, 15, 0, 15, this.Height);
    penLine.Dispose();
}
```

NOTE   For this example to work correctly in C#, don't forget to wire up the Paint event to the LoginWin_Paint method using the techniques described earlier in this chapter, in the "Implementing Enter and Leave Events" section.

In both languages, the code is defined in the Paint event for the form. The code creates a graphics object related to the PaintEventArgs parameter passed into the Paint event procedure. It then sets a pen to define the color and width of the line. The DrawLine method draws the line using the defined pen, beginning at the first two coordinates (15,0) and ending at the second coordinates (15, form's height). Figure 2-6 demonstrates the results.

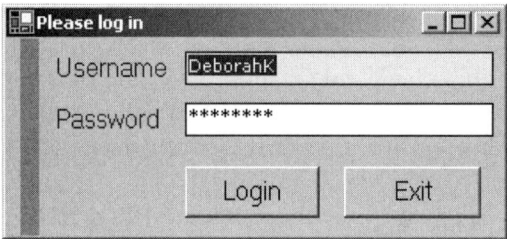

Figure 2-6. A thick line is drawn on the left side of the Login form to provide an interesting visual.

The code for drawing other types of shapes is similar to this example. Paste in the preceding code and type **g.** to display IntelliSense and see the list of shapes that can be drawn.

Resizing Controls for Contents

To make the best use of space on your form, you may want to resize a control, such as a TextBox or ListBox, based on the size of its contents. If the control contains only a few characters, the control size could be resized to be small, but if the control contains many characters, the control size could be expanded. This removes excess empty space within a control and can improve the look of the form when it is displayed with data.

To resize a control to fit its contents, you need to determine the length of the contents, and then size the control appropriately. It seems that this would be straightforward: use the Length property of the string to determine the needed length and set the control's width to that value. But this does not take the font into consideration. Unless the font is fixed-width, the different characters in the string won't be the same width. For example, an *i* has a smaller width than a *W* in most fonts.

To calculate a more precise width of a control's contents, you need to use the .NET graphics library, GDI+.

In VB:

```
Dim g As Graphics = txtName.CreateGraphics()
Dim iWidth As Int32 = CInt(g.MeasureString(txtName.Text, txtName.Font).Width)_+ 5
txtName.Width = iWidth
g.Dispose()
```

In C#:

```
Graphics g  = txtName.CreateGraphics();
int iWidth = (int)g.MeasureString(txtName.Text, txtName.Font).Width + 5;
txtName.Width = iWidth;
g.Dispose();
```

This code creates a graphics object for the TextBox control. It then uses the MeasureString method to measure the contents of the control using the font associated with the control. It adds 5 pixels to provide a little white space after the text in the control, and then sets the control's width to the calculated size.

Use this technique whenever you need to calculate the length of the contents of a control.

Displaying Validation Errors with the ErrorProvider Control

A common Windows Forms requirement is to validate the data entered by the end user. If the data is not valid, you need to inform the end user of the problem and provide information about how to correct the problem. The ErrorProvider control is a standard control that allows you to easily flag the controls that have validation issues, and to display text to provide a description of the problem and how to correct it. This control does not perform the validation; rather, it assists in notifying the end user if the validation failed.

Most controls support a Validating event that you can use to perform validation on the data entered into the control. In the Validating event procedure, you can write code that ensures a required field is entered, a numeric field is a number, a string does not exceed a maximum length, or any other required field-level validation.

If the control's data is not valid, call the SetError method of the ErrorProvider control. This marks the control that failed validation with the ErrorProvider icon and defines the tooltip-style text that the end user can view to aid in resolving the validation issue.

As an example, the following code uses the ErrorProvider control to display a message if the end user left the control named txtName blank.

In VB:

```
Private Sub txt_Validating(ByVal sender As Object, _
    ByVal e As System.ComponentModel.CancelEventArgs) _
    Handles txtName.Validating
    epValidation.SetError(txtName, "")
    If txtName.Text.Length = 0 Then
        epValidation.SetError(txtName, "You must provide a company name.")
    End If
End Sub
```

In C#:

```
private void txt_Validating(object sender,
    System.ComponentModel.CancelEventArgs e)
{
    epValidation.SetError(txtName, "");
    if (txtName.Text.Length == 0)
    {
        epValidation.SetError(txtName, "You must provide a company name.");
    }
}
```

NOTE   For this example to work correctly in C#, don't forget to wire up the Validating event to the txt_Validating method using the techniques described earlier in this chapter, in the "Implementing Enter and Leave Events" section.

The pattern for a Validating event procedure, like the preceding code, is as follows:

- The routine begins by assuming the control will be valid and uses the SetError method of the ErrorProvider control to clear any existing error text for the control. This is needed to ensure that when the end user does enter a valid value and the control is revalidated, the previous error text won't be displayed.

CAUTION If you don't clear the ErrorProvider text and the ErrorProvider control already contains error text for a control, any new error text that you define for the control will be ignored.

- The routine performs the validation on the control contents. In this example, it simply checks the text length to determine whether the end user entered any data into the control.

- If the contents are invalid, the routine sets the error text for the control using the SetError method. The ErrorProvider icon is then displayed next to the control, and this text appears as the icon's tooltip text.

Figure 2-7 presents the result of this code when the end user leaves a required control empty.

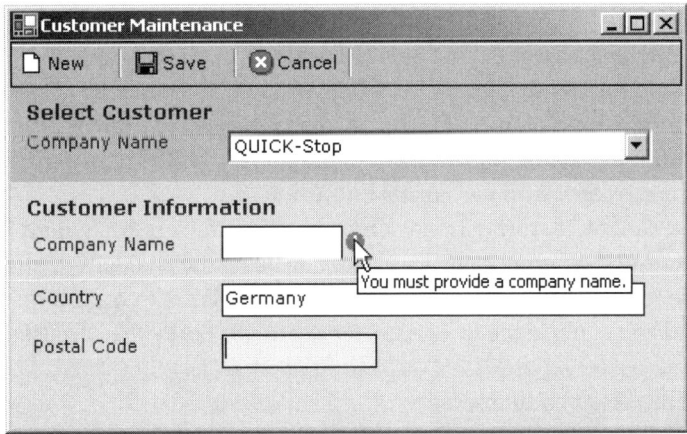

Figure 2-7. The company name and postal code are required, so if the end user leaves either control blank, the ErrorProvider displays an icon next to the control. The end user can view the ErrorProvider's tooltip text for assistance in resolving the validation issue.

Only one ErrorProvider control is needed on the form for use with all of the controls.

TIP If you are familiar with inheritance, you could define one ErrorProvider control in a base form class and use it for all controls on all forms. See the "Implementing Enter and Leave Events" section earlier in this chapter for brief discussion of base form classes.

The ErrorProvider control has a property to define an alternate icon, so that you can tailor the icon for your application. It also has properties for setting the blinking style and rate. The blinking can be very irritating, so usually, you will want to set the blinking style to NeverBlink.

The ErrorProvider control provides an easy way to notify the end user of controls that failed validation and to provide text to aid the end user in correcting the validation error.

What Did This Chapter Cover?

There are many features in Visual Studio that aid in doing Windows Forms.

In the Windows Forms Designer, you can use docking for a better layout, anchoring for better resizing, and aligning for a cleaner look. You can use shortcut keys and Visual Studio commands to edit controls in the Windows Forms Designer without using the mouse. You can get rid of your form centering code by using the appropriate Windows Forms property.

In your code, you can iterate through the controls on your forms, implement Enter and Leave events, and get the results from a dialog using the DialogResult property. You can use the GDI+ library to draw simple lines and resize controls to fit their contents. And you can use the ErrorProvider control to notify the end user of invalid data entry.

The next chapter looks at coding secrets.

Code Tricks

AFTER YOU HAVE BEEN CODING for a while, you'll find that you reuse coding patterns. For example, the code that processes a Toolbar control usually includes a case statement, event procedures contain the standard Try Catch block, and so on. It is easy to get into such a pattern and be so focused on getting the job done that you don't have time to try other coding techniques.

The purpose of this chapter is to present some code tricks to make your coding easier, more productive, and just better. And a few debugging techniques are thrown in, because what good is great code if it has bugs in it?

What Will This Chapter Cover?

This chapter uncovers the following coding secrets:

- Short-circuiting Ands and Ors

- Shortcutting the assignment operator

- Improving string management with StringBuilder

- Declaring on the For

- Strictly converting your data types

- Improving type casting

- Aliasing data types

- Managing regular expressions

- Overloading procedures

- Overloading operators

- Exploring undiscovered regions

- Using XML commenting

- Obsolescing your code

- Expanding your debugging techniques

By the end of this chapter, you'll be able to dazzle your colleagues with these code tricks. You'll find that these techniques will improve your productivity and make your code easier to develop and maintain.

Short-Circuiting Ands and Ors

Logical operators allow you to compare two Boolean (True/False) expressions and return a Boolean result. The most common logical operators are And and Or. To perform an operation when two things are both true, use an And operator (if *A* is true And *B* is true, then . . .). To perform an operation when either of two things are true, use an Or operator (if *A* is true Or *B* is true, then . . .).

To say this more formally, the Or operator evaluates two Boolean expressions. If either expression evaluates to True, the result is True. If neither expression evaluates to True, the result is False. As a simple Or operator example, if the end user-entered username **or** password is blank, then the code should display a message.

In VB, the Or operator is Or:

```
If sUserName = "" Or sPassword = "" then
    Messagebox.Show("You must enter the Username and Password")
End If
```

In C#, the Or operator is |:

```
if (sUserName == "" | sPassword == "")
{
    Messagebox.Show("You must enter the Username and Password");
}
```

The And operator also evaluates two Boolean expressions. If both expressions evaluate to True, the result is True. If either or both expressions evaluate to False, the result is False. As an And operator example, if the number of ordered items is not null **and** greater than 0, then assign it to the Text property of a text box.

In VB, the And operator is And:

```
With m_dsOrder.Tables(Order.TN_OrderHeader).Rows(0)
    If Not .IsNull(Order.FN_ITEM_COUNT) And _
        CType(.Item(Order.FN_ITEM_COUNT), Int32) > 0 Then
        txtItemCount.Text = .Item(Order.FN_ITEM_COUNT).ToString
    End If
End With
```

In C#, the And operator is &:

```
DataRow dr = m_dsOrder.Tables[Order.TN_OrderHeader].Rows[0];
If (!dr.IsNull(Order.FN_ITEM_COUNT) &
    System.Convert.ToInt32(dr[Order.FN_ITEM_COUNT]) > 0)
{
    txtItemCount.Text = dr[Order.FN_ITEM_COUNT].ToString();
}
```

Oops! This example will generate an exception if the item count field is null. In both C# and VB, the logical And and Or operators will cause both expressions to be evaluated. So, even through the item count field is null and the first expression is False, the second expression will be evaluated and will generate an invalid cast exception (a null cannot be cast to an integer).

To prevent this problem, use the conditional logical operators, also called the *short-circuiting* operators. These evaluate the first expression, and then conditionally evaluate the second expression.

In VB, the short-circuiting operators are AndAlso and OrElse. Use AndAlso instead of the And operator in the prior example to prevent execution of the second expression if the first expression is true:

```
With m_dsOrder.Tables(Order.TN_OrderHeader).Rows(0)
    If Not .IsNull(Order.FN_ITEM_COUNT) AndAlso _
        CType(.Item(Order.FN_ITEM_COUNT), Int32) > 0 Then
        txtItemCount.Text = .Item(Order.FN_ITEM_COUNT).ToString
    End If
End With
```

In C#, the short-circuiting operators are && and ||. Use && instead of the & in the prior example to prevent execution of the second expression if the first expression is true:

```
DataRow dr = m_dsOrder.Tables[Order.TN_OrderHeader].Rows[0];
If (!dr.IsNull(Order.FN_ITEM_COUNT) &&
    System.Convert.ToInt32(dr[Order.FN_ITEM_COUNT]) > 0)
{
    txtItemCount.Text = dr[Order.FN_ITEM_COUNT].ToString();
}
```

This is such a seemingly minor change (And to AndAlso or & to &&), yet it offers many benefits. Not only is it more efficient, but it also can prevent errors such as an invalid cast exception.

The short-circuiting operators are conditional versions of the logical operators. They conditionally evaluate the second expression as follows:

- x `AndAlso` y will always evaluate x and will evaluate y only if x is true. (VB)

- x `OrElse` y will always evaluate x and will evaluate y only if x is false. (VB)

- x `&&` y will always evaluate x and will evaluate y only if x is true. (C#)

- x `||` y will always evaluate x and will evaluate y only if x is false. (C#)

When possible, you should use the short-circuiting operators in your application to improve your application's performance. These operators save execution time by bypassing the evaluation of the second expression depending on the result of the evaluation of the first expression.

TIP Check your existing code and replace your logical operators with short-circuiting operators wherever possible.

Since the short-circuiting operators skip the evaluation of the second expression, you should not use them if the second expression calls a function that needs to be executed regardless of the evaluation of the first expression.

Short-circuit operators are especially useful when working with database fields, because you can check for a null value and also check for a specific value within one conditional clause. Think about this trick every time you type And, Or, &, or |.

Shortcutting the Assignment Operator

In both VB and C#, the assignment operator is the equal sign (=). You use the equal sign any time you want to assign the value of an expression to a variable. For example, to accumulate the total number of items to be shipped in an order, each time the end user ordered a product, you would add the requested quantity of that product to the total.

In VB:

```
iOrderItemTotal = iOrderItemTotal + iQuantity
```

In C#:

```
iOrderItemTotal = iOrderItemTotal + iQuantity;
```

Shortcut the + assignment operator, minimizing the amount of typing you need to do, by using the += operator. The += operator adds the value of an expression to the value of a variable and assigns the result to the variable.
In VB:

```
iOrderItemTotal += iQuantity
```

In C#:

```
iOrderItemTotal += iQuantity;
```

Some of the most commonly used shortcut assignment operators are shown in Table 3-1.

Table 3-1. Shortcut Assignment Operators (continued)

OPERATOR	DESCRIPTION WITH EXAMPLE	NOTES
+=	Adds the value of an expression to the value of a variable and assigns the result to the variable. x += 4 Increments x by 4 and assigns the result to x.	In C#, the += operator also concatenates string expressions.
-=	Subtracts the value of an expression from the value of a variable and assigns the result to the variable. x -= 3 Decrements x by 3 and assigns the result to x.	
*=	Multiplies the value of an expression by the value of a variable and assigns the result to the variable. x *= 2 Multiplies x by 2 and assigns the result to x.	

(continued)

Table 3-1. Shortcut Assignment Operators (continued)

OPERATOR	DESCRIPTION WITH EXAMPLE	NOTES
/=	Divides the value of an expression by the value of the variable and assigns the result to the variable. x /= 4 Divides x by 4 and assigns the result to x.	In VB, if Option Strict is On, the variable on the left-hand side (x in this example) must be declared as Double. If Option Strict is Off, the variable on the left-hand side will be implicitly converted to a Double.
\=	Divides the value of an expression by the value of the variable and assigns the *integer* result to the variable. x \= 4 Divides x by 4 and assigns the integer result to x, dropping any remainder.	VB only. If Option Strict is On, the variable must be Byte, Short, Integer, or Long. If Option Strict is Off, the variable is coerced to Long.
&=	Concatenates a string expression to a string variable and assigns the results back to the variable. x &= "World" Appends "World" to the string defined in x and assigns the results to x.	VB only. In C#, use += to concatenate a string expression. In C#, &= performs an And assignment operation. See the Visual Studio help system for more information.

NOTE   See the "Strictly Converting Your Data Types" section later in this chapter for more information about implicit conversions and Option Strict.

Using the shortcut assignment operators reduces the typing you need to do. They are also more efficient at runtime, because the variable (x in the examples in Table 3-1) needs to be evaluated only once.

Improving String Management with StringBuilder

Strings are *immutable*. In other words, a string cannot be changed once it is assigned. When you append a string to an existing string, the .NET Framework actually creates a new string containing the original string and the appended string. If you are thinking that this takes extra processing time, you are correct.

String concatenation has been optimized, so minimal amounts of concatenation won't have a noticeable impact on performance. The impact is noticeable if you are appending a lot of strings; for example, if you are appending many strings to build ASP.NET page contents or to build message text.

In VB:

```
Dim sMessage as String = "This is a message"
sMessage &= " for user "
sMessage &= sUserName
```

In C#:

```
string sMessage = "This is a message";
sMessage += " for user "
sMessage += sUserName;
```

In this example, it appears that an sMessage string is created, and then additional strings are appended to sMessage, modifying the original string. But that is not what is actually happening. In the first line of the example, the string is created and assigned the default value ("This is a message"). In both the second and third lines of the example, the sMessage string is destroyed (marked for deletion by the garbage collector), and a new sMessage string is created to contain the original string plus the appended string.

If the string concatenation is all done as one assignment, the string is not destroyed between concatenations, and there is no performance impact.

In VB:

```
Dim sMessage as String = "This is a message" & " for user " & sUserName
```

In C#:

```
string sMessage = "This is a message" + " for user " + sUserName;
```

However, when concatenating many long strings or building entire ASP.NET page contents using concatenation, appending all of the strings with one assignment may not be practical (or easily readable).

To minimize the impact of string concatenation on performance when you are concatenating many strings, consider using the StringBuilder class. The StringBuilder class creates a string-like object that can be changed. When you have made all of the necessary changes to the string, you can convert the StringBuilder class value to an actual string.

In VB:

```
Imports System.Text
Dim sbMessage As StringBuilder
sbMessage = New StringBuilder("This is a message")
sbMessage.Append(" for user ")
sbMessage.Append(sUserName)
Dim sMessage As String = sbMessage.ToString
```

In C#:

```
using System.Text;
StringBuilder sbMessage = new StringBuilder("This is a message");
sbMessage.Append(" for user ");
sbMessage.Append(sUserName);
string sMessage = sbMessage.ToString();
```

This sample code creates an instance of the StringBuilder class. It then uses the Append method of the StringBuilder class to append text to the StringBuilder. When all of the concatenations are done, the ToString method converts the StringBuilder to a String type. The StringBuilder class has other methods, such as Insert and Replace, to perform various operations on the string.

StringBuilder provides more efficient string concatenation because it creates a buffer that is large enough to contain the original string plus additional space to provide room for the string to grow. However, if the concatenations fill the extra space in the buffer, the buffer size must be extended, causing another performance hit.

 TIP   Use the EnsureCapacity method of the StringBuilder class to further improve performance. EnsureCapacity allows you to set the size of the StringBuilder buffer to the expected size of the final string length. Then StringBuilder won't need to expand the size of the buffer, so you'll avoid a performance hit.

Initializing a StringBuilder object has more of a performance impact than using a string, so you don't want to use StringBuilder if you are appending only a few strings. The generally recommended cutoff number is five. If you have more than five separate string concatenations, StringBuilder is generally more efficient than appending the strings.

TIP   If your string handling needs to perform as efficiently as possible, the only way to know for certain whether using string concatenation or StringBuilder is faster in your situation is to conduct your own performance testing.

Any time you see a lot of string concatenation in your code, consider using the StringBuilder class for better performance.

Declaring on the For

Historically, most coding standards documents have recommended that all method-scoped variables be defined at the top of the method. This can cause problems, however, when variables defined only for the purposes of looping are used somewhere else in the method. The current recommended standard is to declare looping variables as close as possible to where they will be used.

The easiest way to declare a looping variable is to declare it within the loop code itself. You can do this in any For or For Each loop.

For example, a For Each loop in VB:

```
For Each ctrl As Control In pnl.Controls
    ...
Next
```

As another example, a For loop in C#:

```
for (int i = 1; i <= 5; i++)
{
    sResponse = i + sCustomerName;
    ...
}
```

By declaring these variables as part of the loop construct, they won't inadvertently be used anywhere else in the method.

Strictly Converting Your Data Types

Data is not always of the type that you need. For example, your application retrieves an integer from a database and wants to display that integer in a TextBox control. The Text property of the TextBox control requires a string, so the integer must first be converted to a string. Or you have a short integer and a particular method requires a long integer, so the short must first be converted to a long, or vice versa.

Depending on the type of conversion, .NET may handle the conversion for you. When this occurs, it is called an *implicit* conversion because your code does not need to explicitly perform the conversion.

In both VB and C#, widening conversions are performed implicitly. *Widening conversions* occur when converting from a smaller type to a larger type, normally without any loss of information. For example, converting from a short to a long integer is a widening conversion and is handled automatically by VB and C#.

In VB:

```
Dim i As Int16
Dim j As Int32
i = 7
j = i
```

In C#:

```
Int16 i;
Int32 j;
i = 7;
j = i;
```

Notice that in both languages, no casting or conversion was needed in the code. .NET handles the conversion implicitly.

Narrowing conversions occur when converting from a larger type to a smaller type, such as when converting from a long integer to a short integer. Narrowing conversions could result in loss of information, and they normally require that your application perform an *explicit* conversion; that is, your application must specifically define how the conversion is to be performed.

In VB:

```
Dim i As Int16
Dim j As Int32
j = 7
i = CType(j, Int16)
```

In C#:

```
Int16 i;
Int32 j;
j = 7;
i = (Int16)j;
```

In this example, the VB code uses the CType function and the C# code uses the cast operator to explicitly convert to the narrower data type.

Explicit conversion is also required when converting between unrelated data types, such as converting from an integer to a string.

In VB:

```
Dim x As Int32
txtUserName.Text = x.ToString
```

In C#:

```
int x = 7;
txtUserName.Text = x.ToString();
```

In this example, the ToString method was called to explicitly perform the conversion.

By default, VB will attempt to implicitly convert most of your data types for you, including narrowing conversions and conversions between unrelated types. So, by default, the preceding VB examples did not require explicit conversion. Since VB implicitly performs these conversions, you don't control how and when your data types are converted. This can lead to coding errors.

NOTE   C# won't attempt to implicitly perform conversions for narrowing operations or on conversions between unrelated types.

It is much better to explicitly convert your data types yourself. You can enforce this by using the Option Strict statement when coding in VB. Add this statement to the top of every VB code file:

```
Option Strict On
```

NOTE   The Option Strict statement must appear before any other code statements.

When Option Strict is On, you will be required to explicitly convert or cast your data types for narrowing conversions and for conversions between unrelated types. You will then be notified with a compile-time syntax error if you have any of the following in your code:

- Narrowing conversions without an explicit cast operator

- Late binding (when the result of a method call is of type Object instead of a specific type, the call is late bound)

- Operations on type Object other than =, <>, TypeOf...Is, and Is

- Omitting the As clause in a declaration

Set Option Strict to On for an entire project by setting the appropriate Build properties for the project in the project's Property Pages dialog box, as shown in Figure 3-1.

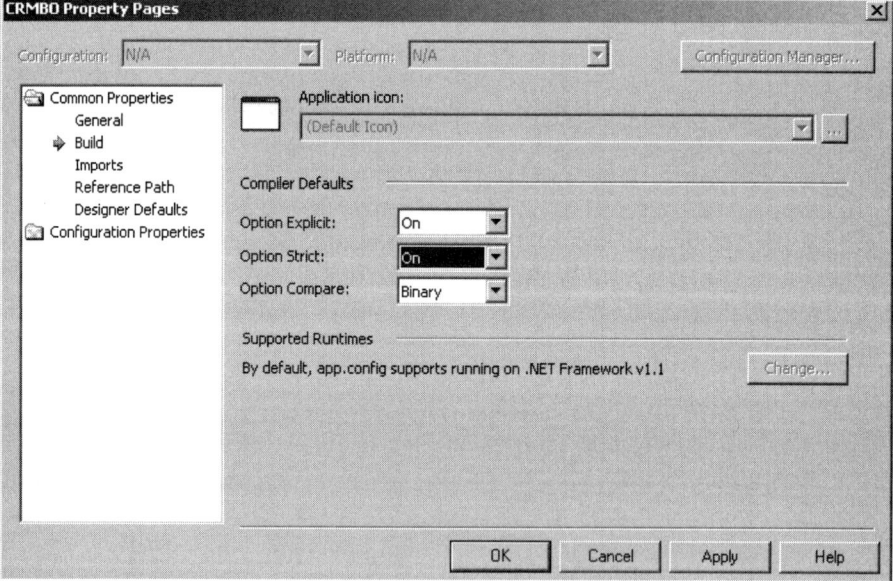

Figure 3-1. Option Strict is Off by default. Set it On for your project in the Property Page dialog box to strictly convert your datatypes. (VB only)

TIP If you are using VB, set Option Strict to On for all of your code by adding the Option Strict statement to each code file or by setting Option Strict On for each project.

Improving Type Casting

Type casting is necessary when you have a variable of one type that needs to be converted to a different type, as described in the previous section. Because the .NET Framework provides many values of type Object, you will find that you frequently need to cast from type Object to a more specific type.

The best way to cast from type Object to another type with VB is to use DirectCast, as follows:

```
Private Sub txt_Enter(ByVal sender As Object, _
    ByVal e As System.EventArgs) Handles txtUserName.Enter
    DirectCast(sender, TextBox).BackColor = Color.BlanchedAlmond
End Sub
```

The DirectCast statement in this example casts the sender variable that is of type Object to a TextBox control in order to access the TextBox properties.

TIP   DirectCast performs better than using CType when casting from an object to a more specific type because it does not use runtime helper functions.

You can use DirectCast only when casting from a type to a related but more specific type, called a *derived* type. For example, you can use DirectCast to cast from type Control to type TextBox because TextBox is derived from Control. You cannot use DirectCast to convert from an Integer to a String type because String is not derived from Integer. DirectCast can always be used to cast from type Object to any other type because all other types derive from type Object.

CAUTION   DirectCast throws an InvalidCastException if you attempt to cast from one type to another when the second type is not derived from the first.

Although C# does not have a direct equivalent to DirectCast, it does have an as operator that performs conversions between compatible types.

```
private void txt_Enter(object sender, System.EventArgs e)
{
    TextBox tb = sender as TextBox;
    tb.BackColor = Color.BlanchedAlmond;
}
```

The as operator is similar to DirectCast with one key difference: it won't generate an exception when it cannot perform the cast; rather, it will return a null. The as operator cannot, however, cast to a value type, such as Int. The as operator can cast only to reference types.

NOTE   In the upcoming Visual Studio 2005 release, VB is expected to get a new operator that is equivalent to the C# as operator. It is currently called TryCast. TryCast tries the cast, and if it succeeds, returns the value cast to the defined type. Otherwise, it returns Nothing.

Aliasing Data Types

Another secret coding feature is data type aliasing. If you want to use a data type, but think you may need to change to a different data type at some time in the future, define an alias for the data type and use the alias throughout the rest of your code.

Say, for example, that you want to use Int16, but think you may want to change to Int32 later. You could define an alias for Int16.

In VB:

```
Imports ChangeableType = System.Int16
```

In C#:

```
using ChangeableType = System.Int16;
```

Anywhere in the code that you want to use that data type, use the alias instead.

In VB:

```
Private m_iSomething As ChangeableType
Debug.WriteLine(m_iSomething.GetTypeCode)
```

In C#:

```
ChangeableType m_iSomething=1;
Debug.WriteLine(m_iSomething.GetTypeCode());
```

If you want to later change to System.Int32, simply change the alias, and then all of the other code will recognize the new type.

In VB:

```
Imports ChangeableType = System.Int32
```

In C#:

```
using ChangeableType = System.Int32;
```

A more common use of this technique is in cases where you don't know the name of the class that you need because another developer is developing that class. You can create a stub for the class, define an alias for the class name, and your application will run. When you get the new class, all you need to do is substitute it in for your stub and change the class name in the alias.

Managing Regular Expressions

A *regular expression* is a pattern for validating that a value, normally a string, conforms to specific criteria. For example, you could use a regular expression to ensure that a phone number contains only numbers or contains numbers and the appropriate parentheses, dashes, or periods to form a valid phone number. This is particularly useful for validating end-user entries. Regular expressions are also useful for replacing or removing portions of a string that match a pattern, such as removing all special characters from a string.

The easiest way to learn regular expressions is by working through a set of examples. These examples provide you with a general idea of how to create regular expressions and how to use them in your code. But it is also important to understand how to build regular expressions using the appropriate syntax.

The following sections first provide several examples of using regular expressions in real-world applications, and then provide details on building your own regular expressions.

Using Regular Expressions

Some of the most common uses of regular expressions are in validating end-user entry. The examples that follow perform validation on numeric postal codes, phone numbers, and U.S. Social Security numbers.

Postal Codes

Starting with a simple example, you can use regular expressions to validate that a string contains only numeric values. Use this technique to validate that an end user-entered postal code is all numeric (for example purposes, this ignores countries with alphanumeric postal codes).

> **NOTE** You could use VB's IsNumeric function, which indicates whether an expression can be evaluated as a number, instead of a regular expression to perform this particular validation. To use VB's IsNumeric function from C#, add a reference to the Microsoft.VisualBasic.dll.

Validate that a particular string contains only numbers using the regular expression pattern:

```
^\d+$
```

The caret (^) defines that the pattern-matching should begin with the first character of the end user-entered string. The \d defines a digit (0-9). The plus sign (+) requires that the preceding character occurs one or more times; in this case, this means one or more digits. The dollar sign ($) specifies that the pattern-matching should end with the last character of the end user-entered string. See Table 3-2 later in this chapter for additional details on regular expression characters.

The System.Text.RegularExpressions namespace in the .NET Framework provides a set of features to assist you in working with regular expressions in your application. Use these features to perform pattern-matching and replacements using regular expressions. The following code demonstrates how to validate an end user-entered postal code to ensure it contains only numbers.

In VB:

```vb
Imports System.Text.RegularExpressions
Dim sRegExPattern As String = "^\d+$"
Dim sTextToValidate As String = txtPostalCode.Text
If Not Regex.IsMatch(sTextToValidate, sRegExPattern) Then
    epValidation.SetError(ctrl, "The postal code must be numeric.")
End If
```

In C#:

```
using System.Text.RegularExpressions;
string sRegExPattern = @"^\d+$";
string sTextToValidate = txtPosalCode.Text;
if (!Regex.IsMatch(sTextToValidate, sRegExPattern))
{
    epValidation.SetError(ctrl, "The postal code must be numeric.");
}
```

The IsMatch method of the RegEx class returns True if the specified text matches the defined pattern. If IsMatch returns False, an ErrorProvider control notifies the end user of the invalid entry. (If you are not familiar with the ErrorProvider control, see the "Displaying Validation Errors with the ErrorProvider Control" section in Chapter 2.) You could generalize the code in this example to validate any regular expression pattern (defined in the sRegExPattern variable) against any string (defined in the sTextToValidate variable).

NOTE   Notice the at sign (@) in the regular expression pattern in the C# code. This is required to prevent C# from attempting to process the escape characters.

Social Security Numbers

As another regular expression example, a common pattern is the U.S. Social Security number. This number is of the form *xxx-xx-xxxx*. If you don't need to validate a Social Security number, you can use this technique to validate any numeric pattern, such as a customer or vendor number.

Ensure that a Social Security number is three digits, a dash, two digits, a dash, and four digits by specifying the following pattern:

```
^\d{3}-\d{2}-\d{4}$
```

This pattern starts matching at the beginning of the pattern (^), matches three digits (\d{3}), a dash (-), two digits (\d{2}), a dash (-), and four digits (\d{4}) to complete the match at the end of the string ($).

To implement this pattern in your application, use code similar to that used to validate postal codes (shown in the previous section), specifying the Social Security number pattern as the regular expression.

Phone Numbers

Any application that stores customer, employee, or contact information needs to validate phone numbers. The issue with phone numbers is that the end user never quite knows whether to put in all of the extra parentheses, dashes, periods, or other special characters. So, before the phone number can be validated, any extraneous characters need to be removed.

The following is the regular expression for a standard U.S. phone number:

```
^\d{10}$
```

The caret (^) and ($) define that the entire value must match the pattern, and the \d{10} syntax implies that the pattern is expecting ten digits.

But before you can validate the phone number, you need to remove any special characters that the end user may have entered by using the Replace method of the Regex class. The code to remove the special characters and then validate the phone number is similar to that used for validating other patterns with one extra line to perform the replacement.

In VB:

```
Imports System.Text.RegularExpressions
Dim sRegExPattern As String = "^\d{10}$"
Dim sTextToValidate As String = txtPhone.Text
sTextToValidate = Regex.Replace(sTextToValidate, "[^0-9]", "")
If Not Regex.IsMatch(sTextToValidate, sRegExPattern) Then
    epValidation.SetError(ctrl, "The phone number must be 10 digits.")
End If
```

In C#:

```
using System.Text.RegularExpressions;
string sRegExPattern = @"^\d{10}$";
string sTextToValidate = txtPhone.Text;
sTextToValidate = Regex.Replace(sTextToValidate, "[^0-9]", "");
if (!Regex.IsMatch(sTextToValidate, sRegExPattern))
{
    epValidation.SetError(ctrl, "The phone number must be 10 digits.");
}
```

This code uses the Replace method of the Regex class to replace any nonnumeric character, specified as not 0 through 9 ([^0-9]), with an empty string. This removes any extraneous characters. The code then uses the IsMatch method to determine if the resulting string matches the pattern for a phone number.

Building Regular Expressions

Once you have a general idea of how to use regular expressions, it is easier to understand how to build some of your own.

Most of the characters in a regular expression are normal characters. Some characters have a special meaning to the regular expression engine, so these characters must be prefixed with an escape character, \ (a backslash), as shown in Table 3-2.

Table 3-2. Common Regular Expression Characters

CHARACTER	MATCHES	EXAMPLE
\b	Word boundary	\bon matches *on* if it is found at the beginning of a word, such as "Come here **on**ce." on\b matches *on* if it is found at the end of a word, such as "I am a pers**on**." \bon\b matches *on* only if a word in the string is *on*, such as "I am **on** top of things".
\B	Nonword boundary	\Bon matches *on* if it is found anywhere but at the beginning of a word, such as "This c**on**tains that."
\b	Backspace	\b represents a backspace when used with a character set defined within [ ] (see Table 3-3). This is used primarily in replacement patterns.
\d	Digits, 0 through 9	\d matches the first digit in a string, such as "**4**44B Privet Drive."
\D	Nondigit	\D matches the first nondigit anywhere in a string, such as "444**B** Privet Drive".
\e	Escape	\e matches an escape character when used with a character set defined within [ ] (see Table 3-3). This is used primarily in replacement patterns.
\f	Form feed	\f matches a form feed character when used with a character set defined within [ ] (see Table 3-3). This is used primarily in replacement patterns.
\n	New line	\n matches a new line character when used with a character set defined within [ ] (see Table 3-3). This is used primarily in replacement patterns.

(continued)

Table 3-2. Common Regular Expression Characters (continued)

CHARACTER	MATCHES	EXAMPLE
\r	Carriage return	\r matches a carriage return character when used with a character set defined within [ ] (see Table 3-3). This is used primarily in replacement patterns.
\s	Space	\s matches the first space, such as "444B Privet Drive."
\S	Nonspace	\S matches the first nonspace, such as "**444**B Privet Drive."
\t	Tab	\t matches a tab character when used with a character set defined within [ ] (see Table 3-3). This is used primarily in replacement patterns.
\v	Vertical tab	\v matches a vertical tab character when used with a character set defined within [ ] (see Table 3-3). This is used primarily in replacement patterns.
\w	Any alphanumeric character including an underscore character	\w matches the first alphanumeric or underscore character, such as "**444**B Privet Drive."
\W	Nonword character	\W matches the first nonalphanumeric or underscore character, such as "444B Privet Drive."

All ordinary characters (without an escape character) match themselves, except for the special characters defined in Table 3-3. To use the special characters themselves, use the escape character before the special character. For example, to validate the string (nnn) use the pattern: ^\(\d{3}\)$, which starts the match at the beginning of the string; matches a left parenthesis, three digits, and a right parenthesis; and ends the match at the end of the string.

Table 3-3. Common Regular Expression Special Characters

CHARACTER	MATCHES	EXAMPLE
.	Any character except new line (\n)	. matches any character, such as "**444**B Privet Drive." This is frequently used to determine if the user entered something in a required field.

(continued)

Table 3-3. Common Regular Expression Special Characters (continued)

CHARACTER	MATCHES	EXAMPLE
[...]	Set of valid characters	[ABC] matches the first occurrence of *a*, *b*, or *c*, such as "444**B** Privet Drive."
[^...]	Set of invalid characters	[^ABC] matches the first occurrence of any character except *a*, *b*, or *c*, such as "**4**44B Privet Drive."
[a-bm-n]	Set of valid character ranges	[0-9a-kA-K] matches the first occurrence of any digits 0–9, letters *a*–*k*, or capital letters *A–K*, such as "**4**44B Privet Drive."
*	Prior character occurs zero or more consecutive times	\d* matches all occurrences of digits, such as "**444**B Privet Drive."
+	Prior character occurs one or more times	\d+ matches all occurrences of digits, such as "**444**B Privet Drive."
?	Prior character occurs zero or one time	\d? matches zero or one occurrence of digits, such as "**4**44B Privet Drive."
{n}	Prior character occurs exactly *n* times	\d{2} matches the first two occurrences of digits, such as "**44**4B Privet Drive."
{n,}	Prior character occurs *n* or more times	\d{2,} matches the first two or more occurrences of digits, such as "**444**B Privet Drive."
{n,m}	Prior character occurs at least *n*, at most *m* times	\d{1,3} matches the first occurrence up to three occurrences, such as "**444**B Privet Drive."
^	Pattern occurs at the beginning of the string	^4 matches the number 4 if it is the first character in the string, such as "**4**44B Privet Drive."
$	Pattern occurs at the end of the string	Drive$ matches the word *Drive* if it is at the end of the string, such as "444B Privet **Drive**."
a|b	a OR b	P | Q matches *P* or *Q*, such as "444B **P**rivet Drive."

Overloading Procedures

This one is not actually a secret; you should already be overloading procedures. If not, here is a quick introduction.

Overloading is defining multiple procedures, instance constructors, or properties in a class that have the same name but different signatures. The primary purpose of overloading is to provide alternative sets of parameters that can be used to perform an operation.

For example, suppose a Customer class has a Retrieve method. You may want to allow all customer key values to be retrieved for use in a drop-down list, all customer key values to be retrieved for a particular region for use in a filtered drop-down list, and all customer data to be retrieved for one customer by ID.

You could implement this functionality in several ways. You could create three different methods with three different names, create one method with optional parameters, or create three different method signatures with the same name. The latter technique uses procedure (or method) overloading.

Using the same name for all three methods makes it is more discoverable to the developers using the method (or yourself). Overloading is also better than using one method with optional parameters, because the method signatures are clear (plus optional parameters are not available in C#).

There is no special technique or keyword that you need to use to take advantage of overloading; just create two or more procedures with the same name and different sets of parameters.

In VB:

```
Public Function Retrieve() As DataSet
    ' Retrieves key data for all customers
End Function


Public Function Retrieve(ByVal sRegion As String) As DataSet
    ' Retrieves key data for all customers in the region
End Function


Public Function Retrieve(ByVal iCustomerID As Int32) As DataSet
    ' Retrieves all data for a specific customer
End Function
```

In C#:

```
public DataSet Retrieve()
{
    // Retrieves key data for all customers
}


public DataSet Retrieve(String sRegion)
{
    // Retrieves key data for all customers in the region
}
```

```
public DataSet Retrieve(int iCustomerID)
{
    // Retrieves all data for a specific customer
}
```

Each of these procedures has a different signature. The first method has no parameters, the second method has only a string parameter, and the third method has only an integer parameter. You can define any number of overloaded procedures with different combinations of parameter types.

TIP In some cases, as in this example, the code in the overloaded methods is different. In other cases, the code may be very similar. In that case, you can put the common code in one of the methods and have all of the other overloaded methods call that method with the appropriate parameters.

When you call an overloaded method, the runtime chooses the correct method to execute based on the parameter types specified in the method call. For example, if you call the Retrieve method and pass it an integer, the Retrieve method with the integer parameter will be executed.

There are some rules for using overloading. The most obvious, of course, is that the procedures need to have the same name. The method signatures (data types of the parameters) must be different; otherwise, the runtime won't know which method to execute. For example, you cannot have two Retrieve methods, each with a single string parameter. The following cannot be used to differentiate method signatures:

- Method return type

- ByVal or ByRef as the only difference

Using overloading can simplify your development and maintenance activities. It can also simplify the use of your methods.

TIP Look at your existing code and determine where you can leverage overloading. Any methods with optional parameters are key targets, as are routines that perform the same basic function but have different sets of parameters and different names.

Overloading Operators

Operator overloading is one of those features that you don't need very often, but when you need it, you *really* need it. It is currently available only in C# (although VB is expected to have operator overloading in Visual Studio 2005).

Operator overloading allows you to define operators, such as +, –, and *, for your data types. Objects created with your data type can then be manipulated using these standard operators. This can make it easier to work with the data types that you define.

As an example, consider an application that works with foreign currency prices. A Price data type supports amounts in any currency. By overloading the mathematical operators for the Price data type, prices in different currencies can be mathematically manipulated. In today's global economy, this is a useful feature.

The Price data type in this example is a structure composed of several fields.

```
public struct Price
{
    public float Amount;
    public string CurrencyCode;
    public float ExchangeRateWRTUSD;
}
```

The Amount field defines the price amount in a defined currency. The CurrencyCode field is the three-character code for the currency, such as USD (U.S. dollars), AUD (Australian dollars), or EUR (European euros).

In a production-level application, the Amount and CurrencyCode fields would be enough. The application would use the CurrencyCode to look up the appropriate currency exchange rates in a table (if current currency rates aren't a requirement) or from a service (if current exchange rates are a requirement).

But writing lookup tables or accessing a service takes away from the focus of this section: operator overloading. So instead, the Price data type in this example has a third field for the exchange rate.

As you know, every currency has an exchange rate with respect to every other currency. The standard way to operate on two prices defined with two different currencies is to find the exchange rate between the two currencies, convert one currency to the other, and then perform the operation. This allows you to add "apples and apples" as the saying goes.

However, any one particular Price object in this example would not know what other currency it may need to convert to. So it would not be enough to store just one exchange rate for the Price data type; it would need to store an exchange rate for every possible other currency.

A better approach in this situation is to define a base currency. The Price data type has a single field that stores the exchange rate with respect to the base currency. The application then converts each Price amount to the base currency, performs the operation, and converts back to the desired currency. This example selected USD as the base currency, but any currency could be used for this purpose.

The constructor for the Price data type structure sets the values of the fields. This constructor allows you to create a Price object with the appropriate data.

```
public Price(float fAmount,
             string sCurrencyCode,
             float fExchangeRateWRTUSD)
{
    this.Amount = fAmount;
    this.CurrencyCode=sCurrencyCode;
    this.ExchangeRateWRTUSD = fExchangeRateWRTUSD;
}
```

Overloading Mathematical Operators

To provide for the addition of two Price objects, you could define an Add method and pass it two Price objects. But it would be more intuitive if you could simply add the two Price objects with the + operator. That is the purpose of operator overloading.

The code to overload an operator uses a static method with the operator keyword to define the method as an overloaded operator.

```
public static Price operator +(Price p1, Price p2)
{
    Price p3;
    if (p1.ExchangeRateWRTUSD == p2.ExchangeRateWRTUSD)
    {
        p3 = new Price(p1.Amount+p2.Amount,
                       p1.CurrencyCode,p1.ExchangeRateWRTUSD);
    }
    else
    {
        float p1InUSD = p1.Amount * p1.ExchangeRateWRTUSD;
        float p2InUSD = p2.Amount * p2.ExchangeRateWRTUSD;
        float p3Converted = (p1InUSD + p2InUSD) / p1.ExchangeRateWRTUSD;
        p3 = new Price(p3Converted,p1.CurrencyCode,p1.ExchangeRateWRTUSD);
    }
    return p3;
}
```

The method first compares the two exchange rates. If the exchange rates are the same, it adds the prices. If the exchange rates aren't the same, each price is converted to the base currency (USD), added, and then converted back to the currency of the first Price object. The resulting Price object is returned, giving you a new Price object that is the sum of the original two Price objects.

You use the overloaded operator with your data type just as you use it with any other data type. Simply add Price objects together.

```
Price keyboardPrice = new Price(40,"AUS",(float).6);
Price mousePrice = new Price(20, "EUR", (float).8);
Price Total = keyboardPrice + mousePrice;
MessageBox.Show("Total Order Price is: " + Total.Amount.ToString());
```

This code first creates the two Price objects. It then adds them using the + operator. Finally, it displays the result for confirmation.

You can write similar code to overload the -, *, /, or other basic operators for this Price object.

Overloading Assignment Operators

Assignment operators, such as equal (=), cannot be overloaded. However, you can achieve operator overloading for the addition assignment operator (+=) and the related assignment operators (-=, *=, /=) using the mathematical operators.

```
Price speakerPrice = new Price(30, "AUS", (float).6);
Price surCharge = new Price(5, "AUS", (float).6);
speakerPrice += surCharge;
MessageBox.Show("Total Cost for Speakers is: " +
    speakerPrice.Amount.ToString());
```

This code defines a surcharge amount and increments the price by the surcharge amount.

If you implemented the other mathematical operators, you can use this technique for their corresponding assignment operators.

Overloading Comparison Operators

You can overload comparison operators, such as equal (= in VB; == in C#), not equal (<> in VB; != in C#), less than (<), greater than (>), less than or equal to (<=), or greater than or equal to (>=).

The code to overload the greater-than operator returns a Boolean value: True or False.

```
public static bool operator >(Price p1, Price p2)
{
    // If both exchange rates are the same type,
    // just compare them
    if (p1.ExchangeRateWRTUSD == p2.ExchangeRateWRTUSD)
    {
        return (p1.Amount > p2.Amount);
    }
    else
    {
        // Convert both currencies to a base currency
        float p1InUSD = p1.Amount * p1.ExchangeRateWRTUSD;
        float p2InUSD = p2.Amount * p2.ExchangeRateWRTUSD;
        return (p1InUSD > p2InUSD);
    }
}
```

This code first compares the exchange rates. If the rates are the same, it returns True if the first Price amount is greater than the second Price amount. If the exchange rates are different, it converts both currencies to the base currency, and then performs the comparison.

Comparison operators must be overloaded in pairs. For example, if you overload ––, you must overload !=. Since the example overloaded the greater-than operator (>), it must also overload the less-than operator (<).

```
public static bool operator <(Price p1, Price p2)
{
    // If both exchange rates are the same type,
    // just compare them
    if (p1.ExchangeRateWRTUSD == p2.ExchangeRateWRTUSD)
    {
        return (p1.Amount < p2.Amount);
    }
    else
    {
        // Convert both currencies to a base currency
        float p1InUSD = p1.Amount * p1.ExchangeRateWRTUSD;
        float p2InUSD = p2.Amount * p2.ExchangeRateWRTUSD;
        return (p1InUSD < p2InUSD);
    }
}
```

This code is similar to the code that overloads the greater-than operator.

> **NOTE**   You cannot overload the conditional logical operators (&& and ||).

Using operator overloading gives your data types an intuitive way to support mathematical and comparison operations. Look for more features for operator overloading in Visual Studio 2005.

Exploring Undiscovered Regions

You have probably noticed the collapsed "Windows Form Designer generated code" sections of your Windows Forms. These collapsed areas are *regions*. Regions can help you organize your code, which aids you in finding the code you need, both during development and maintenance.

You can create a region around a set of code using the Region keyword.
In VB:

```
#Region " Private Methods"
    ' Put any code here
#End Region
```

In C#:

```
#region Private Methods
    // Put any code here
#endregion
```

You can define any number of regions in your code files. You can also nest them, to create regions of regions. Nesting is useful for defining a Private Methods region, for example, and then defining a separate region for each private method.

> **NOTE**   To include closed regions in your searches, be sure to check the Search hidden text check box in the Find dialog box. Otherwise, the Find operation will not look in any closed regions.

If you define regions for all of your code, you will be able to see your entire code file at one time, as shown in Figure 3-2. Expanding or collapsing the regions containing the code you are working on allows you to focus on a particular task.

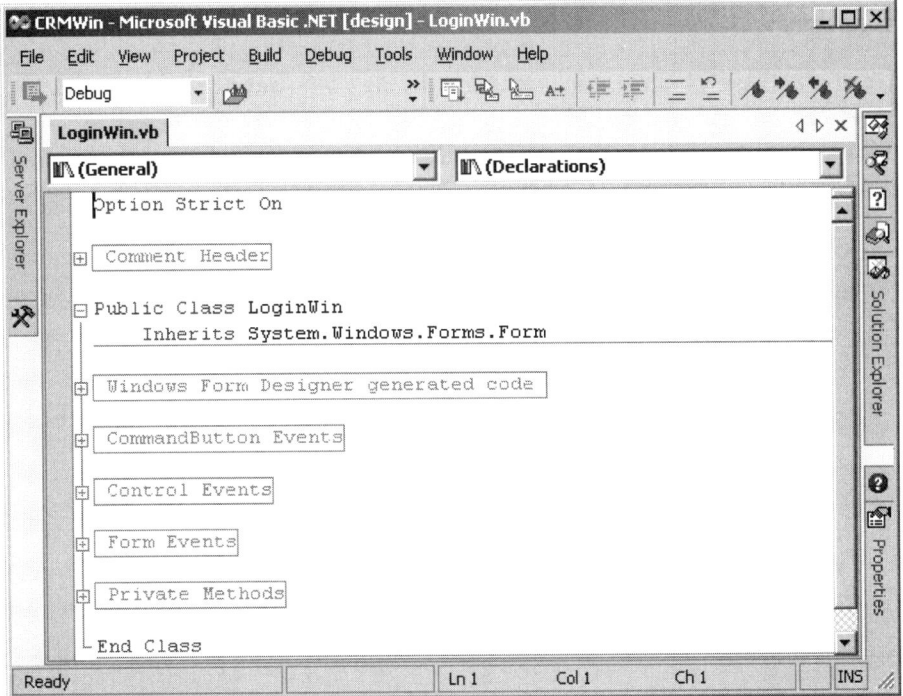

Figure 3-2. The entire set of code in this code file can be viewed all at once. Expand the regions to see the code you need.

TIP   Add regions to your code to make your code easier to manage, both for yourself and future generations of maintenance developers.

Using XML Commenting

C# provides a mechanism for developers to document their code using standard XML elements. This gives the code comments a standard style and allows the Visual Studio IDE to use the comments in IntelliSense. VB developers can also use XML to document their code, but the XML must be entered manually and Visual Studio does not use the comments. (The XML commenting feature is expected to be available for VB when Visual Studio 2005 is released.)

Creating XML Comments

Use the XML commenting tool with C# to create XML comments for classes, delegates, interfaces, fields, events, properties, or methods. To create an XML comment for a particular item, go to the line above the definition of the item in the C# code file and type *///*. When you type the third slash, the XML comments will automatically appear:

```
/// <summary>
///
/// </summary>
/// <param name="pnl"></param>
private void AddEventHandlers(Control pnl)
```

You can enter a summary for the class in the Summary element. Notice that the Param element retrieved the parameter from the method signature and used it as the Name attribute. You can then add a definition for the parameter. A minimal XML comment for a method is as follows:

```
/// <summary>
/// Loops through all of the controls on the form and sets
/// the Enter and Leave event handlers for each Textbox.
/// </summary>
/// <param name="pnl">The form or any control on the form.</param>
private void AddEventHandlers(Control pnl)
```

The XML commenting tool provides additional common elements, including the following:

- **Example:** Allows you to specify an example of how to use a method or other member.

- **Exception:** Allows you to define which exceptions can be thrown from the method.

- **Returns:** Allows you to define the return value from a method.

Search the help system for "XML Documentation tutorial" for a complete discussion of XML commenting for C#.

Viewing XML Comments in IntelliSense

Visual Studio's IntelliSense uses the XML comments that you enter as part of its Quick Info, List Members, and Parameter Info functionality. Although you may not be familiar with these names, you have probably seen all of this functionality.

- **Quick Info:** Displays the declaration and summary for any identifier in your code. Move the mouse so the cursor hovers over any identifier or click the Quick Info button in the Text Editor toolbar to see the Quick Info, as shown in Figure 3-3. Notice that this is the summary text from the XML comment defined in the previous example.

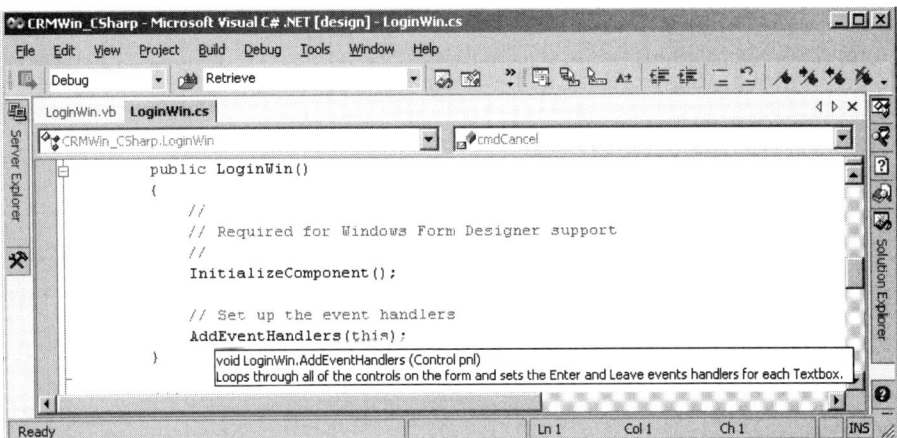

Figure 3-3. Quick Info is the part of IntelliSense that gives you quick information on an identifier in your code. It uses the Summary element of your XML comment to obtain this information for your identifiers.

- **List Members:** Displays the members associated with a particular object in a drop-down list. When you type the object name and a period (.) or select the Member List from the Text Editor toolbar, this list appears. Hover over any of the elements in the list, and the Quick Info appears, as shown in Figure 3-4.

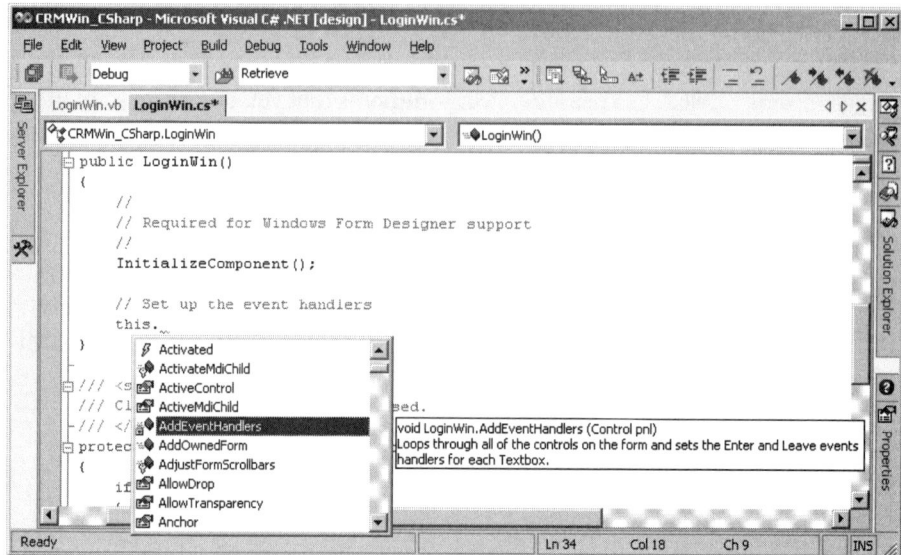

Figure 3-4. The List Members feature of IntelliSense also uses your XML comment.

- **Parameter Info:** Displays information about the parameters of a method. This information appears after you enter the method name and parenthesis or select the Parameter Info button on the Text Editor toolbar (see Figure 3-5).

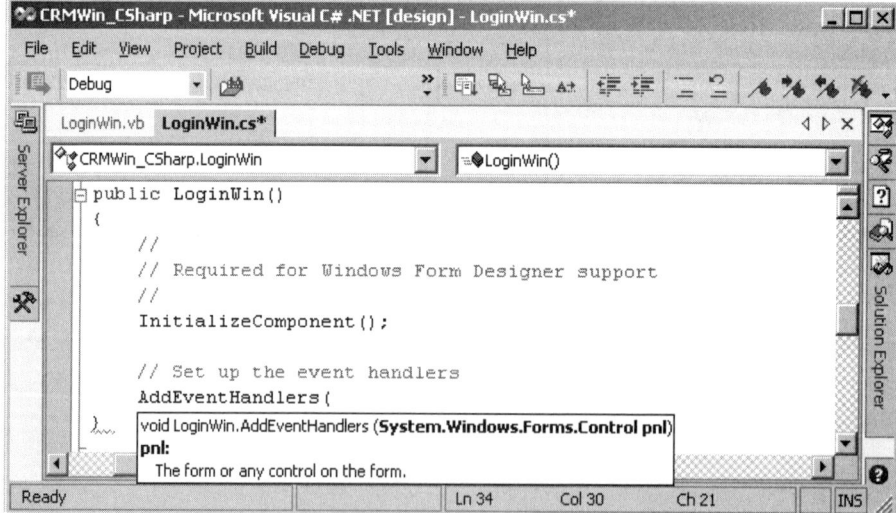

Figure 3-5. The Parameter Info feature of IntelliSense uses the Param elements in your XML comment.

You can generate an external XML file containing all of your XML comments for a project by setting the XML Document File for the project. Select Project ➤ Properties, open the Configuration Properties folder, and choose Build. Then enter a valid file name for the XML Document File in the Outputs node. When you build the project, an XML file is generated. The other advantage to setting this property is that any publicly visible types or methods without XML comments will be listed as warnings in the Task List window as part of the build process. (See the "Managing Your To-Do List" section in Chapter 1 for more information about working with the Task List window.)

TIP   This generated XML file can also be parsed by external tools, such as NDoc (http://sourceforge.net/projects/ndoc) to generate help files containing all of the XML comments from your project.

By using XML comments in each of your methods and other members, you generate the documentation for your future reference, *and* you make it easier to use those methods, because your documentation will appear in the IntelliSense.

TIP   As you add new methods or modify existing methods, add XML comments. If you are a C# developer, Visual Studio will assist you with this process. If you are a VB developer, add the XML-style comments manually using ' ' ' as the delimiter. Although VB developers won't get all of the benefits of XML comments now, they will soon.

Obsolescing Your Code

There is a growing interest in agile methodologies and agile development these days. One of the key tenets of agile development is coding for change; that is, developing code that is adaptive and easily modified as the business changes. This prevents the need to have fixed requirements and allows your software to better meet the changing needs of the corporation and the end users. (If you are not familiar with agile methodologies, see the "Implementing a Methodology for the Design" section in Chapter 5 for more information.)

As you continue to change your code over time, you will find that you need to *refactor* a piece of logic or a routine. Refactoring is the process of rewriting routines or sets of routines to better structure your code. Refactoring is a part of agile development because adaptability requires that code be modified as needed.

Visual Studio 2005 will have many features to make the refactoring process easier. You will be able to convert any piece of code into its own method, for example, using a context menu. This feature will make it easy to break a large routine into smaller routines or separate out a piece of logic so it can more easily be reused.

One feature of refactoring that is available now is the ability to obsolete your properties or methods. Say you have a method (or other member) in your application that is no longer needed or whose signature needs to be changed. You could delete or change the method, and then find and modify all of the code that uses the method. But a better approach is to mark the method as obsolete, basically declaring it to be deprecated. By marking a method as obsolete, instead of deleting or changing it, you avoid needing to modify any of the code that uses the method.

Code that uses the obsolete method will get a warning or a syntax error (depending on how you obsolete the method) the next time that code is compiled. This allows you to define a logical obsolescence path for your code. For example, when building components for a team of developers, your standards may require that you obsolete a method for six months with a warning and another six months with a syntax error, before the method is actually removed from the code.

To mark a routine as obsolete, use the ObsoleteAttribute.

In VB:

```vb
<ObsoleteAttribute("This method is obsolete. Please use Retrieve(iID) instead", _
                    False)> _
Public Function Retrieve(ByVal sProduct As String) As DataSet
    ' Code here performs the retrieve
End Function
```

In C#:

```csharp
[ObsoleteAttribute("This method is obsolete. Please use Retrieve(iID) instead",
                    false)]
public DataSet Retrieve(string sProduct)
{
    // Code here performs the retrieve
}
```

The first parameter of the ObsoleteAttribute is the message text that the developer will see wherever the obsolete method is used. This message text will appear in the Task List window, as shown in Figure 3-6, and in the Quick Info, as shown in Figure 3-7.

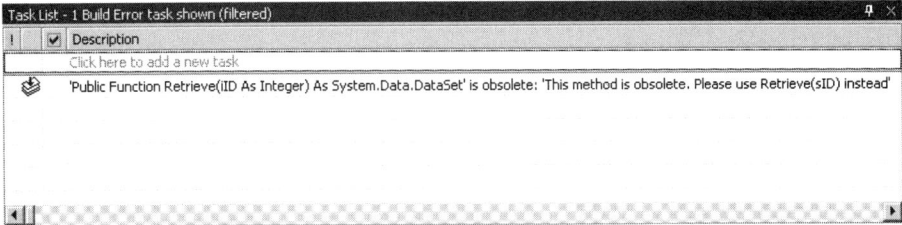

Figure 3-6. When a class member, such as a method, is marked as obsolete, any code that uses the member will appear in the Task List window.

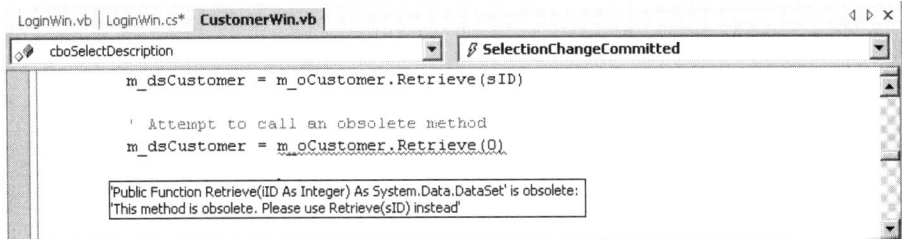

Figure 3-7. Any references to an obsolete member are marked in the code file, and the Quick Info displays the message defined in the ObsoleteAttribute.

The second parameter of the ObsoleteAttribute is whether the obsolete member usage is considered to be an error. Set the parameter to False to specify that the developer using the method will get a warning message in the Task List window, or to True to generate a syntax error if the method is used.

TIP   Plan for change. Define an obsolescence plan in your coding standards, and use the ObsoleteAttribute to help execute the plan.

Expanding Your Debugging Techniques

Once you have your code written, you need to ensure that it compiles. Once the code compiles, you need to ensure it runs. Once the code runs, you need to ensure that it actually performs the operations it needs to perform—that it fulfills its purpose. If the code runs, but does not perform as expected, you need to follow the tried-and-true techniques for figuring out why it does not work. This process is, of course, called *debugging*.

The Visual Studio IDE provides numerous debugging features, many of which you already know about. The beginning of this section lists the well-known debugging techniques that you probably already use. The remainder of this section focuses on the lesser-known, but generally useful debugging techniques available using Visual Studio.

Reviewing the Debugging Techniques You Already Know

It is important to understand what you know before looking at what you may not know. So this section begins with a quick list of the more well-known techniques of debugging with Visual Studio, just for your reference.

- Using the Task List window to view syntax errors (see "Managing Your To-Do List" in Chapter 1 for more information)

- Setting basic breakpoints

- Starting a debugging session (puts you in Debug mode)

- Stepping through the code

- Moving the execution point

- Using the tooltip feature to view values of variables (only available in Debug mode)

- Stopping a debugging session (puts you back into Edit mode)

If you are not familiar with any of these techniques, consult the Visual Studio help system topics under "Debugging."

Working with the Watch Window

You may already know how to use the Watch window to watch variable values. But it is also a great way to change the values of variables during your debugging.

Display a Watch window by selecting Debug ➤ Windows ➤ Watch ➤ Watch 1 from the menu while you are at a breakpoint in Debug mode. You can define up to four different Watch windows.

The Watch window is initially empty. Add any variable or expression to watch by typing the variable or expression into the Name column of the window, or by dragging and dropping a variable from a code file to the Watch window. The result is shown in Figure 3-8.

Watch 1		
Name	Value	Type
sbMessage	Name 'sbMessage' is not declared.	
sUserName	"DeborahK"	String
sPassword	"password"	String
sUserName & sPassword	"DeborahKpassword"	String

Figure 3-8. The Watch window displays the values of variables, indicates when a variable value has changed, and allows you to update variable values.

If the variable or expression that you are watching is not in scope within the code containing the execution point, the value cannot be determined. In this case, the Value column of the Watch window will display a message, as shown in Figure 3-8 with the sbMessage variable.

Modify the value of any variable that is in scope by clicking in the Value column and changing the value. This allows you to adjust variable values as you debug. You cannot change the value of an expression in the Watch window.

To take a quick look at a variable or adjust a variable value that you don't need to watch, use the QuickWatch dialog box by selecting Debug ➤ QuickWatch (see Figure 3-9). You can also access the QuickWatch dialog box by right-clicking a variable or expression and selecting QuickWatch from the context menu.

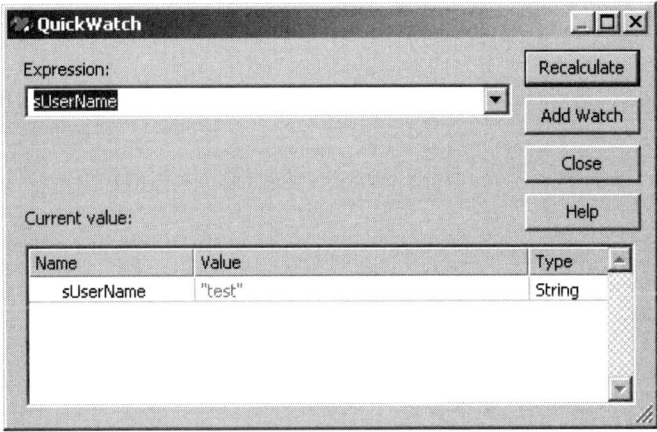

Figure 3-9. The QuickWatch dialog box displays the value of a variable or expression and allows you to update the variable value.

The QuickWatch dialog box is similar in functionality to the Watch window in that it allows you to see the value of a variable or expression and change the value of a variable. However, it is modal, so it does not allow you to watch the variable or expression value as you step through the code. If you decide you want to watch the variable or expression, click the Add Watch button in the QuickWatch dialog box to automatically add the entry to the Watch window.

Use the Watch window or QuickWatch dialog box the next time you want to see a set of variables or expressions, or change the value of a variable while you are debugging.

Working with the Locals Window

The Locals window, shown in Figure 3-10, allows you to watch all of the variables local to the routine containing the execution point. It has many of the same features of the Watch window, except the entries in the Locals window are predefined for you. You cannot add or remove entries from this window.

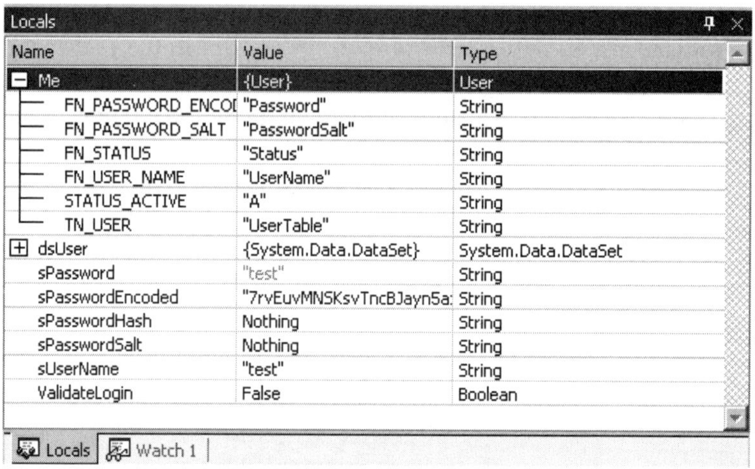

Locals			🔒 ✕
Name	Value	Type	
⊟ Me	{User}	User	
├─ FN_PASSWORD_ENCOI	"Password"	String	
├─ FN_PASSWORD_SALT	"PasswordSalt"	String	
├─ FN_STATUS	"Status"	String	
├─ FN_USER_NAME	"UserName"	String	
├─ STATUS_ACTIVE	"A"	String	
└─ TN_USER	"UserTable"	String	
⊞ dsUser	{System.Data.DataSet}	System.Data.DataSet	
sPassword	"test"	String	
sPasswordEncoded	"7rvEuvMNSKsvTncBJayn5a:	String	
sPasswordHash	Nothing	String	
sPasswordSalt	Nothing	String	
sUserName	"test"	String	
ValidateLogin	False	Boolean	

🖳 Locals | 📉 Watch 1 |

Figure 3-10. The Locals window displays the value of all variables local to the routine containing the execution point.

Use the Locals window to view or edit variable values without needing to add entries to the Watch window.

Working with the Command Window

The Command window is one of the most useful debugging windows available in Visual Studio. The Command window has two modes: Immediate mode and

Command mode. Using this window in Immediate mode, you can view the value of variables, assign variable values, and evaluate expressions. In Command mode, you can execute Visual Studio commands.

To open the Command window in Command mode, select View ➤ Other Windows ➤ Command window. A greater-than sign (>) will indicate that the window is in Command mode. Switch from Command mode to Immediate mode by typing >**immed**.

When the Command window is in Command mode, execute Visual Studio commands by typing the command and pressing the Enter key. For more information about Visual Studio commands, see the "Executing Visual Studio Commands" section in Chapter 1.

Open the Command window in Immediate mode by selecting Debug ➤ Windows ➤ Immediate. The title bar of the Command window will indicate that the window is in Immediate mode, as shown in Figure 3-11. To execute a command while in Immediate mode, precede the command with the greater-than sign (>). Switch from Immediate mode to Command mode by typing **>cmd**.

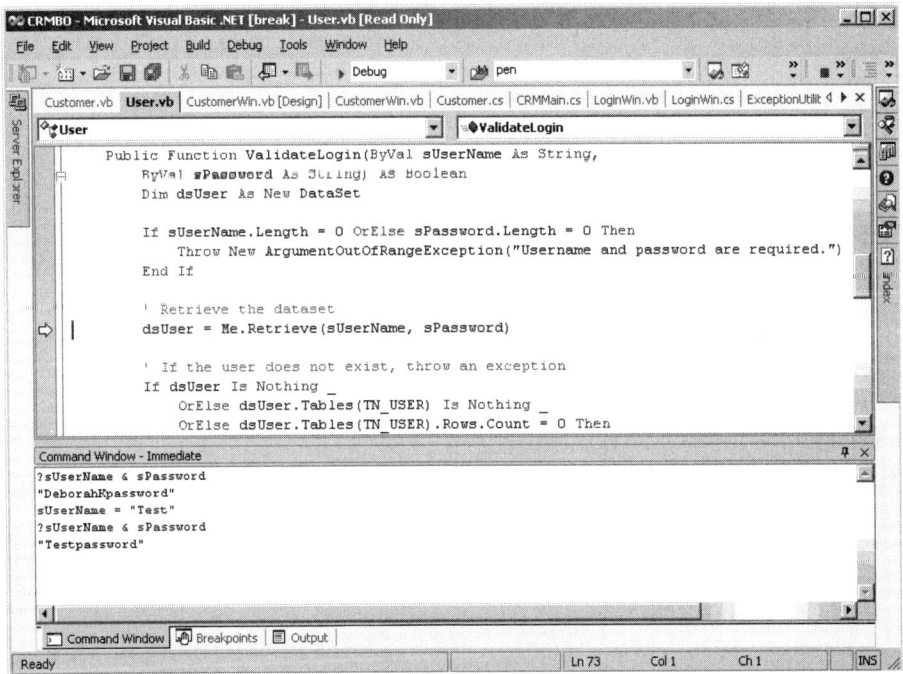

Figure 3-11. When the Command window is in Immediate mode, you can display the value of variables, assign variable values, or evaluate expressions.

When the Command window is in Immediate mode, type a question mark (?) followed by the variable name or expression in the Command window, and then press the Enter key to view the value of the variable or expression without needing to open a Watch or Locals window. To change the value of a variable, type the variable name with the desired assignment and press the Enter key. The result is shown in Figure 3-11.

Clear the contents of the Command window at any time by right-clicking the Command window and selecting Clear All from the context menu.

Working with Breakpoints

Every .NET developer knows how to set a breakpoint by clicking in the left margin of the code window. But many have not found the debugging secrets hidden in the New Breakpoint dialog box. This gem provides a wealth of options for setting breakpoints in your application to make your debugging more efficient.

At first glance, you would think that the Debug ➤ New Breakpoint menu option would simply set a breakpoint in your code file. But instead, it opens the New Breakpoint dialog box.

> **TIP** If you are using C#, you can right-click in a code window and select New Breakpoint from the context menu to open the New Breakpoint dialog box.

The New Breakpoint dialog box allows you to set any of four types of breakpoints: Function, File, Address, and Data. These are discussed in the following sections, along with information about several other breakpoint features.

Setting Function Breakpoints

The Function breakpoint feature of the New Breakpoint dialog box, shown in Figure 3-12, allows you to break the execution of the application at the first line of a specific function.

> **NOTE** Even though it appears that you can set a specific location in the function using the Line and Character text boxes in the New Breakpoint dialog box, you cannot set a Line other than 1, and any entry for Character is ignored.

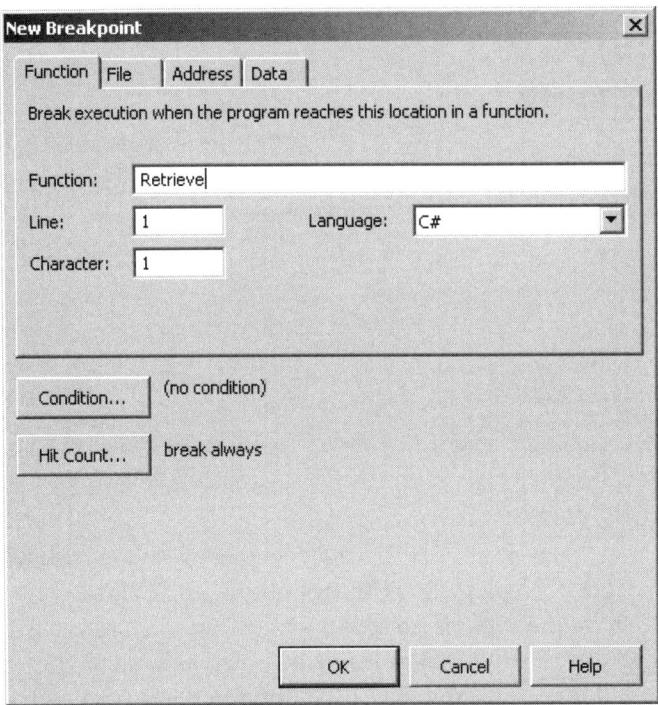

Figure 3-12. The Function breakpoint feature of the New Breakpoint dialog box allows you to set breakpoints at the beginning of specific functions.

To set a breakpoint in a specific function, type the name of the function in the dialog box. For example, type **Retrieve** to set a breakpoint in the Retrieve function. Optionally, prefix the function name with the class name in the format *class.function*. For example, type **User.Retrieve** to set a breakpoint in the Retrieve function in the User class.

 CAUTION   In C#, the case of the function name entered in the New Breakpoint dialog box must match the case of the function in the code file, or the function won't be found to set the breakpoint.

If there is more than one instance of the specified function name in your solution, the Choose Breakpoints dialog box is displayed, as shown in Figure 3-13. Select one or more instances of that function, and a breakpoint will be set in the selected functions.

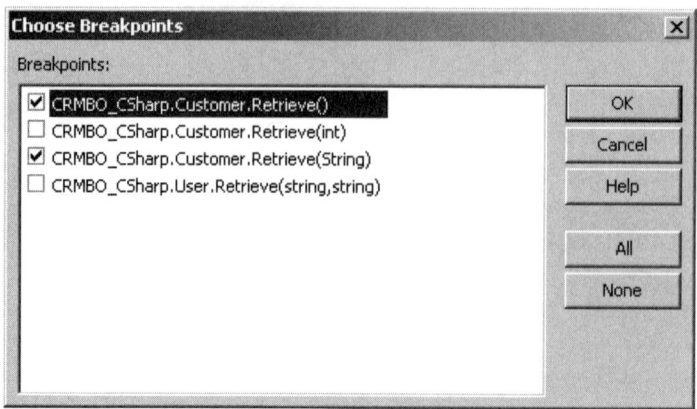

Figure 3-13. The Choose Breakpoints dialog box allows you to set breakpoints in multiple functions at one time.

The Condition and Hit Count buttons in this dialog box allow you to specify additional constraints on the breakpoint. Since these buttons are available for all of the breakpoint types, they are discussed separately later in this chapter.

When you click OK in the New Breakpoint dialog box, a breakpoint is inserted at the beginning of the specified functions, as indicated by a filled red circle icon in the left margin of the associated code file.

The Function breakpoint feature is most useful for setting breakpoints in all overloads of a particular function without needing to locate each function.

Setting File Breakpoints

File breakpoints are the breakpoints that you already use by clicking in the left margin of the code file. A filled red circle icon then appears in the margin. You can also use the New Breakpoint dialog box to set File breakpoints, as shown in Figure 3-14.

To set a breakpoint in a specific file, type the name of the file in the dialog box. For example, type **user.cs** to set a breakpoint in the User.cs file. You can also specify the number of the line and the character position.

NOTE   The character position option for File breakpoints is useful only when you have multiple code lines on a single line in the code file.

When you click OK in the New Breakpoint dialog box, a breakpoint is inserted at the specified line and character position in the specified code file.

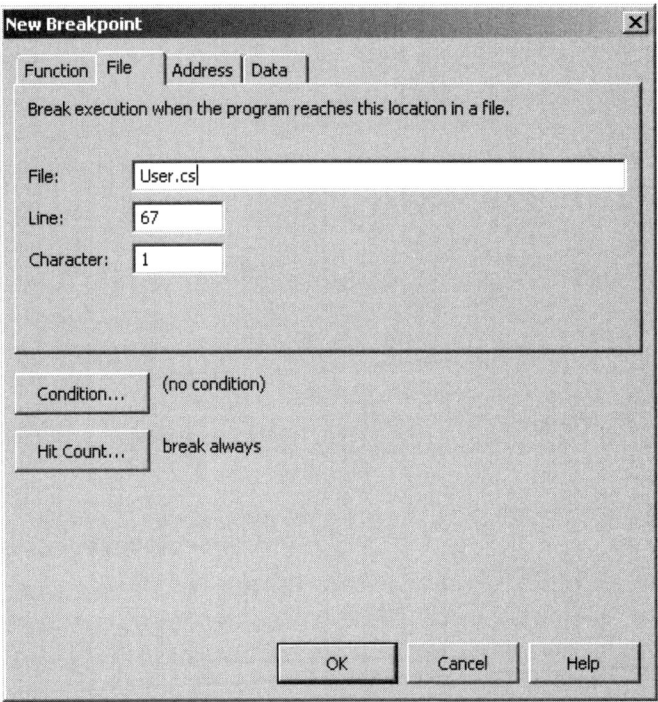

Figure 3-14. The File breakpoint feature of the New Breakpoint dialog box allows you to set breakpoints at any valid breakpoint location in any code file.

NOTE If the specified line number is not a valid line for a breakpoint, you are notified when you click OK in the New Breakpoint dialog box. If the character position is not valid, it assumes the character position closest to the value you entered.

The File breakpoint feature is the most often used breakpoint feature. It becomes even more powerful when used with the Conditions and Hit Count features, discussed later in this chapter.

Setting Address Breakpoints

Address breakpoints are a more advanced feature. They allow you to specify breakpoints based on their disassembled memory address, as shown in Figure 3-15.

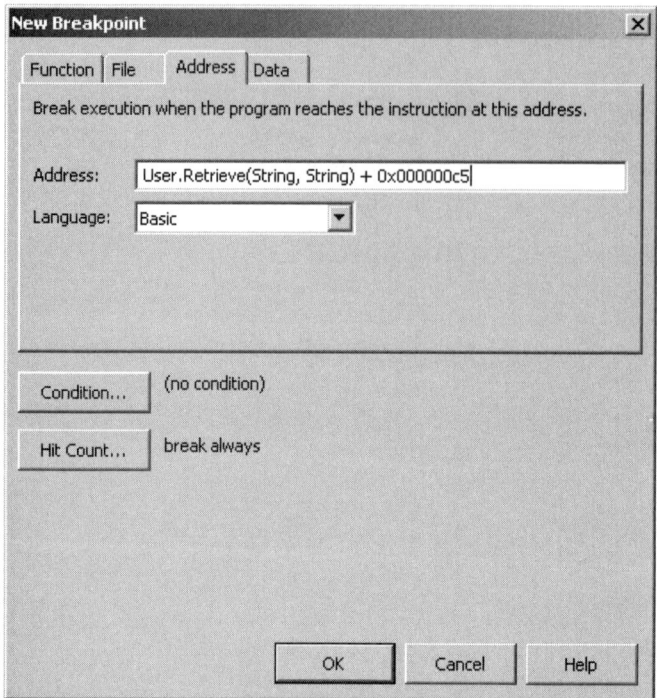

Figure 3-15. The Address breakpoint feature of the New Breakpoint dialog box allows you to set breakpoints based on the memory address.

Most developers don't find the need for this advanced feature, but if you are interested in more information, consult the Visual Studio help system.

Setting Data Breakpoints

Data breakpoints could be exceptionally useful. They cause the execution to break when the value of a variable is changed, without respect to a specific location in the file. The bad news is that neither VB nor C# supports this type of breakpoint, as shown in Figure 3-16.

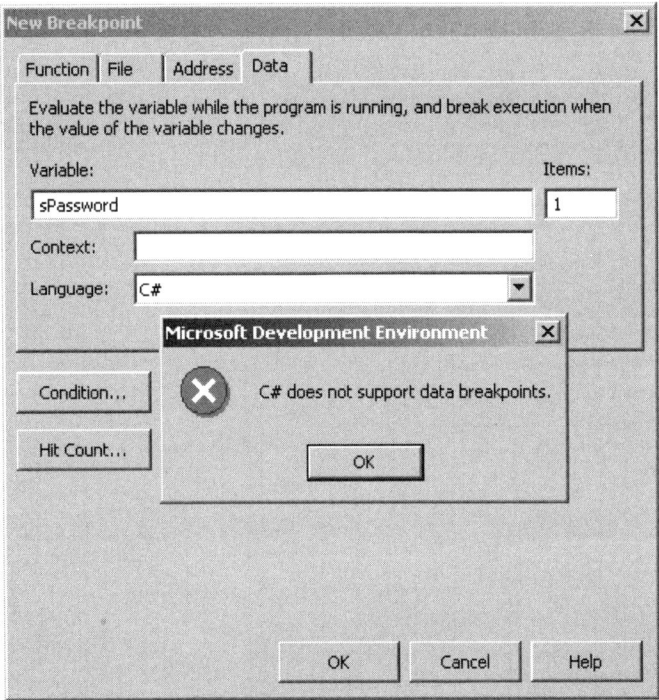

Figure 3-16. The Data breakpoint feature of the New Breakpoint dialog box is not available in VB or C#.

Using Conditional Breakpoints

You can add conditional logic to any breakpoint, regardless of its type, by selecting the Condition button in the New Breakpoint dialog box. This displays the Breakpoint Condition dialog box, shown in Figure 3-17, and allows you to specify that the breakpoint should be in effect only when a specific condition occurs.

In the Breakpoint Condition dialog box, enter a specific expression, and then define whether you want to break when the expression is true or when the expression changes.

Conditional breakpoints are most useful when you want execution to break based on a specific value of a variable or expression. For example, when iterating through a set of items with a For Each loop, you could break when you reach a specific entry using a conditional breakpoint.

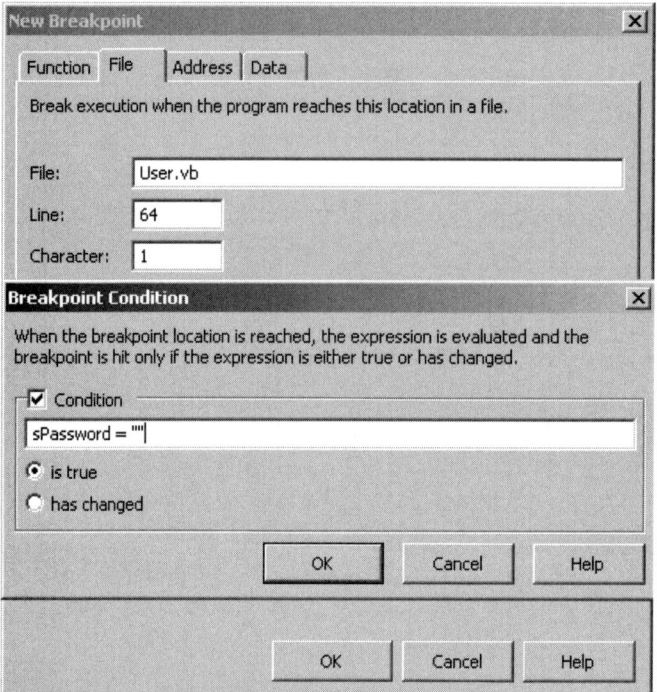

Figure 3-17. The Breakpoint Condition dialog box allows you to define a condition for a breakpoint. This breakpoint will be executed only when the password is empty.

Using Hit Count Breakpoints

The *hit count* defines the number of times that the breakpoint has been reached during the debugging session. Add a hit count condition to any breakpoint by selecting the Hit Count button in the New Breakpoint dialog box. The Breakpoint Hit Count dialog box appears, as shown in Figure 3-18. This dialog box allows you to specify that the breakpoint should be hit a certain number of times before execution actually breaks at that breakpoint.

In the Breakpoint Hit Count dialog box, specify whether to break always, break on a specific hit count, break when the hit count is greater than or equal to a value, or break when the hit count is a multiple of the value. You can also reset the hit count at any time from this dialog box.

Specifying a hit count is most useful when you have a loop and don't want to break each time the loop is executed.

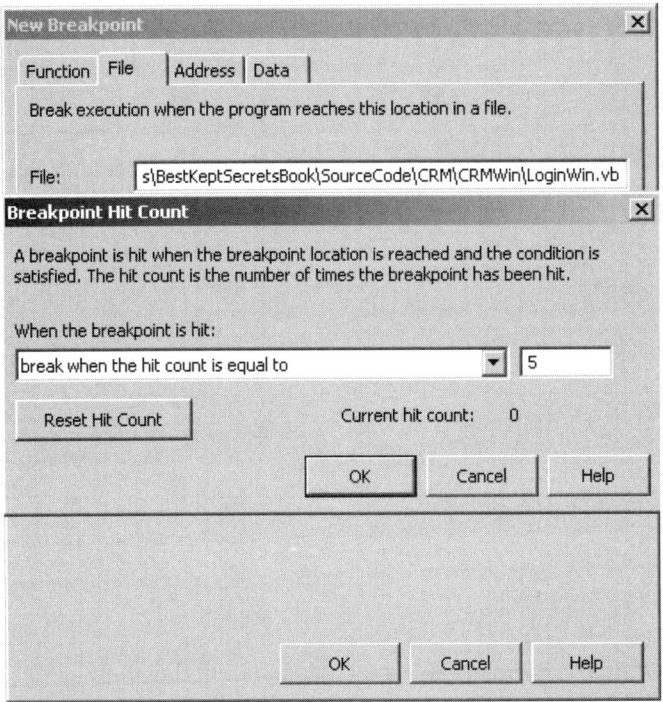

Figure 3-18. The Breakpoint Hit Count dialog box allows you to define the number of times a breakpoint should be hit before execution breaks.

Editing Breakpoint Properties

After you set a breakpoint, it appears as a filled red circle icon in the left margin of the statement at which execution will break. Hover over the icon to view the breakpoint properties, as shown in Figure 3-19.

To edit the breakpoint properties, right-click the line containing the breakpoint and select Breakpoint Properties. The New Breakpoint dialog box appears, with a new title identifying it as the Breakpoint Properties dialog box. You can then edit any of the properties for the breakpoint.

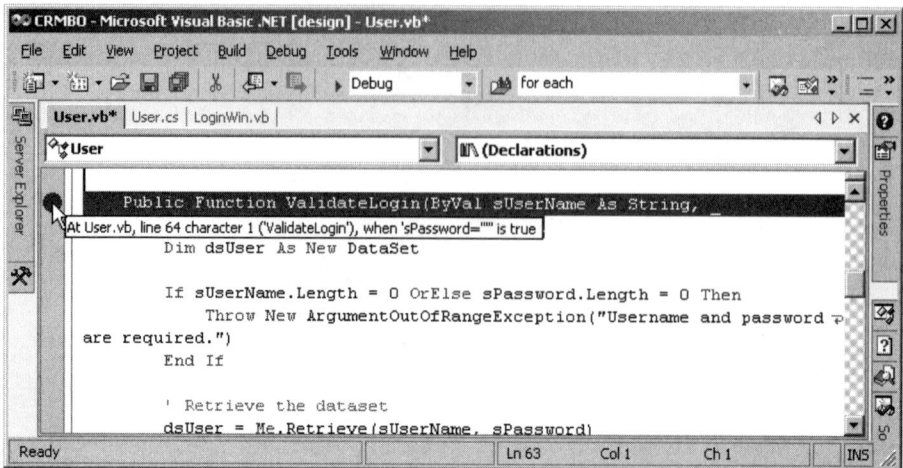

Figure 3-19. Hover over the breakpoint icon to view the breakpoint properties.

Setting Breakpoint State

When you set a breakpoint, the breakpoint is enabled, meaning that your code will stop execution when it reaches the line of code containing the breakpoint. The other breakpoint states are as follows:

- **Disabled:** Disable breakpoints temporarily by selecting Debug ➤ Disable All Breakpoints. Your code will then ignore the breakpoint during execution. Disabled breakpoints appear with an empty red circle icon.

- **Reenabled:** Enable disabled breakpoints by selecting Debug ➤ Enable All Breakpoints. The breakpoints will be enabled and will appear with a filled red circle icon.

- **Error:** A breakpoint will appear with an exclamation point in the icon if the breakpoint cannot be set at the defined line. This normally occurs when you attempt to set a breakpoint at an invalid location or define an invalid condition.

- **Warning:** A breakpoint will appear with a question mark in the icon if the breakpoint cannot be set because the code is not loaded. If the code is loaded later during executing, the breakpoint will be enabled.

- **Cleared:** Clear all breakpoints in the application by selecting Debug ➤ Clear All Breakpoints. To clear a single breakpoint, click the breakpoint icon in the left margin of the code window. The breakpoint icon will be removed.

Knowing how to take full advantage of the breakpoint features of the Visual Studio debugger can make your entire debugging experience more efficient and effective.

What Did This Chapter Cover?

You can improve your code readability, adaptability, and performance if you know a few tricks. This chapter covered several of those tricks.

Short-circuit your logical operators, shortcut your assignment operators, and perform string manipulation with StringBuilder for better performance. Declare the looping variable on the For or For Each statement to keep the variable local to your routine. Strictly convert your data types, perform better type casting, and alias changeable data types so you can easily alter them later.

Leverage regular expressions to validate end-user entry. Overload methods to provide multiple signatures, and overload operators as needed so your data types can perform math and comparison operations. Manage your code better by defining regions, using XML comments, and defining an obsolescence path.

Finally, take full advantage of the debugging features of Visual Studio to expand your debugging techniques and make your debugging experience as effective and efficient as possible.

The next chapter looks at secrets for using ADO.NET and working with data in your application.

Much ADO

MOST APPLICATIONS WORK with some type of data: enterprise data, customer data, experimental data, configuration data, and so on. ADO.NET, which is an intrinsic part of the .NET Framework, supplies the tools for working with data in your application, and Visual Studio provides valuable tools for building your database.

The purpose of this chapter is to show you some of the lesser-known but very useful features of ADO.NET. It also presents a tutorial for working with databases in Visual Studio.

What Will This Chapter Cover?

This chapter uncovers the following ADO.NET and Visual Studio database secrets:

- Working with your database using the Server Explorer

- Managing stored procedures with a database project

- Using the Microsoft Data Access Application Block

- Configuring your connection

- Viewing datasets as XML

- Filtering datasets using data views

- Building smarter datasets using extended properties

By the end of this chapter, you will understand why there is much ado about ADO.NET and the Visual Studio database features.

You will discover how to use Visual Studio's Server Explorer to access your database and view the database structure or contents. You will learn how to create your database, tables, and stored procedures, and how to manage those stored procedures using a database project within Visual Studio.

You will find out the secret to minimizing your data access code using the Microsoft Data Access Application Block. You will see how to use a configuration file for your connection strings. You will learn valuable techniques for working with your dataset, including how to view the dataset as XML to improve your debugging experience and how to filter datasets. Finally, you will discover how to use extended properties to expand the capabilities of your dataset, such as storing validation rules with a database column.

Working with Your Database Using the Server Explorer

If you are an expert at using the Microsoft SQL Server Enterprise Manager (or another database management tool), you may be surprised to hear that the Enterprise Manager database tools that you need for developing an application are available directly within Visual Studio! You don't need two products to work with your database when you can do it all with one.

Using Visual Studio's Server Explorer, you can conveniently access your database to view the database structure or contents directly from within Visual Studio. You can create your database, tables, and stored procedures. You can do everything a developer needs to do with a database without leaving the comfort of your Visual Studio IDE.

NOTE All of the Server Explorer tools described in this section work with the Microsoft SQL Server database. Many of these tools also work with other types of databases, such as Access, MySQL, and Oracle. The best way to determine if a Server Explorer tool works with your particular type of database is to try it.

Since the secret of these tools has been so well hidden, numerous experienced developers have not used the Server Explorer for working with databases. So this section provides an in-depth tutorial on using the Server Explorer database features.

Using the Server Explorer

The Server Explorer allows you to perform database operations that you need during the development phase of a project. It also provides access to system services such as event logs, message queues, and performance counters. But the focus in this section is on the database features available from the Server Explorer.

To access the Server Explorer, select View ➤ Server Explorer. The Server Explorer window appears, as shown in Figure 4-1. By default, the window will appear on the left side of the Visual Studio IDE. The elements of the Server

Explorer relating to databases are the Data Connections node and the SQL Servers node under Servers.

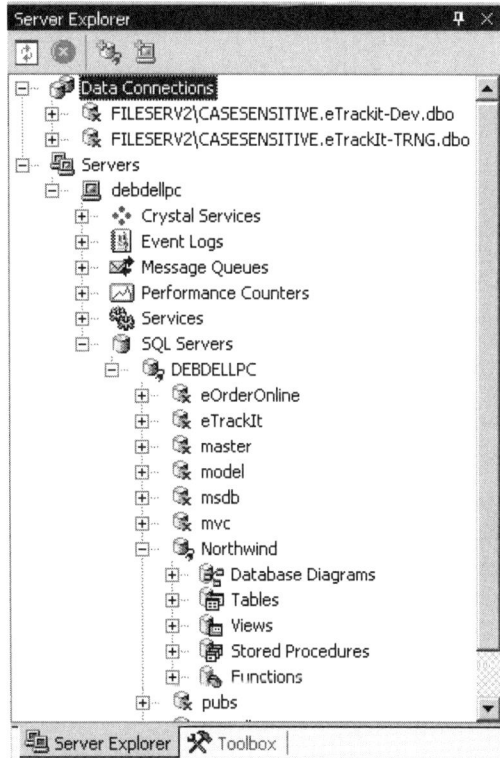

Figure 4-1 The Server Explorer allows you to manage your database connections and view the structure and content of your databases.

The Data Connections node in the Server Explorer allows you to define a connection to any type of database that has a .NET Framework data provider, including SQL Server, Microsoft Access, MySQL, and Oracle running on Windows or UNIX. From the Data Connections node, you can explore or update the database structure and view or edit the database contents.

The Servers node in the Server Explorer provides access to your services and servers, including SQL Servers. You can use the Data Connections node or the SQL Servers node to work with SQL Server databases.

You can build a new database, add new tables, update the database structure, edit data, and build stored procedures from the Server Explorer. The following sections provide detailed instructions on how to use the Server Explorer to perform each of these database operations. You may never need to use the Enterprise Manager again!

Adding a Connection to a Database

A *connection* is how you connect to an existing data source. If you are using any type of database other than SQL Server, you must define a connection to the database under the Data Connections node of the Server Explorer in order to access the database tools. If you are using SQL Server, you can access most of the database tools directly from the SQL Servers node without defining a connection.

To add a connection, right-click the Data Connections node and select Add Connection from the context menu. The Data Link Properties dialog box appears, as shown in Figure 4-2. This feature works with any type of database, as long as it has a .NET data provider or supports OLEDB.

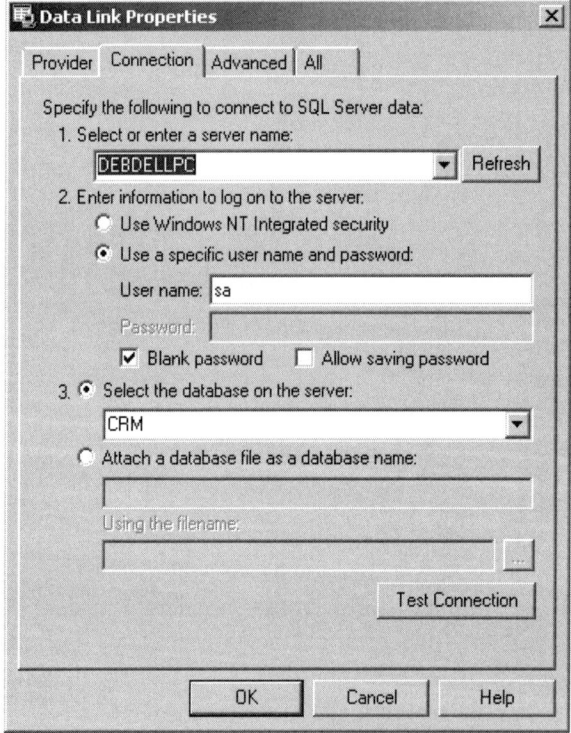

Figure 4-2. Use the Data Link Properties dialog box to define and test a connection to a database.

Once you define a connection, the database appears as a subnode in the Data Connections node, as shown in Figure 4-3. From this node, you can then access the other database tools.

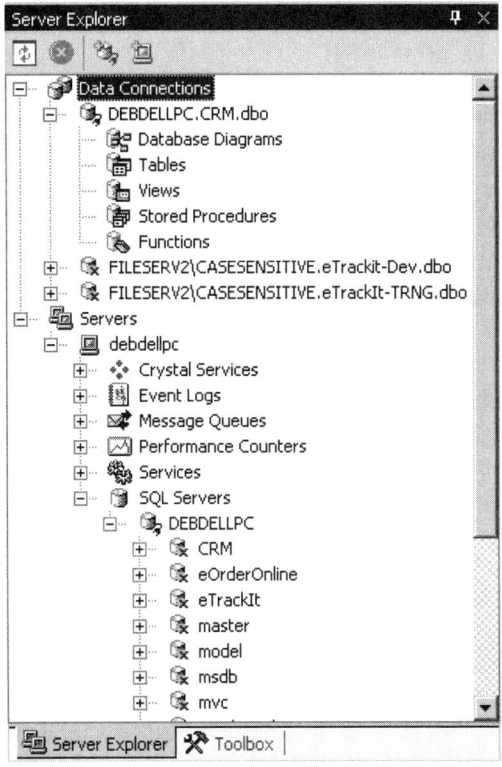

Figure 4-3. Any connection you define in the Server Explorer remains listed in the Data Connections node.

NOTE   You may experience difficulties accessing some of the Server Explorer database tools when there is a firewall between Visual Studio and the database to which you are connecting. See the Microsoft Knowledge Base for more information.

If you use the Visual Studio .NET data designers, you can drag connections from the Data Connections node and drop them onto the designer to precon figure data components. This is useful if you are using data binding or building typed datasets. For more information about data binding or building typed datasets, see the Visual Studio help system.

Create a connection in the Server Explorer any time you want to access a non-SQL Server database directly from Visual Studio, or when you want to predefine connections to SQL Server databases for use within Visual Studio.

Creating a New SQL Server Database

In many cases, your application needs to access existing databases. However, there are times when you need to create a new database for a new project or create a development or test version of a production database. You can create a database directly from within Visual Studio using the Server Explorer.

This section provides the steps for creating a new SQL Server database. Depending on the tools and features provided by your database vendor, you may have similar functionality available to create other types of databases within the Server Explorer.

To create a new SQL Server database, right-click the Data Connections node in the Server Explorer and select Create New SQL Server Database from the context menu, or right-click a SQL Server instance under the SQL Servers node (under Servers) and select New Database. The Create Database dialog box opens, as shown in Figure 4-4.

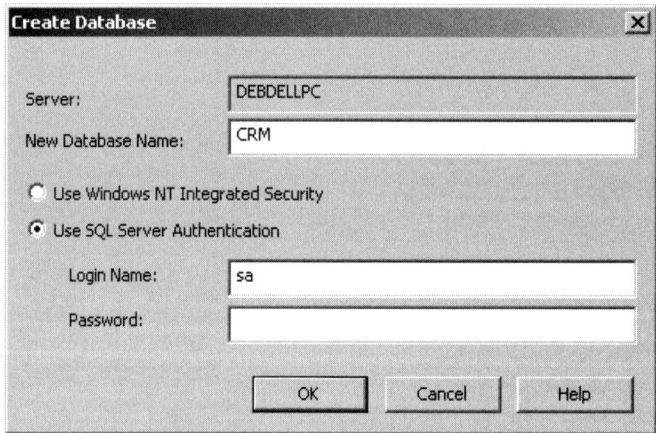

Figure 4-4. Use this dialog box to create a new SQL Server database directly from the Server Explorer.

The new database will then appear as a subnode under the SQL Servers node. If you created the new database from the Data Connections node, a connection to the database will also be created automatically and displayed as a subnode under the Data Connections node.

NOTE If you created the new database from the Data Connections node, you may need to refresh the SQL Servers node before the new database will appear as a subnode.

Use this feature any time you need to create a new SQL Server database for your project.

Creating New Tables

Whether you are creating a new database or working with an existing one, you may need to add tables to the database. Even if you work for an organization where the database administrators (DBAs) are the only people with authority to add tables, you may need to add tables to your development or test version of a database. You can create tables directly from the Server Explorer.

Create a new table within the Data Connections node of the Server Explorer by right-clicking the Tables node under the appropriate connection node. Or create a new table within the SQL Servers node by right-clicking the Tables node under the appropriate SQL Server database. The Table Designer then appears as a tab in the Visual Studio editor, as shown in Figure 4-5.

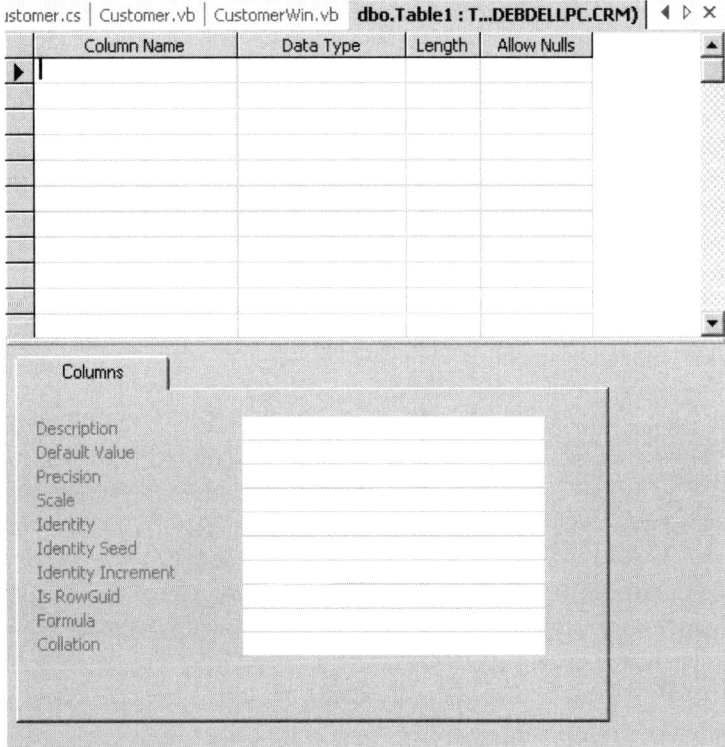

Figure 4-5. Define the columns of your table in the Table Designer.

The Table Designer allows you to view or edit the design of a table. You can define the columns; set their data type, length, and other properties; and define a primary key for the table. From here, you can also access the Property Pages dialog box to define the relationships between your tables, set indexes and keys, and establish database constraints.

Use the Table Designer any time you want to create a new table or edit an existing table in your database.

Viewing a Table's Structure

The Server Explorer exposes the structure for any database listed under the Data Connections node or SQL Servers node. You can view the list of tables, field names, stored procedures, stored procedure parameters, and related information.

View the list of tables defined for a database by expanding the Tables node for the database in the Server Explorer, either under the Data Connections node or the SQL Servers node. As an example, the list of tables in the Northwind database (which comes with Visual Studio) is shown in Figure 4-6.

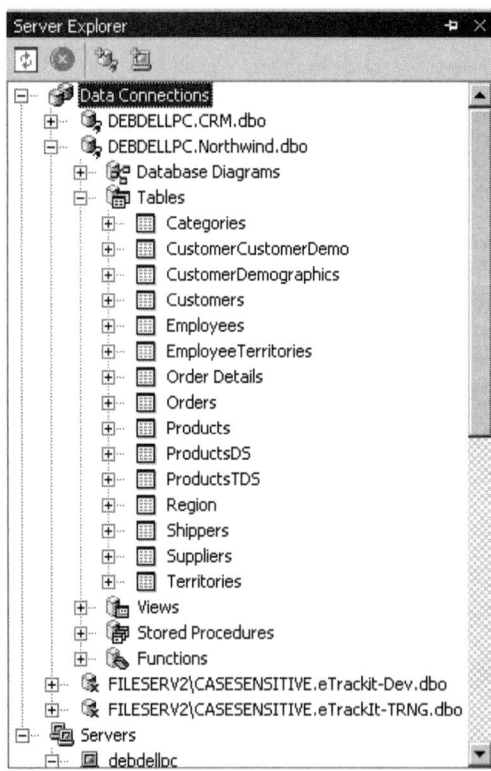

Figure 4-6. The Tables node displays the list of tables and provides access to the features for editing the structure or contents of those tables.

Expand the node for any table to see the list of fields in that table. This is useful when you need to quickly look up a field name while you are writing code within Visual Studio.

Editing a Table's Structure

You can use the Table Designer to add columns, modify columns, change the data type of a column, or change any other aspect of a database table.

To open the Table Designer for a table, expand the Tables node as described in the previous section. Then right-click the table name and select Design Table from the context menu. The Table Designer is then displayed. Figure 4-7 shows the Table Designer for the Customer table of the Northwind database.

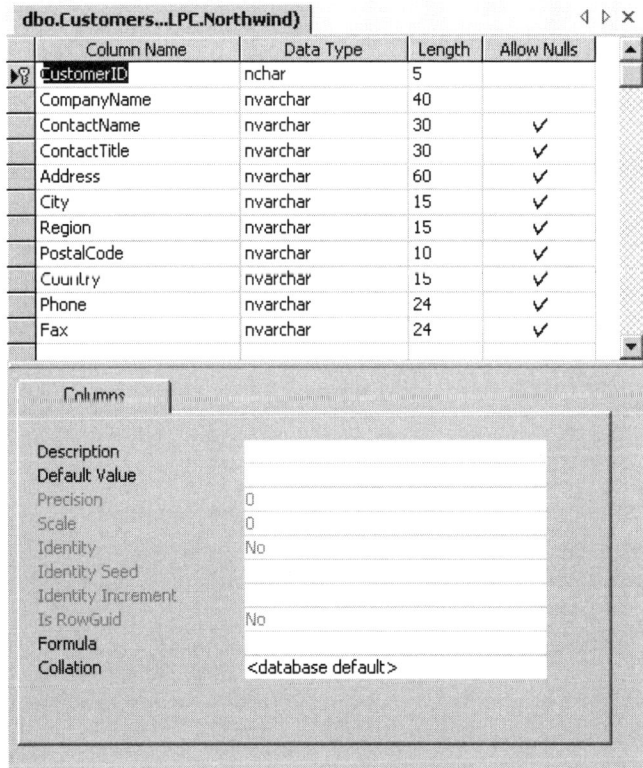

Figure 4-7. Use the Table Designer to edit the structure of a database table.

Editing Table Data

During the development and debugging process, you may want to create test data or examine existing data in your database. You can retrieve and edit the data directly from the Server Explorer.

To view or edit the data in a table, first expand the Tables node for the database in the Server Explorer, either under the Data Connections node or under the SQL Servers node (see Figure 4-6). Then double-click the table name, or right-click the table name and select Retrieve Data from Table from the context menu. The Query Designer Results pane is then displayed in the Visual Studio editor, as shown in Figure 4-8.

CustomerID	CompanyName	ContactName	ContactTitle	Address	City
AAAAA	A Test entry	<NULL>	<NULL>	<NULL>	<NU
ALFKI	Alfreds Futterkiste	Maria Anders	Sales Representati	Obere Str. 57	Berli
ANATR	Ana Trujillo Empare	Ana Trujillo	Owner	Avda. de la Constit	Méx
ANTON	Antonio Moreno Ta	Antonio Moreno	Owner	Mataderos 2312	Méx
AROUT	Around the Horn	Thomas Hardy	Sales Representati	120 Hanover Sq.	Lon
BERGS	Berglunds snabbköj	Christina Berglund	Order Administrato	Berguvsvägen 8	Lule
BLAUS	Blauer See Delikate	Hanna Moos	Sales Representati	Forsterstr. 57	Man
BLONP	Blondesddsl père el	Frédérique Citeaux	Marketing Manager	24, place Kléber	Stra
BOLID	Bólido Comidas prej	Martín Sommer	Owner	C/ Araquil, 67	Mad
BONAP	Bon app'	Laurence Lebihan	Owner	12, rue des Bouche	Mar:
BOTTM	Bottom-Dollar Mark	Elizabeth Lincoln	Accounting Manage	23 Tsawassen Blvd	Tsav
BSBEV	B's Beverages	Victoria Ashworth	Sales Representati	Fauntleroy Circus	Lon
CACTU	Cactus Comidas pa	Patricio Simpson	Sales Agent	Cerrito 333	Buei
CENTC	Centro comercial M	Francisco Chang	Marketing Manager	Sierras de Granada	Méx
CHOPS	Chop-suey Chinese	Yang Wang	Owner	Hauptstr. 29	Berr
COMMI	Comércio Mineiro	Pedro Afonso	Sales Associate	Av. dos Lusíadas, 2	Sao
CONSH	Consolidated Holdir	Elizabeth Brown	Sales Representati	Berkeley Gardens 1	Lon
DRACD	Drachenblut Delikat	Sven Ottlieb	Order Administrato	Walserweg 21	Aacl
DUMON	Du monde entier	Janine Labrune	Owner	67, rue des Cinqua	Nan
EASTC	Eastern Connectior	Ann Devon	Sales Agent	35 King George	Lon
ERNSH	Ernst Handel	Roland Mendel	Sales Manager	Kirchgasse 6	Graz
FAMIA	Familia Arquibaldo	Aria Cruz	Marketing Assistanl	Rua Orós, 92	Sao
FISSA	FISSA Fabrica Intei	Diego Roel	Accounting Manage	C/ Moralzarzal, 86	Mad
FOLIG	Folies gourmandes	Martine Rancé	Assistant Sales Age	184, chaussée de 1	Lille
FOLKO	Folk och fä HB	Maria Larsson	Owner	Åkergatan 24	Bräc
FRANK	Frankenversand	Peter Franken	Marketing Manager	Berliner Platz 43	Mün
FRANR	France restauratior	Carine Schmitt	Marketing Manager	54, rue Royale	Nan
FRANS	Franchi S.p.A.	Paolo Accorti	Sales Representati	Via Monte Bianco 3	Tori
FURIB	Furia Bacalhau e Fr	Lino Rodriguez	Sales Manager	Jardim das rosas n.	Lisb
GALED	Galería del gastrón	Eduardo Saavedra	Marketing Manager	Rambla de Cataluñ	Barc

Figure 4-8. The Query Designer Results pane allows you to view or edit the contents of a table.

From the Query Designer Results pane, you can view or edit any of the data in the table. You can change field values, and you can add and delete rows.

CAUTION Changes made in the Query Designer Results pane are immediately applied to the database, so you must be extremely careful when using this feature with a production database.

The Results pane of the Query Designer is actually presenting the results of a query. When you open the Results pane from a table in the Server Explorer, the query is automatically defined for you as "Select * from table."

The Query Designer has several other panes that allow you to modify this query or build other queries.

- **Diagram pane:** This is a graphical display of the query whose result is presented in the Results pane. To view the Diagram pane, select the Show Diagram Pane button on the Query toolbar. Define a query by checking or unchecking columns in the diagram, adding tables to the diagram, or changing any of the other diagram properties.

- **Grid pane:** This pane displays the fields of the query in a grid format and allows you to specify sorting and filtering criteria. To view the Grid pane, select the Show Grid Pane button on the Query toolbar.

- **SQL pane:** This pane displays the SQL statement for the current query. To view the SQL pane, select the Show SQL Pane button on the Query toolbar.

Modify the contents of the Results pane by first editing the query using the Diagram, Grid, or SQL pane. Changes made in any pane are reflected in the other panes. For example, if you check a field in the Diagram pane to include it in the Results pane, the Grid pane and SQL pane will also show the field.

 TIP Before updating the query, clear the * to remove the selection of all database fields so you can select only those fields that you want to view or edit. The easiest way to clear the * is to delete the * row using the Grid pane.

When you have defined the desired query, click the Run Query button (shown with a red exclamation mark) on the Query toolbar to run the query and update the Results pane. The Query Designer with all four panes is shown in Figure 4-9.

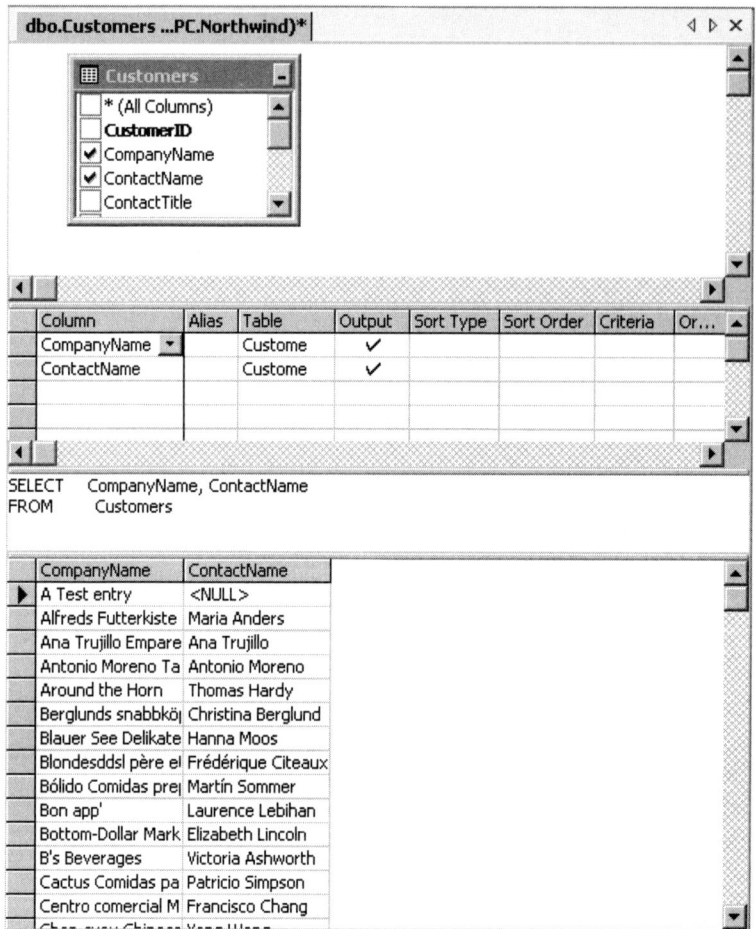

Figure 4-9. The Diagram, Grid, and SQL panes of the Query Designer allow you to define and execute a query against any table listed in the Server Explorer, and the Results pane displays the results of that query.

TIP   If the Query Designer Results pane contents turn gray, this indicates that the data no longer matches the defined query. Use the Run Query button in the Query toolbar to reexecute the query and refresh the data.

Use the Query Designer any time that you want to view or edit data in any table in any database listed in the Server Explorer. You can also use the Query Designer to build or test queries that will later be added to your code or as stored procedures.

Creating or Editing Stored Procedures

Stored procedures are precompiled SQL statements stored within the database that are used to access database data. Stored procedures are primarily used to insert, update, delete, and retrieve data from the database. They can also be used to manipulate and perform calculations on database data. You can create and edit stored procedures from the Server Explorer.

Stored procedures are the recommended technique for accessing data from an application. They offer the following advantages over writing SQL statements in your application:

- **Better execution:** Stored procedures execute faster than SQL statements in your application because they are precompiled and execute directly in the database.

- **Better security:** It is harder for a hacker to break into or inappropriately access a database that is set up to execute only stored procedures.

View the list of all of the stored procedures defined for a database by expanding the Stored Procedures node (either under the Data Connections node or the SQL Servers node) in the Server Explorer. The stored procedures in the Northwind database are shown in Figure 4-10.

To edit an existing stored procedure listed in the Stored Procedures node, double-click it. The Stored Procedure Editor then appears as a tab in the Visual Studio editor. A stored procedure from the Northwind database is shown in Figure 4-11.

To create a new stored procedure within the Server Explorer, right-click the Stored Procedures node, either under the Data Connections node or the SQL Servers node, and select New Stored Procedure from the context menu. The Stored Procedure Editor then appears for entry of the new stored procedure.

Visual Studio provides a code template for your stored procedure. Add any desired SQL statements to the template to complete the stored procedure.

After you have finished creating or editing a stored procedure, you can run it by right-clicking in the editor and selecting Run Stored Procedure from the context menu. This executes the stored procedure, prompting for any parameters, and places the results in the Output window.

Figure 4-10. The Stored Procedures node displays the list of stored procedures with their parameters and provides access to the features for editing the stored procedures.

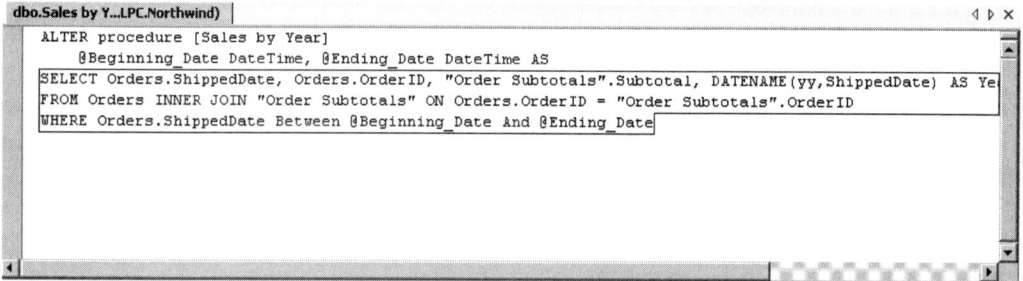

Figure 4-11. The Stored Procedure Editor allows you to create or edit your stored procedures.

Managing Stored Procedures with a Database Project

The previous section described how to create stored procedures directly in the database using Server Explorer features. Although this may be a convenient way to create stored procedures, it may not be the best way for your organization, because it does not provide a way to manage access or track revisions to the stored procedures. A better way to manage your stored procedures is to use stored procedure script files and store those script files as part of your solution. That's the purpose of the database project in Visual Studio.

NOTE   Database projects are not available in all editions of Visual Studio.

A database project is a well-hidden gem that provides a template for managing database scripts within your application's solution. As part of your solution, these scripts are then managed by your source code control tool, along with the other files in your solution. (You are using source code control, right?)

NOTE   A source code control product, such as Microsoft SourceSafe, provides features to ensure that only one developer modifies a project file at a time, and it keeps an edit history to track changes and who made the changes. It also has a checkpoint feature that allows you to checkpoint a specific set of files for a release. By maintaining your database scripts as part of your application solution, you gain all of the same source code control benefits that you have for your other code files.

Because database projects are another feature that few experienced developers are aware of, this section provides a detailed tutorial on how to create and use a database project to manage your database script files.

NOTE   The database project features described in this section work with the Microsoft SQL Server database. Some of these features may also work with other types of databases. The best way to determine which features work with your particular type of database is to try them.

Creating a Database Project

A database project is a specialized project template that allows you to create a project for managing your stored procedure and other database script files.

Add a database project to your solution as follows:

1. Right-click the solution in the Solution Explorer and select Add ➤ New Project from the context menu, or select File ➤ Add Project ➤ New Project from the menu. The Add New Project dialog box is displayed, as shown in Figure 4-12.

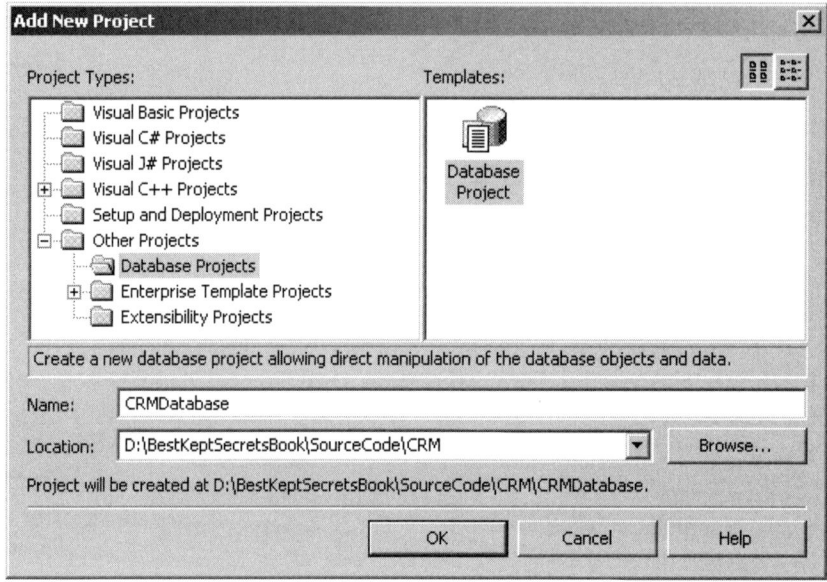

Figure 4-12. The Add New Project dialog box allows you to create a project using a specific project template.

2. Select Database Projects as the project type from the Other Projects node in the Add New Project dialog box.

3. Define a project name for the database project, verify the location, and click OK.

 CAUTION The location of the database project cannot be changed, so ensure that it is correct before clicking OK in the Add New Project dialog box.

4. The Add Database Reference dialog box is displayed, as shown in Figure 4-13. This dialog box lists all of the database connections defined in the Server Explorer Data Connections node. Select the database to be used by the new database project or add a new database connection. Then click OK.

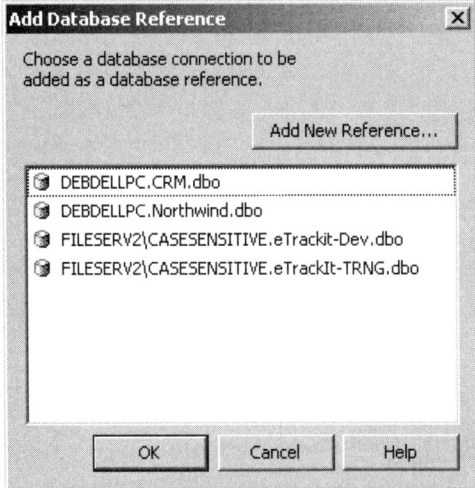

Figure 4-13. The Add Database Reference dialog box allows you to associate a specific database with the database project.

TIP Select one of your existing databases (Northwind is a good example) as your database reference to see how this process works and to try out the many features of a database project, as described in the remainder of this section.

The new database project is then added to your solution and appears in the Solution Explorer, as shown in Figure 4-14.

The resulting database project provides a convenient place to manage your database script files. They are all saved as part of the solution, and if the solution is managed by a source code control product, the database files will be under source code control as well.

Figure 4-14. The Solution Explorer manages the new database project just like any other project.

Use a database project in your application solution if your application needs to manage any database scripts, including scripts to create or update tables and define stored procedures.

Managing Database Project Scripts

When you create a database project, a set of folders is created in the Solution Explorer to aid you in managing your scripts, queries, and database references.

The database project creates the following folders under the database project node in the Solution Explorer:

- **Change Scripts:** Includes scripts for storing modifications that you intend to make to a database.

- **Create Scripts:** Includes scripts for creating the database, including the tables and stored procedures.

- **Queries:** Stores queries to retrieve, create, modify, or delete data in the database. This allows you to store and reexecute queries you defined in the Query Designer. See the "Editing Table Data" section earlier in this chapter for more information about the Query Designer.

- **Database References:** Contains the connection information associated with the scripts and queries. A database project can have multiple database references.

Even though you can have multiple database references, only one is active at a time, indicated by a red arrow in the database link icon (see Figure 4-14). Any action taken within the database project will apply to the currently active database reference only. Change the default database reference by right-clicking the database project and selecting Set Default Reference from the context menu.

Initially, the script and query folders are empty, and the Database References folder contains the link to the database defined when the database project was created (see Figure 4-13).

Use the folders within the database project to manage your scripts, as described in the following sections.

Generating Create Scripts

The purpose of the database project's Create Scripts folder is to manage the set of scripts that can be used to generate your database. This provides an easy way to re-create your database for testing or when the application is ready for production.

To define the create scripts for a database (as defined by the active database reference), right-click the Create Scripts folder in the Solution Explorer and select Generate Create Script from the context menu. After you log in to the database, the Generate Create Scripts dialog box is displayed, as shown in Figure 4-15.

If you are creating the scripts for the first time, you will most likely want to script all of your database objects, so check the Script all objects check box on the General tab, and then click OK. The scripts to create your database tables, stored procedures, and other objects are generated from the existing database structure and inserted in the Create Scripts folder, as shown in Figure 4-16.

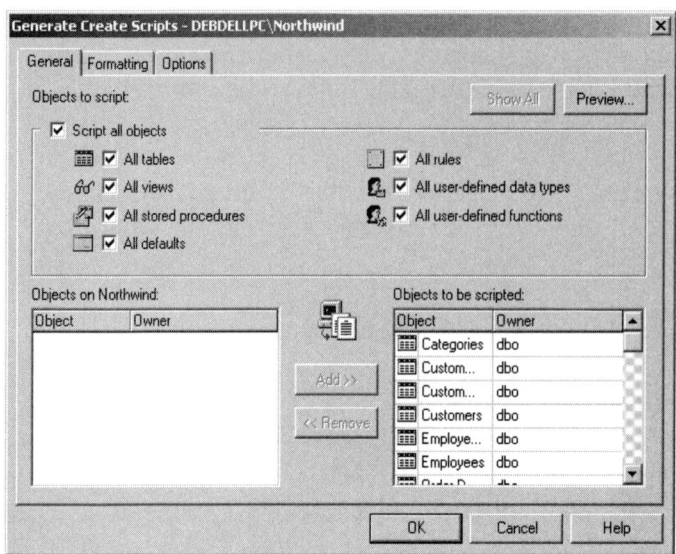

Figure 4-15. The Generate Create Scripts dialog box allows you to define the criteria for generating your database create scripts.

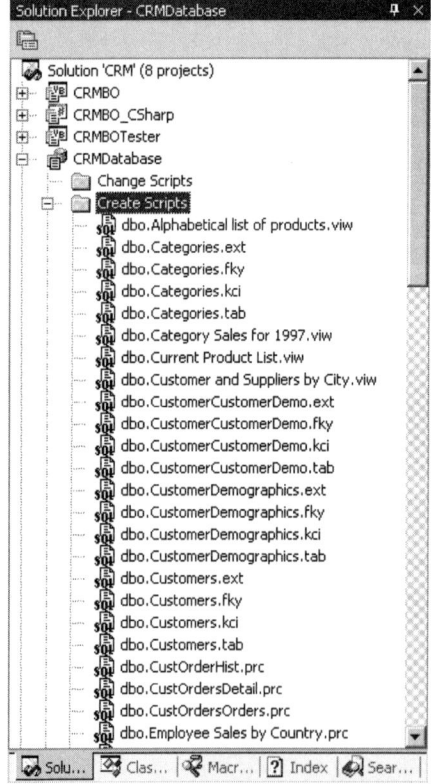

Figure 4-16. The generated scripts all appear in the Solution Explorer.

TIP   If you want to keep your scripts more organized, create sub-folders within the Create Scripts folder, and then generate each type of scripting object into its own folder. This makes it easier to manage your scripting objects, such as your stored procedures.

The resulting scripts can be used to re-create your database structure. You can then manage these scripts with your source code control product.

If you script all of your stored procedures in this way, you can update your stored procedures through these scripts instead of directly in the database. See the "Working with Stored Procedure Scripts" section later in this chapter for more information.

Generating a Command File

Since you may have many script files, it is easier to re-create your database if you group the scripts into one command file.

Create a command file for your scripts by right-clicking the Create Scripts folder in the Solution Explorer and selecting Create Command File from the context menu. The Create Command File dialog box is displayed, as shown in Figure 4-17.

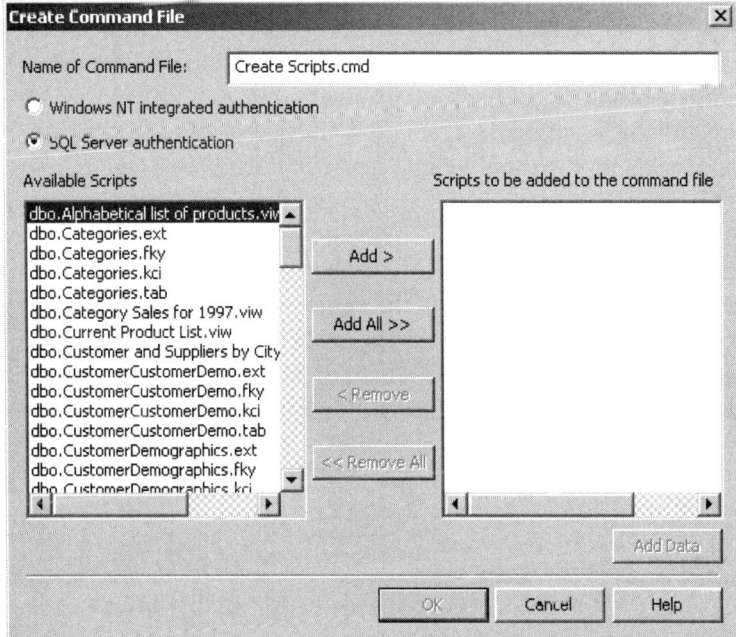

Figure 4-17. The Create Command File dialog box allows you to create a command file to execute any set of scripts defined in your Create Scripts folder.

Select the scripts you wish to include in the command file. You can use this feature to produce any set of scripts for creating the objects in your database. You can also set up one command file to create your entire database with one command.

You can run the set of scripts directly from the Solution Explorer by right-clicking the command file and selecting Run On from the context menu. The command file will execute against the database defined by the active database reference.

Use this technique to script out your development database, create a command file, and run the resulting command file on the test database server to create the database for your quality assurance (QA) staff. After passing QA, you can provide the command file and scripts to your DBA for execution on the production database server.

Working with Stored Procedure Scripts

Using the database project to create, edit, and test your stored procedure as script files has many benefits over editing the stored procedures directly in the database. It is much safer to edit and test a script than to make changes to the stored procedure directly in the database, especially if other developers are using the same database. The scripts can be managed by source code control, whereas changes directly to the database are not tracked and cannot easily be undone. The Find in Files and other Visual Studio Find features will search through the scripts (see the "Finding Code" section in Chapter 1 for more information). You can also more easily apply stored procedure changes that you make to another database, such as the QA or production system.

After you generate the create scripts for your database, as described earlier in this chapter, any existing stored procedures in the database are listed in the Create Scripts folder of the Solution Explorer. The stored procedures have a .prc extension.

Open a stored procedure file by double-clicking it, or by right-clicking it and selecting Open from the context menu. Edit the contents of the stored procedure in this file, instead of editing the file directly in the database. Test any part of the stored procedure by selecting it, right-clicking, and choosing Run Selection. This will execute the selected portion of the stored procedure and display the results in the Output window, as shown in Figure 4-18.

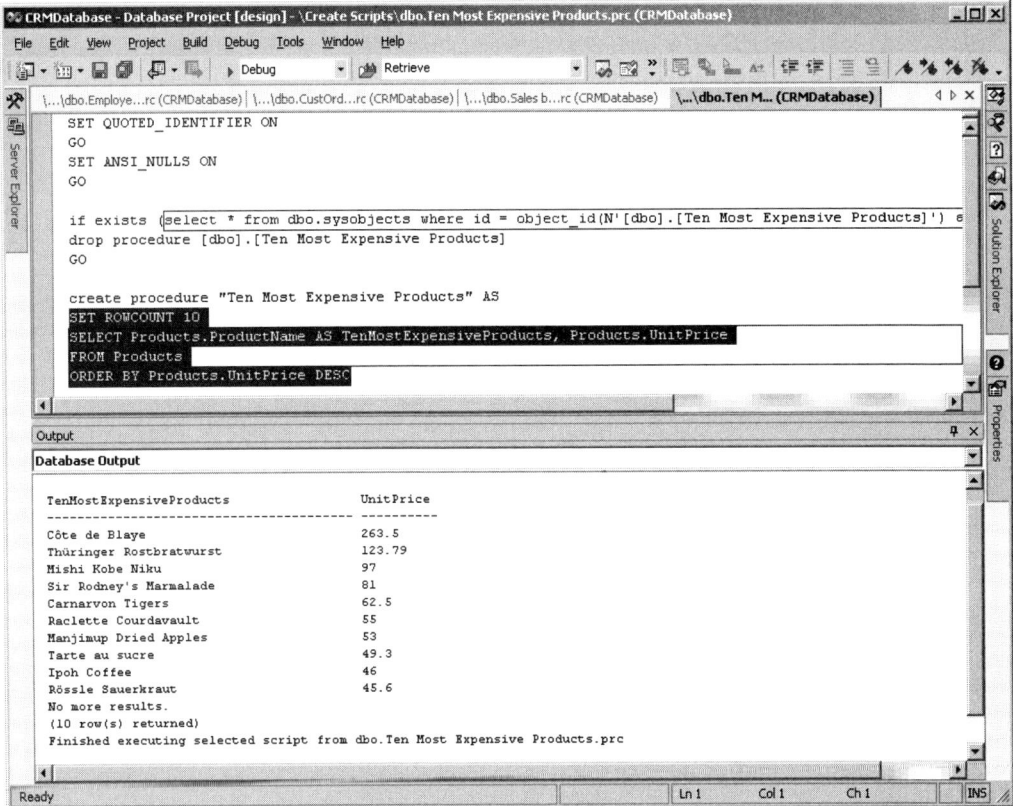

Figure 4-18. Execute any portion of the stored procedure and see the results in the Output window.

When you want to apply the updated stored procedure to the database (as defined by the default database reference), right-click in the stored procedure script file and select Run from the context menu. This won't run the stored procedure, but will instead run the stored procedure script, which applies the revised script to the database. You can also use your stored procedure scripts to apply your stored procedure changes to the QA or production database.

Creating New Stored Procedure Scripts

Now that you have a database project with all of your stored procedure scripts, any new stored procedure should be created with a script in the database project and tested before it is applied to the database.

Create new stored procedures in the Create Scripts folder of the Solution Explorer by right-clicking Create Scripts and selecting Add SQL Script. The Add New Item dialog box is then displayed, as shown in Figure 4-19.

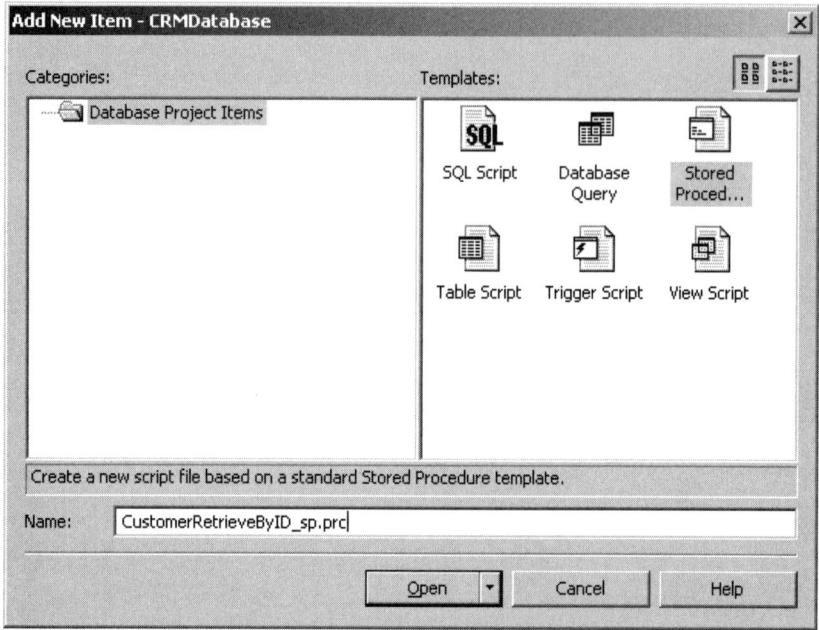

Figure 4-19. Add any type of database script to the Create Scripts folder.

To create a new stored procedure, select Stored Procedure Script. A stored procedure script template is then displayed as a tab in the Visual Studio editor.

TIP   If you don't like the stored procedure script template, you can create your own and add it to the Database Project Items subdirectory of your templates directory (for example, C:\Program Files\Microsoft Visual Studio .NET 2003\Common7\ Tools\ Templates\Database Project Items). Your template will then appear in the Add New Item dialog box (shown in Figure 4-19).

Use the template as a starting point for your stored procedure. When the stored procedure is complete, test it by right-clicking it and choosing Run Selection. Apply it to the database by right-clicking in the stored procedure script file and choosing Run.

TIP If you need help creating your stored procedure, right-click the stored procedure script template and select Insert SQL from the context menu. The Query Designer is then displayed to assist you with building your query.

Using a database project is a great way to manage the database scripts, including the stored procedure scripts, for your project.

Using the Microsoft Data Access Application Block

So far, this chapter has discussed the little-known tools available within Visual Studio to assist you with working with your database and stored procedures. But to use the database within your application, you need to write the code to access that database. Or do you?

Microsoft has developed a project that encapsulates all of the code needed to access a SQL Server database using the .NET Framework data access library, better known as ADO.NET. This project is called the Microsoft Data Access Application Block, and it is available, with full source, from `http://msdn.microsoft.com/patterns` (search for "Data Access Application Block").

This project is basically the data access component (DAC) portion of a multitilayered architecture, encapsulating all of the code that accesses the database into one component. If you use this component, you don't need to have any code in your application to establish a connection, set up a transaction, execute a stored procedure, or fill a dataset. Everything you need for database access is in the Data Access Application Block.

To use this application block, download and install the Data Access Application Block from the Microsoft web site. Then add the project to your solution by right-clicking the solution and selecting Add ➤ Existing Project from the context menu. The project then appears within the solution in the Solution Explorer. Finally, set a reference to the Data Access Application Block project from any project that needs to use it. That's it!

The SQLHelper class in the Data Access Application Block contains the data access code that can call stored procedures or execute SQL commands against a SQL Server database. The methods within the SQLHelper class can return data as a DataSet, a DataReader, or an XMLReader object.

TIP Even if you want to write your own data access component, save time by starting with the Data Access Application Block code and updating it to suit your needs. Since you have the full source, you can enhance it however you wish.

Once you have the Data Access Application Block in your solution, use it to access your data. The code to use the SQLHelper ExecuteDataset method to retrieve a DataSet object given a SQL statement follows.

In VB:

```
Imports Microsoft.ApplicationBlocks.Data
Public Function Retrieve() As DataSet
    Dim dsCustomer As DataSet
    dsCustomer = SqlHelper.ExecuteDataset(sConn, _
    CommandType.Text, _
    "Select CustomerID, CompanyName from Customers Order by CompanyName")
    Return dsCustomer
End Function
```

In C#:

```
using Microsoft.ApplicationBlocks.Data;
public DataSet Retrieve()
{
    DataSet dsCustomer = SqlHelper.ExecuteDataset(sConn,
    CommandType.Text,
  "Select CustomerID, CompanyName from Customers Order by CompanyName");
    return dsCustomer;
}
```

The first parameter to the ExecuteDataset method of the SQLHelper class is the connection string. See the "Configuring Your Connection" section later in this chapter for more information about defining the connection string.

The second parameter defines the type of command that is to be executed. In this case, it is a text command. The last parameter is the command text. In this example, the CustomerID and CompanyName fields are retrieved from the Customers table, the results are sorted by the CompanyName field, and the results are returned in a DataSet object.

You can use the SQLHelper class to execute a stored procedure instead of a text command. The code to use the SQLHelper class to call a stored procedure with parameters is shown in the following example.

In VB:

```
Public Function Retrieve(ByVal sCustomerID As String) As DataSet
    Dim dsCustomer As DataSet
    dsCustomer = SqlHelper.ExecuteDataset(sConn, _
        CommandType.StoredProcedure, _
        "CustomerRetrieveByID_sp", _
        New SqlClient.SqlParameter("@sID", sCustomerID))
```

```
        Return dsCustomer
End Function
```

In C#:

```
public DataSet Retrieve(String sCustomerID)
{
    DataSet dsCustomer = SqlHelper.ExecuteDataset(sConn,
        CommandType.StoredProcedure,
        "CustomerRetrieveByID_sp",
        new System.Data.SqlClient.SqlParameter("@sID", sCustomerID));
    return dsCustomer;
}
```

The first parameter is again the connection string. The second parameter defines the command type as a stored procedure. The third parameter is the name of the stored procedure.

NOTE   The Northwind database provided with Visual Studio does not contain a CustomerRetrieveByID stored procedure. If you want to try this code, you will need to either replace the stored procedure name with one from the Northwind database or write a stored procedure with this name.

The last parameter of the ExecuteDataset method defines the parameter(s) that are passed to the stored procedure. In this case, there is only one parameter, which is the customer ID. The constructor for the SqlParameter object has two parameters. The first is the name of the stored procedure parameter (@sID), and the second is the value of the parameter (sCustomerID).

Use the Microsoft Data Access Application Block to minimize the amount of code you need to write to access your database.

Configuring Your Connection

For your application to access a database, it needs to establish a connection to that database. The code to establish this connection is built into the Data Access Application Block, as discussed in the previous section, but you are still responsible for configuring the connection string.

A connection string defines the source database name and any other parameters needed to establish the initial connection to the database. For example, the following string is a valid connection string for accessing the Northwind database:

```
data source=(local);initial catalog=Northwind;user ID=sa;password=
```

This string defines the data source as local, meaning it is accessing the SQL Server database on the local computer. This is frequently the case when working with your development server. The initial catalog is the name of the database; in this case, it is Northwind. The user ID is sa, and the password is blank.

 CAUTION   When you create your own databases for your application, create a user ID and password to ensure that your database is secure. Do *not* use a user ID of sa and blank password. Anyone with any programming or database knowledge knows that ID and could hack your database.

You could create a constant in your application to store the connection string. But a better choice is to store it in the application's configuration file. This approach offers the following benefits:

- You can easily change the application configuration file connection string without recompiling the application. This allows you to change the connection string from the development database to the test database without recompiling.

- The DBA or other person responsible for the production system can easily change the application configuration file to contain the connection string for the production database. That person can also change the user ID and password in the connection string as needed.

 CAUTION   For security reasons, you may want to store the connection string encrypted on your production system and decrypt it in your production code. For more information about encryption, see the Visual Studio help system.

If you don't already have a configuration file defined for your application, create one by right-clicking the project containing the startup code for your application and selecting Add ➤ Add New Item from the context menu. The Add New Item dialog box is displayed, as shown in Figure 4-20. Select the

Application Configuration File item and click OK. Visual Studio then adds an App.config file to your project.

NOTE   If you are developing a web application, a Web.config file is already created for you. Use that file instead of a separate App.config file.

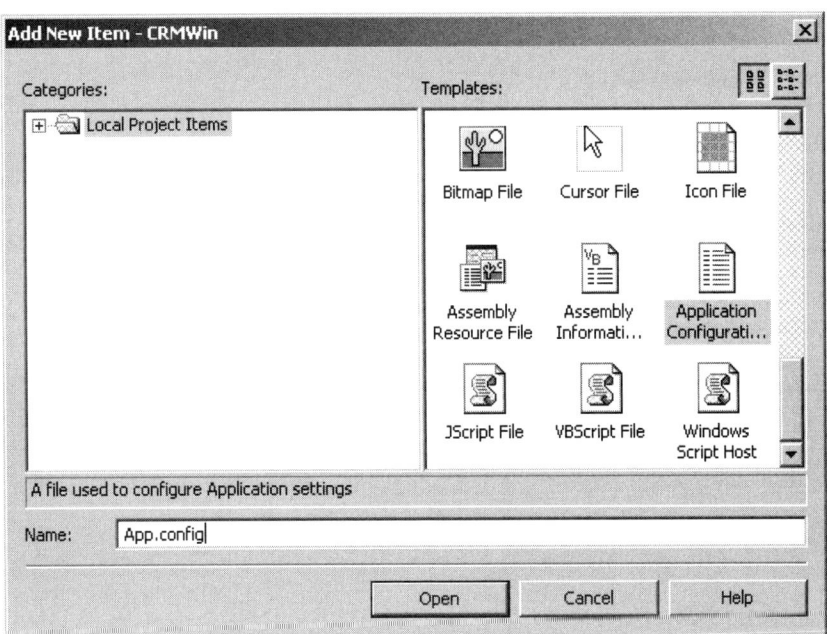

Figure 4-20. The Add New Item dialog box provides an Application Configuration File template.

Double-click the App.config file in the Solution Explorer to edit it. Insert the connection string in the AppSettings section of the file as follows:

```
<?xml version="1.0" encoding="utf-8"?>
<configuration>
  <appSettings>
    <add key="CONN" value="data source=(local);initial catalog=Northwind; ↵
user ID=sa;password=" />
  </appSettings>
</configuration>
```

CAUTION   The App.config file is an XML file and is case-sensitive. Ensure that the element and attribute names, such as appSettings, are defined with the correct uppercase and lower-case letters.

CAUTION   The value string in the App.config file must be defined on one line. It cannot contain extraneous characters, such as a carriage return.

The appSettings element in the App.config file is easy to access from your code using the System.Configuration.ConfigurationSettings class.

In VB:

```
sConn = Configuration.ConfigurationSettings.AppSettings("CONN").ToString()
```

In C#:

```
string sConn = System.Configuration.ConfigurationSettings.AppSettings["CONN"];
```

This code retrieves the value of the appSettings configuration file entry that is defined with a key of CONN.

Configuring your connection with a configuration file makes it easy to work with your connection string, as well as any other application settings that you want to define for your application.

Viewing Datasets As XML

Have you ever tried to use the Watch or Locals window to view the contents of your dataset? You end up with something like Figure 4-21. It is very difficult to find your data in there!

It is much easier to view your dataset using the XML features provided in ADO.NET. Use the GetXML method to display the XML associated with your dataset.

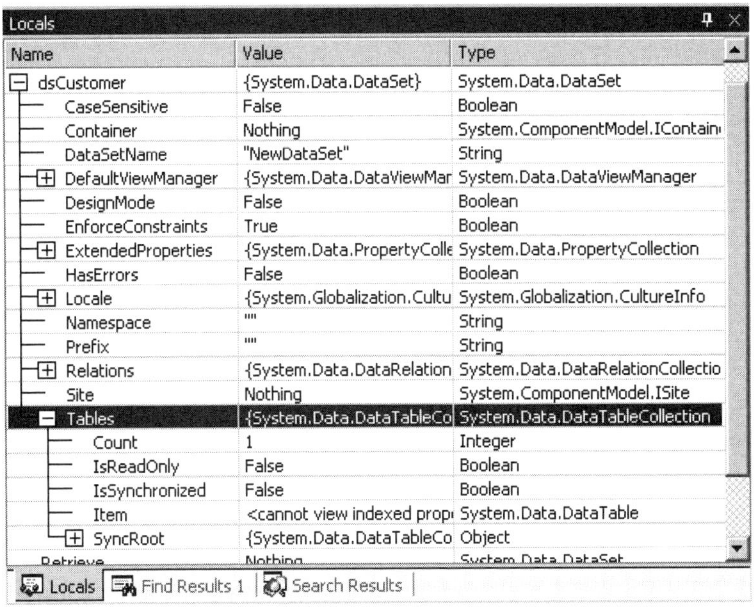

Figure 4-21. The Locals window is very useful for debugging, but not when it comes to viewing the contents of your dataset.

In VB:

```
Debug.WriteLine(dsCustomer.GetXml())
```

In C#:

```
Debug.WriteLine(dsCustomer.GetXml());
```

In this example, dsCustomer is the dataset containing fields for a particular customer in the Northwind database's Customers table. The GetXML method displays the contents of the dsCustomer dataset in XML format, as follows:

```
<NewDataSet>
  <Customer>
    <CustomerID>AROUT</CustomerID>
    <CompanyName>Around the Horn</CompanyName>
    <Country>UK</Country>
    <PostalCode>WA1 1DP</PostalCode>
  </Customer>
</NewDataSet>
```

You can also use the GetXML method from the Command window to view the dataset while you are debugging, as shown in Figure 4-22.

Figure 4-22. Using the GetXML method in the Command window provides a nicer view of the dataset than using the Locals or Watch window.

If the dataset is large or if you want to output the XML to a file that you can search, use the WriteXML method instead to write the dataset to a defined file.
In VB:

```
dsCustomer.WriteXml("c:\temp\customerDataset.xml")
```

In C#:

```
dsCustomer.WriteXml("c:\temp\customerDataset.xml");
```

And if you want to see the structure of the database, view the schema in XML format using the GetXMLSchema method.
In VB:

```
dsCustomer.GetXmlSchema()
```

In C#:

```
dsCustomer.GetXmlSchema();
```

As an example, the schema definition for the dsCustomer dataset is as follows:

```
<?xml version="1.0" encoding="utf-16"?>
<xs:schema id="NewDataSet" xmlns="" xmlns:xs="http://www.w3.org/2001/XMLSchema" ⮐
xmlns:msdata="urn:schemas-microsoft-com:xml-msdata">
  <xs:element name="NewDataSet" msdata:IsDataSet="true">
    <xs:complexType>
      <xs:choice maxOccurs="unbounded">
        <xs:element name="Customer">
          <xs:complexType>
            <xs:sequence>
              <xs:element name="CustomerID" type="xs:string" minOccurs="0" />
              <xs:element name="CompanyName" type="xs:string" minOccurs="0" />
              <xs:element name="Country" type="xs:string" minOccurs="0" />
              <xs:element name="PostalCode" type="xs:string" minOccurs="0" />
            </xs:sequence>
          </xs:complexType>
        </xs:element>
      </xs:choice>
    </xs:complexType>
  </xs:element>
</xs:schema>
```

The schema lists each field of the dataset as an XML element. Within each element, it lists the name and properties of each field as an XML attribute. In this example, the dataset contains the CustomerID, CompanyName, Country, and PostalCode fields.

Use these XML features of the dataset to assist you in debugging your data access code.

Filtering Datasets Using Data Views

When your application has retrieved data into a dataset, you may need to sort or filter that data. It is often more efficient to work with the dataset you already have than to go back to the database. Sort and filter an existing dataset in your application using a data view.

As an example, suppose you have a grid containing all customers within a specified region. The end user wants to filter the grid contents to only those customers within a particular postal code. Your application could do this by executing another stored procedure or SQL statement to collect the appropriate data from the database, or you could simply filter the dataset that you already have.

Each table in a dataset has a default data view that you can access, as shown in the following example.

In VB:

```
Dim dv As DataView = dsCustomer.Tables(0).DefaultView
```

In C#:

```
DataView dv = dsCustomer.Tables[0].DefaultView;
```

If you need to display the same dataset in different ways, you can create additional data views and sort or filter each data view separately.
In VB:

```
Dim dv As DataView = New DataView(dsCustomer.Tables(0))
```

In C#:

```
DataView dv = new DataView(dsCustomer.Tables[0]);
```

Regardless of the data view you use, you define a filter by setting the RowFilter property of the DataView class. The filter can contain operators such as =, >, <, >=, and <=. You can also use the Like keyword with or without wild-card characters, such as these:

- % (percent) for zero or more characters in that position

- _ (underscore) for one character in that position

You can also use aggregates such as Count, Max, Min, Sum, and Ave. The syntax for using aggregates is a little unnatural because the RowFilter must be an expression. So you need to assign the aggregate to the field name, as shown in the examples in this section.

The following are several RowFilter property examples. The first example filters the dataset to all customers with a specific postal code. The second example filters the dataset to all customers with a postal code that begins with a 9. The third example filters the dataset to the single customer that contains the largest postal code.
In VB:

```
dv.RowFilter = "PostalCode=" & sPostalCodeSelection
dv.RowFilter = "PostalCode like '9%'"
dv.RowFilter = "PostalCode = Max(PostalCode)"
```

In C#:

```
dv.RowFilter = "PostalCode=" + sPostalCodeSelection;
dv.RowFilter = "PostalCode like '9%'";
dv.RowFilter = "PostalCode = Max(PostalCode)";
```

Define the sort order for a data view using the Sort property.
In VB:

```
dv.Sort = " PostalCode ASC, CompanyName DESC"
```

In C#:

```
dv.Sort = " PostalCode ASC, CompanyName DESC";
```

You can define any number of sort columns, separated by commas. You can also define the direction of the sort for each column: use ASC for ascending or DESC for descending.

By binding to the resulting DataView object instead of the DataSet object, the bound control will display the sorted and filtered data.

Use the data view to sort a dataset or for filtering any time you need to view or process a subset of the dataset. This normally performs better than executing another SQL statement or query to retrieve a new dataset.

Building Smarter Datasets Using Extended Properties

You may have heard people say that datasets are dumb data containers. That is not necessarily true. They have intelligence in that each table knows its column names and appropriate types. You can make the dataset even smarter by using extended properties.

Defining Extended Properties

Extended properties are developer-defined properties that can be added to some of the ADO.NET objects. You can add extended properties to datasets, tables, columns, data relations, and constraints. You can use these extended properties to add information to the dataset, making it "smarter."

The use of extended properties is limitless. This section focuses on adding extended properties to the dataset Column object to provide an example of how you can take advantage of extended properties. The following are some of the more common uses of extended properties on the Column object:

- **Defining a column to be uppercase or proper case.** This property can then be used within the user interface to convert the end user-entered value to the appropriate case. In practice, end users frequently request this conversion to get a consistent look for names and addresses when printing orders, invoices, and other external documents.

- **Defining a regular expression associated with a column.** Regular expressions define a pattern that can be used to validate an end user-entered value. Some common examples are phone numbers, Social Security numbers, and e-mail addresses. See the "Managing Regular Expressions" section in Chapter 3 for more information about defining regular expressions.

- **Defining validation criteria associated with a column.** By defining the validation criteria for a column as an extended property of the column, the dataset contains the knowledge it needs to validate the end user-entered data. Define the validation criteria in your business objects by adding the extended properties. Use the extended properties when performing the validation in the user interface to provide immediate feedback to the end user when something invalid is entered.

Adding extended properties is an effortless process. First, pick a name for each extended property. In the following example, the extended properties are named ValidateRequired and ConvertToProperCase.

It is always good practice to define any string constant as a constant in the application. The primary benefit of defining the strings as constants is that you get compile-time checking of the constant, whereas a typographical error in a string won't be found until runtime.

In VB:

```
Public Const EP_VAL_REQUIRED As String = "ValidateRequired"
Public Const EP_CONV_PROPER As String = "ConvertToProperCase"
```

In C#:

```
public const String EP_VAL_REQUIRED = "ValidateRequired";
public const String EP_CONV_PROPER = "ConvertToProperCase";
```

The most logical place to set the extended properties is after you have retrieved the desired dataset from the data access component. In the example that follows, the customer name column is set to be required and converted to proper case. The postal code column is set to required.

In VB:

```
With dsCustomer.Tables(TN_CUSTOMER)
  .Columns(FN_CUSTOMER_NAME).ExtendedProperties.Add(EP_VAL_REQUIRED, True)
  .Columns(FN_CUSTOMER_NAME).ExtendedProperties.Add(EP_CONV_PROPER, True)
  .Columns(FN_POSTALCODE).ExtendedProperties.Add(EP_VAL_REQUIRED, True)
End With
```

In C#:

```
DataTable tb = dsCustomer.Tables[TN_CUSTOMER];
tb.Columns[FN_CUSTOMER_NAME].ExtendedProperties.Add(EP_VAL_REQUIRED, true);
tb.Columns[FN_CUSTOMER_NAME].ExtendedProperties.Add(EP_CONV_PROPER, true);
tb.Columns[FN_POSTALCODE].ExtendedProperties.Add(EP_VAL_REQUIRED, true);
```

The Add method of the column's ExtendedProperties object allows you to define the name of the extended property and its value. In this example, the extended property names were defined with constants, as shown earlier in this section. The extended property value could be any desired value. For both the ValidateRequired and ConvertToProperCase, the most logical value is True when setting the extended property for a column.

If you look at the schema of the dataset at this point using the GetXMLSchema method (see the "Viewing Datasets As XML" section earlier in this chapter), you can see the extended properties defined with the keyword msprop:

```
<?xml version="1.0" encoding="utf-16"?>
<xs:schema id="NewDataSet" xmlns="" xmlns:xs="http://www.w3.org/2001/XMLSchema" ⤷
xmlns:msdata="urn:schemas-microsoft-com:xml-msdata" ⤷
xmlns:msprop="urn:schemas-microsoft-com:xml-msprop">
  <xs:element name="NewDataSet" msdata:IsDataSet="true">
    <xs:complexType>
      <xs:choice maxOccurs="unbounded">
        <xs:element name="Customer">
          <xs:complexType>
            <xs:sequence>
              <xs:element name="CustomerID" type="xs:string" minOccurs="0" />
              <xs:element name="CompanyName" msprop:ValidateRequired="True"
              msprop:ConvertToProperCase="True" type="xs:string" minOccurs="0" />
              <xs:element name="Country" type="xs:string" minOccurs="0" />
              <xs:element name="PostalCode" msprop:ValidateRequired="True"
                          type="xs:string" minOccurs="0" />
            </xs:sequence>
          </xs:complexType>
```

```
            </xs:element>
        </xs:choice>
      </xs:complexType>
    </xs:element>
</xs:schema>
```

Define extended properties for any of the dataset objects to expand their capabilities. You'll see the benefits of these properties in the next section.

Using Extended Properties

After you have defined extended properties for any of the dataset objects, those properties remain with the dataset. Use them anywhere in your code that can access the dataset.

If you pass the dataset to your user interface, you can use the extended properties to perform the desired data conversion and validation on the values entered by end users. For example, if the ConvertToProperCase extended property is set, convert the entered value to proper case. If the ValidateRequired extended property is set, define an error message if a value is not entered.

To build a routine that performs these actions, create a new function. The new function can perform both conversion and validation.

In VB:

```
Public Shared Function ValidateColumn(ByRef sTextToValidate As String, _
    ByVal dcCol As DataColumn) As String
    Dim sErrorText As String = ""
    If CType(dcCol.ExtendedProperties(EP_CONV_PROPER), Boolean) = True Then
        sTextToValidate = StrConv(sTextToValidate, VbStrConv.ProperCase)
    End If
    If CType(dcCol.ExtendedProperties(EP_VAL_REQUIRED), Boolean) = True _
        AndAlso sTextToValidate.Length = 0 Then
        sErrorText = "You must provide a response."
    End If
    Return sErrorText
End Function
```

In C#:

```
using Microsoft.VisualBasic;
public static string ValidateColumn(ref string sTextToValidate, DataColumn
dcCol)
{
    string sErrorText = "";
```

```
    if (Convert.ToBoolean(dcCol.ExtendedProperties[EP_CONV_PROPER])== true)
    {
     sTextToValidate = Strings.StrConv(sTextToValidate, VbStrConv.ProperCase,0);
    }
    if (Convert.ToBoolean(dcCol.ExtendedProperties[EP_VAL_REQUIRED])
        == true && sTextToValidate.Length == 0)
    {
        sErrorText = "You must provide a response.";
    }
    return sErrorText;
}
```

NOTE   This C# code "cheats" by using the VisualBasic library's StrConv method. To use this library, you need to set a reference to Microsoft.VisualBasic. If you don't wish to access the VisualBasic library from your C# code, you will need to write your own function to proper case the entered string.

This routine takes the text from the control to be validated and the associated data column from the dataset, and performs the conversion and validation. It first checks the value of the column's EP_CONV_PROPER extended property. If that property is true, then the column is converted to proper case using the StrConv function.

NOTE   If the extended property is not defined for the column, no error is generated. You don't need to check for the extended property on the column before checking the value of the extended property.

The routine then checks the value of the column's EP_VAL_REQUIRED extended property. If that property is true and the length of the text is zero, meaning that the end user did not enter any data into the field, an error text string is created.

You could add conversion or validation logic to this method to support any other extended properties that you define. The error text string could be accumulated to contain any and all error text. At the end of the routine, the error text string is returned.

This code could reside in a standard validation component and be reused in any application that needs to perform similar types of conversion and validation.

Call this routine from the Validating or similar method and pass in the control's text and the associated column. Use a case statement to determine the appropriate column associated with the control.

In VB:

```
Dim dcCust As DataColumn
Select Case ctrl.Name
    Case txtName.Name
        dcCust = _
    m_dsCustomer.Tables(Customer.TN_CUSTOMER).Columns(Customer.FN_CUSTOMER_NAME)
    Case txtPostalCode.Name
        dcCust = _
    m_dsCustomer.Tables(Customer.TN_CUSTOMER).Columns(Customer.FN_POSTALCODE)
End Select
Dim sErrorText As String
sErrorText = ValidateUtility.ValidateColumn(ctrl.Text, dcCust)
```

In C#:

```
DataColumn dcCust;
switch(ctrl.Name)
{
    case txtName.Name:
        dcCust =
    m_dsCustomer.Tables[Customer.TN_CUSTOMER].Columns[Customer.FN_CUSTOMER_NAME];
        break;

    case txtPostalCode.Name:
        dcCust =
    m_dsCustomer.Tables[Customer.TN_CUSTOMER].Columns[Customer.FN_POSTALCODE];
        break;

    default:
        dcCust = null;
        break;
}
string sErrorText = ValidateUtility.ValidateColumn(ctrl.Text, dcCust);
```

This code sets the appropriate column variable based on the name of the control. For example, the txtPostalCode control is associated with the column defined by FN_POSTALCODE. This code could use the error text returned from the function to display the ErrorProvider control icon. (See the "Displaying Validation Errors with the ErrorProvider Control" section in Chapter 2 for more information.)

In VB:

```
If sErrorText.Length <> 0 Then
    epValidation.SetError(ctrl, sErrorText)
End If
```

In C#:

```
if (sErrorText.Length == 0)
{
    epValidation.SetError(ctrl, sErrorText);
}
```

Using extended properties, you can write more general code to perform validation, because the dataset itself can contain the information it needs to validate its own columns. But the usefulness of extended properties is not limited to just validation. It is limited only by your imagination.

What Did This Chapter Cover?

With the many database features of Visual Studio and ADO.NET described in this chapter, you can see why there is much ado about data access in .NET.

You can perform many database operations, such as viewing a database structure, updating data, creating a database, creating tables, defining columns, and writing stored procedures directly from the Server Explorer in Visual Studio. No more swapping back and forth between Visual Studio and the SQL Server Enterprise Manager or other database management tools. You can use the database project to manage a set of database and stored procedure scripts within your solution.

You can use the Microsoft Data Access Application Block as a quick way to define a data access component, you can configure your connection string with an application configuration file, and you can view your dataset as XML to aid in debugging. You can sort and filter datasets using a data view. And you can build a smarter dataset by defining extended properties for the dataset objects. For example, you can define extended properties for a column and use these extended properties to convert and validate the end user-entered information associated with the column.

The next chapter exposes defensive development secrets.

Defensive Development

THE KEY TO A GOOD OFFENSE is a good defense. When you build your software, you define its features and implementation so that it can attack the business problem at hand, but what about your defensive line? To build robust applications, you need to incorporate development techniques that defend against unanticipated system crashes, bugs in third-party controls, bad data, developer errors, and (of course) end user errors.

The purpose of this chapter is to uncover the secrets of how to use .NET to design and build your application so it can defend itself against the perils awaiting it in production.

What Will This Chapter Cover?

This chapter uncovers secrets for defensive development in the following areas:

- Anticipating failures

- Implementing a methodology for the design

- Preventing unauthorized application access

- Verifying data

- Following good programming practices

- Managing application failures

- Developing a notification mechanism

- Performing unit testing

By the end of this chapter, you will have the tools to arm your application so it can defend itself against common failures.

You will learn how to anticipate where application failures can occur. You will discover how to create a design and development infrastructure that minimizes failures. You will see how to use damage-control techniques to manage application failures. You will learn how to develop a notification mechanism to collect information useful for diagnosing failures when they do occur. Finally, you will understand the benefits of unit testing for testing your defenses.

Anticipating Failures

The first step in developing a good defense for your application is to define your application's potential weaknesses. By first looking at where problems could occur, you are better able to defend against those problems.

The most common areas of failure include the following:

- Design errors

- Unauthorized application access

- Invalid end user entry

- Bad data

- Coding errors

- System crashes

By anticipating these failures, you can build a defensive infrastructure to aid in preventing them. The techniques for building that defensive infrastructure are covered in the remaining sections of this chapter.

NOTE You may have noticed that system attacks are not included in this list. Threat modeling and countermeasures are a very important topic, and the security features of .NET are extensive. For more information about these topics, see `msdn.microsoft.com/library/default.asp?url=/library/enus/dnnetsec/html/ThreatCounter.asp`.

Implementing a Methodology for the Design

It's no secret that every application is designed. Even for an application that doesn't have an official design phase, you are designing it as you are deciding on the appropriate rules and constructs that the application requires.

If you make an incorrect assumption about a business rule during the design process, the application will not execute as the end users expect. If you didn't know that a particular operation had to follow specific business rules, the application will not execute as the end users expect. Even though the application executes as per the design, an incomplete or inaccurate design can cause a failure in your application, at least from the end users' point of view.

Because it's almost impossible to get perfect information about the application before building that application, it's nearly impossible to prevent all design failures. But there is something you can do to minimize the number of design failures: implement a design methodology.

The secrets of implementing a design methodology include selecting the appropriate methodology for your project and your company, sufficiently documenting the design, and appropriately including end users. These secrets are uncovered in the following sections.

Selecting a Methodology

To minimize design failures, select a methodology for your design. A *design methodology* is a set of practices, procedures, and rules that provides a path through the design of an application. By using a methodology, you can leverage the accumulated knowledge of the experts who defined the methodology. This gives you best practices and a proven set of tools and techniques for designing your application. It also helps the end users understand the process and ensures that all of the desired design steps are completed.

Selecting the appropriate design methodology for your project is an important step toward successfully implementing that methodology. Defining which methodology is right for your project depends on many factors, including the scope of the application, the size of the development team, the skills of your end users, and your corporate culture. Based on these factors, decide on the level of formality that your design requires.

Formal methodologies are process- and documentation-intensive. They normally require a significant time investment—sometimes as much as 50% of the total project budget. A formal methodology is best for applications that are very complex or are mission-critical, and when the corporate culture is more formal in its design approach. One of the most well-known formal methodologies is the Rational Unified Process (RUP). For more information about this methodology, see `http://www-306.ibm.com/software/rational`.

Over the past several years, the software industry has been moving away from documentation-intensive formal design processes and toward light, or *agile*, methodologies. Agile methodologies are based on the idea that applications should be designed and built in small increments over many iterations.

Agile principles allow you to focus on a small set of features, and design and build those features so the end user can work with them as quickly as possible, normally within three to six weeks. You then do another iteration with the next set of features, making the design and development processes iterative.

Some of the more common agile methodologies are as follows:

- Extreme programming: `www.extremeprogramming.org`

- Design by contract: `www.eiffel.com`

- Microsoft Solutions Framework (MSF): `www.microsoft.com/msf`

NOTE   Although it's more of an adaptable framework than a methodology, MSF can be tailored to most any level of formality. Expect to see a lot more on MSF in Visual Studio 2005.

Selecting a design methodology helps you minimize software failure by ensuring that a design process is followed. By using an agile design process and agile development methods, you can react quickly to resolve design failures when they do occur.

TIP   For a good discussion on the reasons for agile methods and an overview of several agile methodologies, see `http://www.martinfowler.com/articles/newMethodology.html`.

Automated Software Construction

The software industry is frequently compared to the building construction industry regarding the processes and steps required to accomplish an objective. The design process is viewed as the step that requires a small number of people with intelligence and creativity: the architects. The development process requires a large number of worker bees who can just pound out the work: the builders. The large movement to offshore development supports this comparison.

Some people in the agile design and development community believe that if the software industry is going to be compared with the construction industry, then the software design phase actually extends through the code development, since coding is also a creative activity. They also purport that the software construction phase is the time at which a developer literally selects to build the solution and the compiler takes over converting the design (code) into the built application (executable). So the entire software construction process is fully automated.

Documenting the Design

The amount of documentation that is required as part of the design process depends on the design methodology you selected for your project. Even with an agile approach, however, it is best to have some written documentation. You need some way to record the features and business rules that are to be included in the application, both to feed back to the end users and to share with the development team. The secret here is to keep some amount of design documentation so that you can minimize design failures.

In most cases, you can limit the documentation during the design process to a set of use cases or stories and a user interface design document. You can then augment this documentation with the technical specifications, which can be done using code comments during the development phase. See the "Using XML Commenting" section in Chapter 3 for more information about code comments.

NOTE As part of your design process, you will need to define the architecture and framework of your application, but most agile methodologies do not require a formal document to describe that part of the design. Rather, this information is also documented using code comments.

Developing Stories

A use case describes a specific use of the application. Because the term *use case* is used in documentation-intensive methodologies, it sometimes has a negative connotation, especially in agile methodologies. The term *story* is often used instead.

The purpose of a story is to define a feature of the application along with its detailed requirements, specified as business rules. *Business rules* are the rules that define what valid data is and what valid processes can occur on that data. You may already be collecting this information, but may be calling this process by a different name, such as requirements analysis or feature specifications.

The best way to document a story is to write a narrative providing an overview of the feature and then a bulleted list of the associated business rules. Here is a sample, albeit simple, story:

Create a New Customer

A customer is any person or company that places an order for our products.

A customer record must exist for the customer to place an order. A customer record can be created by the customers themselves when placing an order online. A customer record can be created by a sales representative when placing an order by phone.

A customer record requires the following:

- The customer name must be defined and must be proper case.

- If the customer is representing a company and the company will be billed for the order, the company name must be defined.

- The customer shipping address must be defined.

- The customer phone number must be defined.

- A customer number must be generated in the accounting system and added to the customer record before the order is shipped.

- And so on . . .

By documenting each story, you will be collecting the set of features and business rules that your application must implement. The more accurate this documentation is, the less chance for design failures in the resulting application.

Developing a User Interface Document

The user interface is, of course, the way that the end user will see the application. By documenting the user interface, you are putting the story into pictures. A picture is worth a thousand words, as the saying goes. Most end users find it much easier to look at the pictures than to read all of the words in the story. So the user interface design document provides a communication tool for feeding the stories back to the end users for review, thus further reducing the possibility of design failures.

The user interface design document contains the screenshots of the forms or pages of the application. With each screenshot is text describing the elements on the screen and any business rules related to processing the information on the screen. Because this document is more end user-focused, it is much easier for the end users to review, understand, and evaluate. It can also be used as the first cut of the end user documentation.

You can use .NET to rough out the Windows forms or web pages, and then take screenshots to create the user interface design document. By showing the end users the document instead of running software, you don't need to implement any functionality. This greatly reduces the time it takes to create the document and prevents the end users from thinking that you are almost finished with the application.

As you make design changes that require end user review, you can extract sections from this document. It is much easier for an end user to review a few new or revised pages than to look at the entire user interface design document for each iteration or change request.

Including End Users

Yes, it would be much easier if developers could just define the requirements for the application, and then go off and build it without interference from the pesky end users. But if the developers build something that the end users won't use, then what was the point? Only with end user participation in the process can you minimize design failures and make the application a success.

The end users can be of particular good use at several specific times during the design process:

- **When writing stories:** The end users are the best source of information for defining the requirements and providing input into the stories. The secret here is to pick a small number of key end users who are knowledgeable and articulate to assist with writing the stories

- **When validating the design:** The end users are the best source for validating the design. As mentioned in the previous section, this is best done with a user interface design document. You can provide this document to your key end users or to an expanded group for review.

- **During development:** To ensure that the development team can keep the development process moving forward efficiently and get responsive feedback, it's a good idea to identify one key end user or a small set of end users who can answer business process questions.

- **During application reviews:** With agile methodologies, frequent end user reviews of the written software are imperative. Use the same set of key end users for this process.

In some companies, there is a business analyst or subject matter expert available to provide these services instead of including end users. In other situations, there is a set of key end users who have the background to answer business process questions and review the resulting application features. It is important that these resources are knowledgeable in the business issues that the application will support and that they are readily available.

By following a design methodology, documenting the design, and including end users in the process, you can minimize the number of design failures in your application.

Preventing Unauthorized Application Access

After your application has been designed, developed, and tested, it is deployed. Your application is then ready to be used by the appropriate set of end users. At this point, the application must defend itself against unauthorized access.

If you want to sell your car, you want to have flyers with information about your car easily accessible so people can take them. But you don't leave your car with the keys easily accessible to anyone. The amount of security and ease of accessibility are based on who should have access to the resource and the value of the resource.

If you have a web-based application that sells products, like gap.com, you want to ensure that everyone can get access to the catalog of products. However, you don't want just anyone to have access to customer or order information, especially credit card numbers.

If you are building a Windows-based application that supports business operations, you don't want the cleaning crew to be able to access the application. And key business functions, such as payroll and accounting, should be restricted to a very limited number of end users.

The most common way to limit access to an application is with a login form or page, as shown in Figure 5-1.

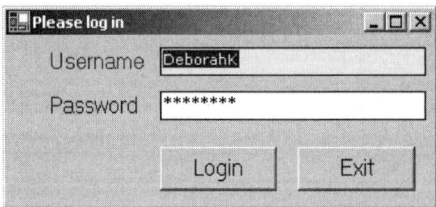

Figure 5-1. A login form limits access to an application.

Notice that the password appears as a series of asterisks to prevent anyone from seeing the characters that the end user enters. This is done by setting the PasswordChar property of the password TextBox control for Windows forms and by setting the TextMode property to Password for web forms.

But you need to do more than display a login form and hide the password. To help prevent unauthorized application access, you need to protect the password in the database, and you need to validate the end user's username and password.

Hashing the Password

It is no secret that an application needs a username and password to be secure. The secret is in how the password should be handled. The password should not be stored in the database as a string. Rather, it should be converted to an unrecognizable value that is unique for any defined password. This value is called a *hash*. Hashing algorithms are defined so that any string that is hashed to a unique value will always be hashed to that unique value.

When an end user defines a password, the password should be hashed to a unique value, and that unique value should be stored in the database. When the end user logs in with the password, the password can be hashed again using the same algorithm. The resulting value can be compared with the hashed value stored in the database to validate the login.

Hashed values cannot be "unhashed," so there is no way to get the original password back from the hashed value. This provides an additional level of security, because if someone obtains hashed passwords from the database, they cannot be converted back to the original passwords. A side effect of this is that if an end user forgets the password, a new password would need to be assigned.

The System.Security.Cryptography library in the .NET Framework provides a set of classes that assist with hashing. Two primary hashing schemes are provided in this library:

- **MD5:** The Message Digest 5 (MD5) hash digest uses an MD5 algorithm to hash a value, such as an end user password. This algorithm provides better performance than SHA1.

- **SHA1:** The Secure Hash Algorithm-1 (SHA1) hash digest uses a SHA1 algorithm to hash a value, such as an end user password. This algorithm provides better security than MD5.

A password such as "password" will have a hash that looks something like W6ph5Mm5Pz8GgiULbPgzG37mj9g=.

The following code uses the SHA1 algorithm to hash a password:
In VB:

```
Imports System.Security.Cryptography
Public Function ComputeHash(ByVal textToHash As String) As String
    Dim SHA1 As SHA1CryptoServiceProvider = New SHA1CryptoServiceProvider
```

```
        Dim byteValue As Byte() = System.Text.Encoding.UTF8.GetBytes(textToHash)
        Dim byteHash As Byte() = SHA1.ComputeHash(byteValue)
        SHA1.Clear()
        Return Convert.ToBase64String(byteHash)
    End Function
```

In C#:

```
using System.Security.Cryptography;
public static String ComputeHash(string textToHash)
{
    SHA1CryptoServiceProvider SHA1 = new SHA1CryptoServiceProvider();
    byte[] byteValue = System.Text.Encoding.UTF8.GetBytes(textToHash);
    byte[] byteHash = SHA1.ComputeHash(byteValue);
    SHA1.Clear();
    return Convert.ToBase64String(byteHash);
}
```

You can put this code in a utility component and reuse it in every application that needs to store a password or other secure information.

But hashing a password does not protect the application from a dictionary attack. For further security, salt the password as well, as described in the next section.

Salting the Password

Hashed passwords provide much better security than storing passwords in the database as simple text. They are, however, potentially vulnerable to a dictionary attack. In a *dictionary attack*, the attacker attempts to guess passwords by using software to iteratively hash all words in a large dictionary and compare the generated hashes to the stored hash values.

You can help prevent dictionary attacks by requiring the end users to define passwords that are not common words and that contain some numbers or other nonalphanumeric characters.

In addition, you can add a random set of bytes at the beginning or end of the password before hashing it. This random set of bytes is called a *salt*. You then store this salt value in the table along with the password.

There are many ways to generate a salt value. One way is to generate a globally unique ID, or GUID, as follows.

In VB:

```
Public Function ComputeSalt() As String
    Dim GuidValue As System.Guid = System.Guid.NewGuid()
    Return GuidValue.ToString()
End Function
```

In C#:

```
public static String ComputeSalt()
{
    System.Guid GuidValue = System.Guid.NewGuid();
    return GuidValue.ToString();
}
```

This code can also be included in your utility component so it can be reused.

By using both the hash and the salt, you can minimize the possibility of an unauthorized user accessing your application.

Validating the Login

Hash and salt—sounds more like breakfast than password management. The code in this section puts all of these concepts together to demonstrate a generic ValidateLogin method. This method uses both the hash and salt techniques described in the previous sections.

In VB:

```
Public Function ValidateLogin(ByVal sUserName As String, _
    ByVal sPassword As String) As Boolean
    Dim dsUser As New DataSet
    If sUserName.Length = 0 OrElse sPassword.Length = 0 Then
     Throw New ArgumentOutOfRangeException("Username and password are required.")
    End If
    dsUser = Me.Retrieve(sUserName)

    ' If the user does not exist, throw an exception
    If dsUser Is Nothing _
       OrElse dsUser.Tables(TN_USER) Is Nothing _
       OrElse dsUser.Tables(TN_USER).Rows.Count = 0 Then
        Throw New UsernameNotFoundException("Invalid username")
    End If
```

```
' If the user does exist, verify the password
' A hash value is generated using a salt and the user-entered password
With dsUser.Tables(TN_USER).Rows(0)
    Dim sPasswordEncoded As String = CType(.Item(FN_PASSWORD_ENCODED), String)
    Dim sPasswordSalt As String = CType(.Item(FN_PASSWORD_SALT), String)
    Dim sPasswordHash As String = SecurityUtility.ComputeHash(sPasswordSalt & _
                                                    sPassword)

    ' does the computed hash match the database hash?
    If String.Compare(sPasswordEncoded, sPasswordHash) <> 0 Then
        Throw New PasswordInvalidException("Invalid password")
    End If

    Return True
End Function
```

In C#:

```
public bool ValidateLogin(string sUserName, string sPassword)
{
    DataSet dsUser;
    if (sUserName.Length == 0 || sPassword.Length == 0)
    {
    throw new ArgumentOutOfRangeException("Username and password are required.");
    }
    dsUser = this.Retrieve(sUserName);

    // If the user does not exist, throw an exception
    if (dsUser == null || dsUser.Tables[TN_USER] == null
       || dsUser.Tables[TN_USER].Rows.Count == 0)
    {
        throw new UsernameNotFoundException("Invalid username");
    }

    // If the user does exist, verify the password
    // A hash value is generated using a salt and the user-entered password
    DataRow dr =  dsUser.Tables[TN_USER].Rows[0];
    string sPasswordEncoded  = dr[FN_PASSWORD_ENCODED].ToString();
    string sPasswordSalt = dr[FN_PASSWORD_SALT].ToString();
    string sPasswordHash = SecurityUtility.ComputeHash(sPasswordSalt +
                                                    sPassword);

    // does the computed hash match the database hash?
    if (String.Compare(sPasswordEncoded, sPasswordHash) != 0)
```

```
    {
        throw new PasswordInvalidException("Invalid password");
    }

    return true;
}
```

NOTE UsernameNotFoundException and PasswordInvalidException are developer-defined exceptions. See the "Managing Application Failures" section later in this chapter for more information about creating developer-defined exceptions.

This method takes the end user-entered username and password as parameters. If the parameters are empty, the code throws an exception. The username is then passed to a Retrieve method (not shown), which retrieves a dataset from the database that contains the record for the defined end user. The code throws an exception if the dataset is empty.

The salt is retrieved from the dataset and appended to the end user-entered password. The result is passed to the ComputeHash method to compute the hash value. The resulting hash is compared with the hash retrieved from the dataset. The code throws an exception if the two hash values don't match.

You can use this method as a pattern for your login validation to help prevent unauthorized access to your application.

Verifying Data

Once an end user has access to your application, the most common task is to enter or retrieve data. In addition to receiving data from the end user, your application can receive data from other places, such as a database, providing many opportunities to obtain bad data. And as we all know, bad data is, well, bad. The secret to minimizing the effect of bad data in your application is to develop an infrastructure that verifies data at every entry point.

The sections that follow define the most common data-entry points in an application and the secrets for preventing bad data from coming into those entry points and causing a failure in your application.

Verifying End User Entered Data

When you think of data entry, the first thing that probably comes to mind is data entered by the end user. Although that's not the only way for your application to receive data, it does have the greatest possibility for invalid data.

End users have a job to do, and that job is not normally focused on getting correct data into your application. Rather, they are using your application as a tool to get a specific result. For example, salespeople use an application to enter customer and order information to achieve their sales goals. Help desk people use an application to track help calls to achieve their support goals. Administrative personnel use an application to enter financials so management can get a financial picture of the organization. The end users are not necessarily focused on entering correct data, so it is up to the application to ensure that the entered data is valid.

There are two basic ways to assist the end users in entering valid data:

- **Restriction:** An application can restrict end user entry to a defined set of possibilities, thereby significantly increasing the probability of obtaining correct information. The easiest way to restrict entry is by using the appropriate user interface controls. Use a check box to restrict entry to a yes/no choice. Use a set of radio buttons to restrict the choices to a small set. For a larger set of choices, use a combo box to restrict input, and so on.

- **Validation:** If the end user must type in a response, the application can validate the entry with code in the application. The validation code evaluates the information entered by the end user and ensures that it meets defined criteria.

 TIP Validate the entered field length as well to prevent overflow issues.

For web pages, a set of validation server controls is available to assist with this validation. Validation controls provide an easy way to perform standard validation on data entered by the end user on a web page.

For Windows forms, you can write code to respond to the Validating event or the DataChanged event (if you're using data binding). By combining your validation code with the ErrorProvider control, you make it easy for the end users to see any validation error so they can correct it. See the "Displaying Validation Errors with the ErrorProvider Control" section in Chapter 2 for more information and an example.

Verifying Database Data

If your application includes careful restriction and validation on end users' data entry, you can feel confident that the data your application puts into the database is valid. But can you assume that the data coming out of the database is valid? Maybe, maybe not. Bad data can get into your database in other ways. And garbage in, garbage out, as the saying goes. So if there are other ways that bad data can get into your database, this bad data could be retrieved from the database and cause a failure in your application.

The best way to defend your application against bad data coming from your database is to do everything you can to prevent bad data from getting into your database. In addition to invalid end user entry, the most common ways bad data can get into your database include the following:

- **Other applications:** If your application shares its database with other applications, you cannot be certain that the other applications use the same care in validating entry into the database. Define corporate standards on validation and, where possible, restrict all database access to a shared component for consistent data validation.

- **Translation:** Your application may require data that has been translated into your database from another source. To minimize errors from translation issues, allocate the appropriate time to work on the translation task. This task is often significantly more difficult than you would estimate. The better job that is done in performing the translation, the better that translated data will be.

- **Database changes:** Using agile development techniques and an iterative development process, you may be changing your data structures as you add and change features in the application. These changes could introduce potential problems with data already in your database. For example, a new feature requires a new field in the Customer table to store the customer's assigned sales representative. Any new customer records that are added will have a valid value in this new field, but any existing customer record won't have a value in the new field.

- **Programming errors:** One inaccurate calculation or incorrect field name in your application, and your application can put bad data into your database. To help minimize this type of problem, be sure to review the records that your application creates as part of the testing process (see the "Expanding Your Debugging Techniques" section in Chapter 3). Just because you can enter a customer record and bring up that customer record during testing does not necessarily mean that all of the data stored in that record is valid.

By considering each of these scenarios, you can take steps to minimize the amount of invalid data getting into your database. But you still cannot assume that your application will never receive invalid data from the database. Your second line of defense, then, is to code your application so that it does not assume that data from the database is valid.

Your application should validate data before it is used. The biggest problem with data from the database is often null values, so ensure that your application checks for nulls before using any value from a database.

Self-Healing Systems

The software industry is not quite at the point where it can build software that heals itself, like Commander Data's software on *Star Trek: The Next Generation*. But there has been some progress in the area of self-healing systems.

The large software vendors all have some initiatives that take a first step toward self-healing systems, specifically related to managing distributed systems in the IT enterprise:

- IBM's Autonomic Blueprint: `http://www-306.ibm.com/autonomic`

- HP's Adaptive Enterprise strategy: `http://www.hp.com/enterprise`

- Microsoft's Dynamic Systems Initiative (DSI):
  `http://www.microsoft.com/windowsserversystem/dsi`

Although these initiatives focus on managing enterprise-wide systems, you can include some self-healing features in your own applications. For example, instead of just notifying the end user of a problem with the data, your application could actually correct the data.

In many cases, your application could have the intelligence to not only determine that data is bad, but also to figure out what is wrong with it and update it. For example, if your application found a null in a column that should not be null, it could potentially figure out the correct value for that column and update it. Your application may not have enough information to do this in all cases, but it could heal itself when possible.

The downside of this is time. Making the application smart enough to heal itself requires additional development time. Management may feel that the time should be spent on ensuring that the data is correct to begin with and not spend time on code to find and fix invalid data.

But the thought of building software that can fix its own data, thereby minimizing support costs, has some appeal.

Verifying Application Data

Most methods in your application have parameters. Data is passed to the method using the parameters. That method often makes assumptions as to the validity of those parameters. If those assumptions are not verified, the application could fail.

For example, if an object variable is passed as one of the parameters to a method, the method may make the assumption that the object variable is assigned to a valid object. If the object variable is null (nothing), the method might fail, thereby causing the application to fail.

To defend your application against this possibility, devote the first few lines of each method in your application to checking the parameters passed in to the method. All assumptions that are made regarding the parameter values should be verified.

As another example, the ValidateLogin method shown earlier in the "Validating the Login" section assumes that the entered username and password are not empty. The first few lines of code in the method are written such that the method won't even attempt to validate the login if the values are empty.

In VB:

```
Public Function ValidateLogin(ByVal sUserName As String, _
   ByVal sPassword As String) As Boolean
   If sUserName.Length = 0 OrElse sPassword.Length = 0 Then
     Throw New ArgumentOutOfRangeException("Username and password are
required.")
   End If
```

In C#:

```
public bool ValidateLogin(string sUserName, string sPassword)
{
   if (sUserName.Length == 0 || sPassword.Length == 0)
   {
     throw new ArgumentOutOfRangeException("Username and password are
required.");
   }
```

Parameter checking is one of the key tenets of defensive development, because it can prevent inappropriate application execution and minimize the amount of invalid data used by your application.

By using validation techniques to verify end user data, verifying data from the database before using it, and performing parameter checking, you can protect your application from invalid data.

Following Good Programming Practices

Even if your data is valid, if the code processing that data is not correct, your application can fail. Coding mistakes can cause invalid business processes to occur, such as shipping an item to the wrong address. They can cause data corruption, such as saving an order for the wrong customer. And most visibly, coding errors can cause your application to generate an exception. You can minimize the number of coding errors in your applications by defining, and then following, good programming practices.

If you don't already have a set of coding standards and best practices for your development team, take the time to create a best practices document. This can really save you time in the long run, because your team won't make mistakes caused by bad practices.

If you do have an existing document, review it from time to time to ensure that it is still appropriate for the way that you code your applications. This is especially true when new versions of Visual Studio are released, because good practices in one version may not be the best ones in future versions.

Finally, be sure to follow the coding standards and practices defined in your document. If you have a team of developers, a code review with one of the other team members helps with this process.

The following sections cover a few items to include in your best practices document.

Specifying Commenting Standards

Comments provide code documentation. By specifying commenting standards in your best practices document, you ensure that all of the code is documented, and documented consistently.

Code comments should minimally describe the purpose of the class, method, or other member and should detail any assumptions that the code makes. The best way to comment your application is to use XML comments, as described in the "Using XML Commenting" section of Chapter 3.

By commenting your code, you provide information to yourself and any future maintenance developer about the code, including its purpose and assumptions. This reduces the possibility of coding errors caused by changes to the code that were done without understanding the original purpose of the code and the effect of the change.

In your best practices document, define the parts of the application that must be commented, how the comments should be defined, and the information that must be included in the comments.

Including Code Efficiency Practices

The best practices document should include coding practices that can make the code more efficient. One such practice is to short-circuit And and Or operations.

By short-circuiting the Ands and Ors in your application, you can improve your application's performance. These short-circuiting operators are also great for checking for null values in a database column before working with that column. See the "Short-Circuiting Ands and Ors" section in Chapter 3 for more information.

There are many other best practices for making your code more efficient, some of which were described in Chapter 3, such as using StringBuilder instead of appending strings. Add these types of best practices to your document to ensure that the application is developed with efficiency in mind.

Documenting Data Validation Practices

The best practices document should include coding practices for data validation. For example, if your code is expecting one of a set of values, include code that handles a value that is not one within the valid set of values. This is most often done using a case statement.

Every case statement (Select in VB; switch in C#) should have a default case. If there is no valid default case, then the default case should throw an exception.

In VB:

```
Select Case ctrl.Name
    Case txtName.Name
        ' Do something
    Case txtPostalCode.Name
        ' Do something
    Case Else
        ' Throw an exception
End Select
```

In C#:

```
switch(ctrl.Name)
{
    case txtName.Name:
        // Do something
        break;
```

```
case txtPostalCode.Name:
    // Do something
    break;
default:
    // Throw an exception
    break;
}
```

Adding a default case ensures that the code never "falls through" the case statement, thereby creating errors that are difficult to find.

Other data validation practices were covered earlier in this chapter, such as validating method parameters. By including best practices for data validation within your best practices document, you ensure that data is validated and that this validation is done in a consistent manner.

Specifying Coding Conventions

Include standard coding conventions in your best practices document. Coding conventions are industry-defined standards that aid in minimizing coding errors. One such standard is to define constants in place of quoted text strings.

Using quoted text strings in your application for names of items, such as field names, is a common source of coding errors, because the quoted string cannot be validated at compile time. It is much better to define any unchanging quoted strings as constants in the application. If you then mistype the constant name, it is caught at compile time and won't be a source of runtime errors.

For example, suppose that your Customer table has fields named "CustomerID" and "CompanyName." You could use these quoted strings everywhere you wanted to reference the field. But then you would need to remember the correct text to type in each time (or look them up in the Server Explorer; see Chapter 4 for more information). And if you mistyped the text ("CustID," for example), the compiler wouldn't catch the mistake. You wouldn't know that you had an error until you ran the application. Even then, it might not be easy to figure out why the application did not work.

By creating constants, you define a standard set of symbols that can be verified at compile time.

In VB:

```
Public Const FN_CUSTOMER_ID As String = "CustomerID"
Public Const FN_CUSTOMER_NAME As String = "CompanyName"
```

In C#:

```
public const String FN_CUSTOMER_ID = "CustomerID";
public const String FN_CUSTOMER_NAME = "CompanyName";
```

You type the quoted text string in only one time; the rest of the time, you use the constants.

In VB:

```
txtName.Text = dr.Item(Customer.FN_CUSTOMER_NAME).ToString
```

In C#:

```
txtName.Text = dr[Customer.FN_CUSTOMER_NAME].ToString();
```

Another benefit of using constants is that you get IntelliSense, so you don't need to remember the name of the constant. In this example, you could type **FN_**, and then press Ctrl+spacebar to see the list of all constants that begin with FN_.

TIP   By prefixing each of your constants with the same characters, such as *FN* for field name, you can easily see all of your constants grouped together using IntelliSense.

Other coding conventions to specify in your best practices document are described in Chapter 3, including the conventions for data type conversion in the "Strictly Converting Your Data Types" section.

Specify coding conventions in your best practices document to ensure that your code follows industry-standard best practices. This minimizes potential coding errors and reduces your debugging time.

Managing Application Failures

Application failures will occur, and that is not necessarily a bad thing. For example, if your application determines that a particular business rule is not met, the application may define a failure. The secret is in managing these failures appropriately.

Some application failures can be more anticipated than others. Say, for example, you need to open a file. File processing is prone to many different types of errors—everything from file not found to disk read errors. You can anticipate these and code appropriately. Other failures, such as your database server crashing, are harder to anticipate.

Knowing that application failures can occur, you can protect your code by implementing damage-control techniques. The best damage-control technique that your application can use is exception handling. Exception handling provides a mechanism for catching failures that occur in your application (anticipated and unanticipated) and gives your application an opportunity to handle the failure.

 TIP Microsoft has published the Exception Management Application Block to provide an extensible framework for handling and logging exceptions. See msdn.microsoft.com/patterns for more information about this application block.

The techniques for exception handling should be included in your best practices document, discussed in the previous section, to ensure that your exception handling is implemented consistently throughout your application.

Handling Anticipated Failures

Anticipated failures are those failures for which you can plan. Since you can plan for them, you can develop code to handle them.

In some cases, the anticipated failures are *business rule violations*. As described earlier in this section, business rules are normally defined in the story for the associated feature. For example, the story may say, "If the customer record cannot be found, the order cannot be processed." This statement defines a business rule. If a business rule is not met, the failure is a business rule violation. A business rule violation will occur, for example, if the customer record is not found when attempting to process the order.

Other anticipated failures are system-oriented rather than business-oriented. These are frequently anticipated based on your past experience. Opening a file is an example; you know from past experience that opening a file can cause certain failures.

In either case, you can use exception-handling techniques for managing anticipated application failures. An *exception* is any error condition, business rule violation, or failure in your application. *Exception handling* is the process by which your application can define the exception and respond accordingly to either correct the problem or to notify the end user.

Exception handling requires two basic steps:

1. Throw an exception when the failure occurs.

2. Catch the exception and handle it.

These steps are described in the following sections.

Throwing an Exception

The first step for managing anticipated application failures is to write code to check for the possible failure, and then throw an exception if the failure occurs.

As a common example, consider the code required to validate an end user's login. The business rules require that the username and password are entered, that the username exists, that the password is correct for the defined end user, and so on. If any of these rules are not met, the code should generate an exception. The code for the ValidateLogin method was shown in its entirety in the "Preventing Unauthorized Application Access" section earlier in this chapter. Snippets from this code example demonstrate how to throw an exception.

In VB:

```
If sUserName.Length = 0 OrElse sPassword.Length = 0 Then
    Throw New ArgumentOutOfRangeException("Username and password are required.")
End If
```

In C#:

```
if (sUserName.Length == 0 || sPassword.Length == 0)
{
    throw new ArgumentOutOfRangeException("Username and password are required.");
}
```

This code throws the standard .NET Framework ArgumentOutOfRangeException if the parameters passed to the method are blank.

But the .NET Framework does not have specific exceptions for every business rule that you may have in your application. For example, if the end user-entered username is not found in the database, the code should generate an exception.

In VB:

```
If dsUser Is Nothing _
    OrElse dsUser.Tables(TN_USER) Is Nothing _
    OrElse dsUser.Tables(TN_USER).Rows.Count = 0 Then
      Throw New UsernameNotFoundException("Invalid username")
End If
```

In C#:

```
if (dsUser == null || dsUser.Tables[TN_USER] == null
    || dsUser.Tables[TN_USER].Rows.Count == 0)
{
    throw new UsernameNotFoundException("Invalid username");
}
```

Notice that this code generates a UsernameNotFoundException. This is not a .NET Framework exception; it is a developer-defined exception.

Before you can throw a developer-defined exception, you must define it. For your exception to act like a .NET Framework exception, you define your exception class as a subclass of a .NET Framework exception class. Most often, this is the .NET Framework Exception class.

In VB:

```
Public Class UsernameNotFoundException : Inherits Exception
    Public Sub New()
        MyBase.New()
    End Sub
    Public Sub New(ByVal message As String)
        MyBase.New(message)
    End Sub
    Public Sub New(ByVal message As String, ByVal innerEx As Exception)
        MyBase.New(message, innerEx)
    End Sub
End Class
```

In C#:

```
public class UsernameNotFoundException : Exception
{
    public UsernameNotFoundException()
        : base()
    {
    }
```

```
public UsernameNotFoundException(string message)
    : base(message)
{
}
public UsernameNotFoundException(string message, Exception innerEx)
    : base(message, innerEx)
{
}
}
```

NOTE Until recently, the recommended technique was to sub-
class your exception classes from the ApplicationException class.
This is no longer recommended. You should subclass from the
Exception class instead.

Since your exception class inherits from the Exception class, it automatically has all of the properties and methods of the Exception class, such as
Message and Source. The only things that your exception class cannot inherit
are the constructors. So the only code that your exception class needs is for the
three different overloaded constructors that are defined for the standard .NET
Framework exception. In each case, the overloaded constructor simply calls the
base class's constructor.

TIP You can do so much more with developer-defined exceptions than what is shown here. You can give them more
properties and methods or other constructors. For example, you
could define an exception class that allowed exception messages
to accumulate in a string array, so that all of the business rule violations could be accumulated into one exception generated from
the business object.

In summary, the first step for managing anticipated failures in your applications is to develop code to check for the possible failure, and then throw an
exception if the failure occurs. In some cases, such as when you're checking
your parameter arguments, you may throw a standard .NET exception. In other
cases, such as business-process checking, you may want to define your own
exception and throw it. There are also cases when the anticipated failure will
automatically throw a .NET Framework exception. For example, the Open
method of the File object has many standard .NET Framework exceptions that
it throws.

In all of these cases, you will want to add code to your application to catch any exception that you throw. Otherwise, the end user will see an unhandled exception, which is never desired.

Catching an Exception

After you throw an exception, you will want to have code that catches the exception. You catch an exception with a Try Catch block. The Try block allows your application to try executing a set of code. If the code fails, control is returned to the Catch block. This is called *structured exception handling* (SEH).

The secret here is not in how to use structured exception handling, since you probably are already using it throughout your application. The trick here is in knowing where you should put that exception-handling code.

The following is the basic structure of an exception handler.

In VB:

```
Try
    ' Code here that could generate an error
Catch ex As Exception
    ' Code here to handle the error
Finally
    ' Optional cleanup code
End Try
```

 TIP You should be using this style of structured exception handling in your VB applications rather than the old style, unstructured exception handling that uses On Error.

In C#:

```
try
{
    // Code here that could generate an error
}
catch (Exception ex)
{
    // Code here to handle that error
}
finally
{
    // Optional cleanup code
}
```

Add a Catch block for every type of exception that you want to catch. Add code in the Finally block to perform any cleanup that needs to occur, whether or not the code caught an exception.

> **TIP** You can use the Finally block without the Catch block if you have cleanup code that needs to run but you don't want to catch any exceptions.

One of the benefits of using developer-defined exceptions is that you can catch each exception separately and process it differently. For example, a ValidateLogin method could generate a UsernameNotFoundException if the username is not found, a PasswordInvalidException if the password is not valid, a UserIsInactiveException if the user's record is inactive, and so on. The user interface code could then respond appropriately, based on the specific exception.

In VB:

```
Dim bValid As Boolean
Try
    Dim oUser As New User
    bValid = oUser.ValidateLogin(txtUserName.Text, txtPassword.Text)
    DialogResult = DialogResult.OK

Catch ex As UsernameNotFoundException
    MessageBox.Show(ex.Message)
    txtUserName.Focus()

Catch ex As PasswordInvalidException
    MessageBox.Show(ex.Message)
    txtPassword.Focus()

Catch ex As Exception
    MessageBox.Show(ex.Message)
End Try
```

In C#:

```
bool bValid = false;
try
{
    User oUser = new User();
    bValid = oUser.ValidateLogin(txtUserName.Text, txtPassword.Text);
```

```
        DialogResult = DialogResult.OK;
    }
    catch (UsernameNotFoundException ex)
    {
        MessageBox.Show(ex.Message);
        txtUserName.Focus();
    }
    catch (PasswordInvalidException ex)
    {
        MessageBox.Show(ex.Message);
        txtPassword.Focus();
    }
    catch (Exception ex)
    {
        MessageBox.Show(ex.Message);
    }
```

In this example, the code is checking for two specific developer-defined exceptions. It also has a Catch block for any other exception that could be generated. This provides a good design pattern for you to use when defining your exceptions.

The more controversial discussion is where this exception-handling code should reside. The general rule of thumb is to put it as close to the end user-generated event that caused the issue as possible, but still retain enough information to handle the exception as needed. For example, the structured error handler just shown would be in the Click event procedure for the Login button.

Another rule of thumb is to never catch an exception unless you plan to do something with it. You should not catch an exception and then simply rethrow it. That has a negative impact on performance and provides no benefit.

Handling Unanticipated Failures

Unanticipated failures are system crashes that cause the application to abort. These crashes can be caused by a number of different sources:

- Coding errors

- The .NET Framework itself

- Any third-party controls you are using

- The database (such as connectivity or locking issues)

- The network

The best kept secret for exception handling is the ability to set up a global exception handler for your application. This global exception handler can handle any unanticipated failure that occurs in your application.

To create a global exception handler, define a method that will process unanticipated exceptions. Depending on your application, this method may allow the end user to try again, or it may simply notify the end user of the problem, clean up, and exit the application. The following class gives the end user the option to retry or exit.

In VB:

```vb
Private Class GlobalExceptionHandler
    Public Sub OnThreadException(ByVal sender As Object, _
        ByVal t As System.Threading.ThreadExceptionEventArgs)
        Dim result As DialogResult = DialogResult.Cancel
        Try
            result = MessageBox.Show("Unhandled exception in application", _
                    "Application Error", _
                    MessageBoxButtons.AbortRetryIgnore, MessageBoxIcon.Stop)
        Catch
            Try
                MessageBox.Show("Fatal Error", "Fatal Error", _
                        MessageBoxButtons.OK, MessageBoxIcon.Stop)
            Finally
                Application.Exit()
            End Try
        End Try

        ' Exits the program when the user clicks Abort.
        If result = DialogResult.Abort Then
            Application.Exit()
        End If
    End Sub
End Class
```

In C#:

```csharp
internal class GlobalExceptionHandler
{
    public void OnThreadException(object sender,
        System.Threading.ThreadExceptionEventArgs t)
    {
        DialogResult result = DialogResult.Cancel;
        try
        {
```

```
        result = MessageBox.Show("Unhandled exception in application",
                    "Application Error",
                    MessageBoxButtons.AbortRetryIgnore, MessageBoxIcon.Stop);
    }
    catch
    {
        try
        {
            MessageBox.Show("Fatal Error", "Fatal Error",
                    MessageBoxButtons.OK, MessageBoxIcon.Stop);
        }
        finally
        {
            Application.Exit();
        }
    }

    // Exits the program when the user clicks Abort.
    if (result == DialogResult.Abort)
    {
        Application.Exit();
    }
}
}
```

This code executes when there is a thread exception. First, it notifies the end user that an unhandled exception occurred. The end user can then abort, retry, or ignore the message. If the end user selects to abort, the code after the exception-handling block exits the application.

If there is an error in attempting to process the first message box, a second message is displayed, stating that there is a fatal error. The Finally block code causes the application to terminate.

To complete implementation of this global exception handler, you need to wire up the Application.ThreadException event to it. You can add the following code to the Main method of the application.

In VB:

```
' Creates an instance of the class that will handle the exception.
Dim gEx As New GlobalExceptionHandler
' Adds the event handler to to the event.
AddHandler Application.ThreadException, _
New System.Threading.ThreadExceptionEventHandler(AddressOf gEx.OnThreadException)
```

In C#:

```
// Creates an instance of the class that will handle the exception.
GlobalExceptionHandler gEx = new GlobalExceptionHandler();
// Adds the event handler to to the event.
Application.ThreadException +=
    new System.Threading.ThreadExceptionEventHandler(gEx.OnThreadException);
```

This code adds an event handler that will execute the OnThreadException code if the ThreadException event occurs for the application.

You can try out this code by throwing an exception anywhere in your application that does not have an exception handler. The exception should then be caught by your global exception-handling code.

Developing a Notification Mechanism

When an unanticipated application failure does occur, do you trust the end users to report the failure to you correctly and with all of the detailed information you need? That's doubtful. If you have code to recover from a failure without end user participation, how will you ever know about it? And how will you know if an unauthorized end user is attempting to access the application? To ensure that you get the information you need where there is a problem with your defenses, you develop a notification mechanism. Your application can use this mechanism to notify you or the application support personnel when a failure occurs.

You need a notification mechanism in your application for several reasons:

- You cannot assume that the end users will notify you when a failure occurs.

- The end users often don't recall the exact steps they executed prior to the failure.

- You cannot expect the end users to remember all of the information in the error message that they saw and dismissed.

- Your application may recover from a failure without the end users even knowing about it.

- You need to know when an unauthorized end user is attempting to access your application.

The key to developing a good notification mechanism is to write all of the information for the failure somewhere, so you can retrieve it without the end user's help.

You could store information about the failure in the database, but that won't work if the database is causing the failure. You could use a file, which the application sends to you when a failure occurs. You could use an e-mail message and put all of the information into a text message. Another option is to use the system event log to store failure information.

The following code demonstrates how to write text to the system event log. You could modify this code to write to any output type that you desire.

In VB:

```
Private Shared Sub AddEventLogEntry(ByVal sText As String, _
    ByVal eEntryType As EventLogEntryType)

    ' Get the current executing Assembly
    Dim asm As System.Reflection.Assembly
    asm = System.Reflection.Assembly.GetExecutingAssembly

    ' Get the Title Attribute
    Dim AppName As String
    AppName = DirectCast(asm.GetCustomAttributes(GetType(System.Reflection. _
        AssemblyTitleAttribute), False)(0), _
        System.Reflection.AssemblyTitleAttribute).Title

    ' Ensure application is registered in event log
    If Not EventLog.SourceExists(AppName) Then
        EventLog.CreateEventSource(AppName, "Application")
    End If

    ' Add entry
    EventLog.WriteEntry(AppName, sText, eEntryType)
End Sub
```

In C#:

```
public static void AddEventLogEntry(string sText, EventLogEntryType eEntryType)
{
    // Get the current executing Assembly
    System.Reflection.Assembly asm =
        System.Reflection.Assembly.GetExecutingAssembly();

    // Get the Title Attribute
    System.Reflection.AssemblyTitleAttribute assTitleAttr =
        (System.Reflection.AssemblyTitleAttribute)asm.
    GetCustomAttributes(typeof(System.Reflection.AssemblyTitleAttribute),false)[0];
        string AppName = assTitleAttr.Title;
```

```
    // Ensure application is registered in event log
    if (!EventLog.SourceExists(AppName))
    {
        EventLog.CreateEventSource(AppName, "Application");
    }

    // Add entry
    EventLog.WriteEntry(AppName, sText, eEntryType);
}
```

You can add a call to this method in any routine that you wish to log information. For example, you could include it in an exception handler for any unanticipated exception. You could also include it in the code that validates the end user's login to log every invalid login attempt. Pass to this method a text string that includes all of the information you need to understand the failure.

TIP   Don't use this technique to log end-user entry validation errors. Simply report that type of error to the end users so that they can correct the error. Use this technique to log only the information that you would want to review.

Information written to the event log will then appear in the log, as shown in Figure 5-2. If you want notification each time that an exception occurs, you can add code to this method to send an e-mail message to you or a support person.

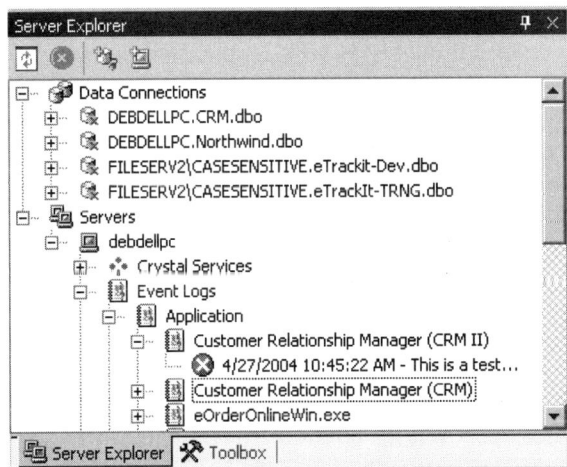

Figure 5-2. The Server Explorer in Visual Studio provides easy access to the event log.

By using a notification mechanism, you won't be counting on the end users to notify you when a failure occurs or when there is a problem with your defenses. Add any relevant information to the notification to aid you in determining the location and scope of the failure.

Performing Unit Testing

You defined and followed a design methodology. You developed the application ensuring that you validated the end user access, verified application data, followed best practices, implemented exception handling, and incorporated a notification mechanism. It would seem that you are finished, but you really have one more task to do: testing.

Testing is the final step in defensive development. Testing ensures that the application performs the functions that it is supposed to do, and verifies its operation with both valid and invalid data.

You can perform many types of tests on an application. Some of these, such as a functional test, may be done by someone other than the developer. The key end users may be best for this type of test. This section focuses on the testing that *must* be executed by the developer: unit testing.

Unit testing is the testing performed on one particular unit, or feature, of the application. This testing is done by the developer after a feature compiles and before it is defined to be finished by the developer. This step is often rushed, with only a quick run to ensure that the feature executes. To minimize coding errors found during production, spend more time on the unit testing step.

Some agile development methodologies, such as Extreme Programming, view unit testing as so important that the process requires building the unit test *before* building the feature. The feature can then be fully tested using the unit test that was developed. The basic reasoning behind this is that the unit testing code will help clarify what the feature needs to do and what the boundary conditions are, making it easier to build the feature.

Regardless of whether you develop the unit test before or after you develop the feature, it is important to perform the unit testing. Your unit testing should use the stories defined during the design process to test each possible way that the feature could be used. It should also test all boundary conditions and invalid data conditions.

The most common mistake in unit testing is to test only the primary story, thinking that "someone else" will test the details of the other stories, the boundary conditions, and other cases. This "someone else" frequently becomes the end users after the application has gone into production. There are many issues with using the end users as your unit testers:

- End users have a primary job, and it is not to provide feedback on your application. Unless the application prevents them from doing their job, they will ignore or work around the problem. So you may not be aware of the problem until it has corrupted data or caused enough frustration for the end user to go to management. That is not normally a good thing for you.

- When end users do call with a problem, they often do not remember details about what they were doing or what happened beyond "it doesn't work." So you won't get much helpful information.

- It is much better to spend the time unit testing and debugging the feature while it is fresh in your mind than to get a call from an end user when you are at a ball game, and attempt to debug the feature from there.

The bottom line is that it is much more efficient and causes much less bad will with the end users if you spend the requisite time performing unit testing.

There are two basic approaches to unit testing: manual and automated. With the manual approach, you can read through the stories and execute the code using the debugger to assist in executing each case. See the "Expanding Your Debugging Techniques" section in Chapter 3 for information about using the debugger. If you later change a feature of the application, you need to recall all of the possible cases and manually retest them.

A more automated approach requires the development of unit testing code. The primary benefit of building code to perform the testing is that code can be easily reexecuted as the feature is modified for regression testing.

The testing code can be created as part of the application itself. For example, you can change a class library into a console application, and then for the console application, define a Main procedure that executes each method of the class library, including all boundary conditions. You just need to remember to change the code back to a class library before deploying the application.

Alternatively, many developers use a unit testing tool, such as NUnit, to assist in creating the testing code. By using a testing tool, you can more easily keep the testing code separated from the production code, and you can run suites of tests on multiple components all at one time.

 TIP NUnit is a free tool that is available from `http://sourceforge.net/projects/nunit`.

Without adequate unit testing, the support costs for the application can be astronomical. And even if your application includes every feature the end users could ever want, if the application does not work correctly, it will be viewed as a failure.

What Did This Chapter Cover?

To build a strong defense, you need to know your application's weak points, you need to build an infrastructure to compensate for the weak points, you need to have a damage-control procedure in place to repair any failures, you need a reliable notification mechanism so you can quickly respond to any failures, and you need to perform unit testing to test your defenses.

This chapter included a set of common failure points, along with tips for building an infrastructure to minimize failures. It also included information about using exception handling for damage control and using the system event log and e-mail for reliable notification. Finally, it included some information about the importance of unit testing.

Did you say, "I didn't know that!" at least once while reading this book? If so, it met its objective of revealing the best kept secrets in .NET.

Index

Symbols

&& operator, C#, 81–82, 106

$ (dollar sign), regular expressions, 94–96, 99

% (percent) wildcard character, Like operator, 162

( ) (casting operator) in C#, 64, 89

''' as delimiter, 111

/// as delimiter, 108

@ (at sign), regular expressions in C#, 95

\d, regular expressions, 94–96, 97

^ (caret), regular expressions, 94–96, 99

_ (underscore) wildcard character, Like operator, 162

|| operator, C#, 81–82, 106

+ (plus sign), regular expressions, 94–96

= (equal sign), assignment operator, 82, 104

= (equal sign), comparison operator in VB, 104

== (equal signs), comparison operator in C#, 104

!=, not equal operator in C#, 104

<>, not equal operator in VB, 104

> (greater than character), and commands, 21

A

Adaptive Enterprise strategy, HP, 186

Add Database Reference dialog box, 145

Add New Item dialog box, 152, 156–157

Add New Project dialog box, 144

AddHandler statement, 65–66

address breakpoints, setting, 121–122

ADO.NET, 153–169

    connections, configuring, 155–158

    datasets, 158–169

        extended properties, 163–169

        filtering, 161–163

        sorting, 163

        viewing as XML, 158–161

    Microsoft Data Access Application Block, 153–155

agile methodologies

    coding for change and, 111–112

    described, 173–175

    unit testing and, 204

alias

    data types and, 92–93

    Visual Studio commands and, 49–50

aligning, and Windows Forms, 57–59

Anchor property, Windows Forms, 56

anchoring, and Windows Forms, 55–57

And operators, short-circuiting, 80–82

AndAlso operator, 81–82

App.config files, 157–158

ArgumentOutOfRangeException, 181–182, 187, 193

as operator, in C#, 64, 91–92

assignment operators, 82–84, 104

at sign (@), regular expressions in C#, 95

automated software construction, 174

Autonomic Blueprint, IBM, 186

B

BackColor property, Windows Forms, 63, 64

bookmarks, 15, 26

Boolean expressions, 80

breakpoints, 118–127

    address breakpoints, 121–122

    breakpoint state, 126–127

    conditional breakpoints, 123–124

    data breakpoints, 122–123

    editing breakpoints, 125–126

    file breakpoints, 120–121

    function breakpoints, 118–120

    hit count breakpoints, 124–125

build error tasks, viewing, 11, 14

business rules

    business rule violations, 192

    defined, 175, 192

buttons

    Condition button, New Breakpoint dialog box, 120, 123

    DialogResult property, setting for, 71

    Hit Count button, New Breakpoint dialog box, 120, 124

    navigate buttons, Visual Studio, 27–28

    Reset Window Layout button, Visual Studio, 8

    Run Query button, Query Designer, 139, 140

forums.apress.com

FOR PROFESSIONALS BY PROFESSIONALS™

JOIN THE APRESS FORUMS AND BE PART OF OUR COMMUNITY. You'll find discussions that cover topics of interest to IT professionals, programmers, and enthusiasts just like you. If you post a query to one of our forums, you can expect that some of the best minds in the business—especially Apress authors, who all write with *The Expert's Voice™*—will chime in to help you. Why not aim to become one of our most valuable participants (MVPs) and win cool stuff? Here's a sampling of what you'll find:

DATABASES
Data drives everything.

Share information, exchange ideas, and discuss any database programming or administration issues.

INTERNET TECHNOLOGIES AND NETWORKING
Try living without plumbing (and eventually IPv6).

Talk about networking topics including protocols, design, administration, wireless, wired, storage, backup, certifications, trends, and new technologies.

JAVA
We've come a long way from the old Oak tree.

Hang out and discuss Java in whatever flavor you choose: J2SE, J2EE, J2ME, Jakarta, and so on.

MAC OS X
All about the Zen of OS X.

OS X is both the present and the future for Mac apps. Make suggestions, offer up ideas, or boast about your new hardware.

OPEN SOURCE
Source code is good; understanding (open) source is better.

Discuss open source technologies and related topics such as PHP, MySQL, Linux, Perl, Apache, Python, and more.

PROGRAMMING/BUSINESS
Unfortunately, it is.

Talk about the Apress line of books that cover software methodology, best practices, and how programmers interact with the "suits."

WEB DEVELOPMENT/DESIGN
Ugly doesn't cut it anymore, and CGI is absurd.

Help is in sight for your site. Find design solutions for your projects and get ideas for building an interactive Web site.

SECURITY
Lots of bad guys out there—the good guys need help.

Discuss computer and network security issues here. Just don't let anyone else know the answers!

TECHNOLOGY IN ACTION
Cool things. Fun things.

It's after hours. It's time to play. Whether you're into LEGO® MINDSTORMS™ or turning an old PC into a DVR, this is where technology turns into fun.

WINDOWS
No defenestration here.

Ask questions about all aspects of Windows programming, get help on Microsoft technologies covered in Apress books, or provide feedback on any Apress Windows book.

HOW TO PARTICIPATE:
Go to the Apress Forums site at **http://forums.apress.com/**.
Click the New User link.